Do you keep a running list of go-to restaurants for your favorite flavorbombs? Can you articulate exactly what it is about those dishes that you find so addictive? Would you like to reproduce the same explosive flavors at home? If your answer is yes . . .

Flavorbomb will change the way you cook forever.

Flavorbomb

Flavorbomb

A rogue guide to making everything taste better

Bob Blumer

appetite
by RANDOM HOUSE

Appetite by Random House® and colophon are registered trademarks of Penguin Random House LLC.

Library and Archives Canada Cataloguing in Publication is available upon request.
ISBN: 978-0-525-61089-2
eBook ISBN: 978-0-525-61090-8

Photography by Suzi Q. Varin
Food Styling by Bob Blumer

Book and cover design by Andrew Roberts
Printed and bound in China

Published in Canada by Appetite by Random House®,
a division of Penguin Random House Canada Limited.

www.penguinrandomhouse.ca

10 9 8 7 6 5 4 3 2 1

For all the chefs,
prep-cooks, street
food vendors,
winemakers, and
on-camera mentors
who patiently and
selflessly shared their
skills and trade
secrets with me.

Contents

A crash course in cranking up the heat,
seasoning with wild abandon,
and making every bite count

Addictive, bombastic, life-affirming
flavorbombs

The Flavorbomb Manifesto

If you live for wildly addictive, life-affirming taste sensations that knock you off your feet, pin you to the ground, and pleasure you with layers of intense flavors, welcome to the club. You have just found your kindred culinary spirit.

If this describes you, I'm willing to bet you keep a running list of restaurants you go to for your favorite flavorbombs—such as a vibrant, pungent Caesar salad, extra crispy garlic fries, or a spicy puttanesca pasta. I'll also guess that you might be able to articulate exactly what it is about those dishes that you find so addictive. But when you try to reproduce the same flavors at home, do you find yourself falling short? That's what I hear from so many of my friends. And that's why they are curious about why food always tastes better at my house (their words, not mine). Hence this book.

I'm a culinary charlatan. Thinking about food 24/7 is my job—and making it taste good without playing by the rules is my game. For the past 25 years I've eaten my way around the globe, traveling millions of miles in search of culinary adventures and inspiring foods for my three TV series and six cookbooks. Along the way, I've broken eight food-related Guinness World Records, competed in some of the most outrageous food competitions on the planet, cooked alongside countless amazing chefs, harvested grapes at legendary wineries, and sampled every local street food imaginable at ramshackle carts, hawker stalls, and night markets from Italy to India.

Before I wrote my first cookbook, I managed and toured with international recording artists. So why should you look to a rock-manager-turned-culinary-adventurer for guidance instead of a restaurant chef or a Cordon Bleu instructor? Because rock 'n' roll and cooking are based on the same two principles: there are no rules (and any rules that do exist are meant to be broken), and the only thing that matters is leaving your audience in a state of euphoria.

The collective experiences from my travels, adventures, and competitions, combined with the tricks, techniques, and hacks that I've learned from observing street vendors and working with talented chefs all over the world, have formed the backbone of my cooking in ways that culinary school can't begin to teach.

If you are familiar with my previous cookbooks, you know that in the past I have been known to play with my food. As the self-christened "Surreal Gourmet," I made edible creations that fooled the eye into thinking you were eating something you were not (think savory "cupcakes" made with braised lamb shanks, topped with beet-dyed pink mashed potato icing). While I would like to think that I was making Salvador Dalí proud, I was also leaning heavily on a highly styled surreal presentation that in retrospect was a work-around for not having a formal culinary education.

I no longer feel the need to apologize for that, and now the gloves are off. The single focus of this book is to channel everything I have gleaned into recipes and practical tips that will help you create bold, stimulating flavors that leave you and those you cook for in a state of bliss. Simply stated, this book is the distillation of my life's journey. It is how I cook at home every day for my wife and friends. And my goal is to share everything I have learned, in practical, applicable ways that will make you a rock star in your own kitchen.

Any time I set foot in my kitchen, I challenge myself to maximize the flavor potential of every bite. And when I write a recipe, I strive to make it addictive *and* foolproof for anyone who makes it. Because I get more excited by tacos than truffles, my outsider approach to creating addictive flavors won't require you to buy frivolous top-shelf ingredients or use super-sophisticated techniques. Nor will it rely on gratuitous amounts of butter, salt, and sugar.

Instead, we will start every recipe together by building a foundation, and then we'll add layers of flavors and textures at every step of the way. We'll add complexity with some simple techniques (like my favorite, caramelization), and then finish it with some of the final flourishes I've learned in professional kitchens. If there's a hack or a simple trick that can save you time or up the ante—believe me, I'll share it with you. Each individual step is easy to wrap your head around, and when you start pulling them all together at the same time, your cooking will be forever changed.

Here's the real secret: once you have quality ingredients on hand, creating Flavorbombs (dishes that explode with flavor and texture), is all about the execution. Learning to execute well will become second nature to you when you become comfortable with harnessing the full potential of each step of the flavor-building process. We're talking about developing the courage to season with wild abandon, brown your food to within an inch of its life, double down on the ingredients that can increase the pleasure factor, and taste and adjust on the fly.

The confidence to cook like this is what differentiates a dish that is *the bomb* from one that bombs. None of it is very hard—after all, I'm a rogue, not a rocket scientist.

The first half of the book is the real "money." It's full of tips, strategies, ingredients, techniques, and gear that will help you crack the code—and gain the confidence to take the leap on your own and turn any dish into a Flavorbomb. The second half consists of step-by-step recipes that use all the tricks in my rogue arsenal to deliver the addictive, life-affirming dishes we all crave.

Now that you know I've got your back, the only things standing between you and a kick-ass dinner are a basic kitchen setup, a reasonable amount of active cooking time (as defined by the amount of time during which you have to put down your glass of wine, beer, or joint), and the will to make every bite count like it's your last.

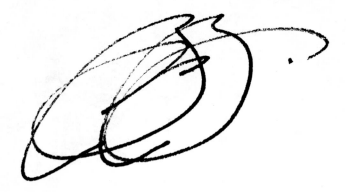

Terms of Service

(Promises, Disclaimers, and Rules of Engagement)

Limited warranty The recipes herein are designed to provide intense, addictive flavors for those occasions when you want every bite to count. My rule of thumb in deciding which recipes made the cut was simple: all killer, no filler. With that said, I'm not going to ask you to break the bank on ingredients like truffles or *foie gras*, and I'm not going to call for excessive amounts of fat or salt that will lead you to an early demise. I won't send you on a wild goose chase for an obscure ingredient that isn't going to make much difference anyway, or base a recipe on a seasonal ingredient that renders the recipe useless for the other 11 months of the year. Nor will I ask you to dedicate your entire weekend to making a meal.

Simply stated, my goal is to help you coax the maximum amount of flavor out of your ingredients, with the least amount of time and effort. Do I break my own rules? Sometimes. But only when the extra effort will be rewarded exponentially.

Information technology Since I wrote my last book, the web has exploded with granular details on anything and everything in the food world that could possibly pique your curiosity. Within the pages of this book I have shared the best of my personal experiences, distilled the information I think you will care about, and divulged the shortcuts that I believe will be the most helpful to you—without sucking up more space on your mental hard drive than is necessary. If you want to go deeper, I encourage you to let your fingers do the googling.

Policy and practice It should be noted that I have only written about ingredients, techniques, and equipment that I am intimately familiar with. Consequently, my lists and musings are not always exhaustive. For example, I've never used an Instant Pot or a pressure cooker, so I'm not going to read the Cliff's Notes, then start dispensing advice.

Repetition Where I feel it's justified, I have returned to the subject of salt, acidity, and some specific ingredients in several sections of the book. In each section, I approach the subject from a different perspective.

On the subject of duplication, you may notice that I rely on a similar universe of ingredients for many of the recipes in this book. That's because they are the ingredients I use myself, and the ones I see in most of my friends' kitchens. With these ingredients and the recipes I use them in, my goal is to add bigger, bolder flavors to your repertoire, not reinvent modern cuisine.

Methodology In several recipes, I have provided two cooking methods (for example, grilling and pan-searing). Both options will deliver the desired results, but all things being equal, my preference is listed first.

Optics All of the dishes are presented in the same manner that I would serve them at home. The wayward bits of shrapnel you see in some of the photos, and the occasional drips or oil stains, are your license to not sweat the small stuff. In my book (literally and figuratively), the emphasis is on flavor, not fussiness.

Waste management For the past decade I have been an ambassador for Second Harvest, a perishable-food bank in Toronto that rescues unloved food and delivers it to those in need within 48 hours. And in 2019, I was appointed as ambassador for a national Canadian zero-waste initiative called Love Food Hate Waste. Its mission is to reduce the amount of kitchen waste that we all produce, thereby reducing consumption, minimizing the impact on landfills, and protecting what's left of the fragile ecosystem. I now look at every dish I prepare through this lens. Where relevant in these pages, I have provided suggestions for how to use more of an ingredient—and when you can't use it all, what to do with the kitchen scraps and leftovers. I hope you will do your best to minimize your kitchen waste when you are making anything from this book.

○ **I agree to the terms of service**

○ **I do not agree**

Verbiage

Glossary (The decoder ring)

Flavorbomb = An addictive dish that explodes with tongue-twisting flavors you can't stop thinking about long after you have finished it.

Rogue = Lawless, cunning, crafty, and artful (there are many other less flattering definitions, but these are the ones I choose to be defined by).

Mouthfeel = The sensory perception created by the physical characteristics of things we jam into our pieholes.

Racy = A bright, tangy flavor profile created by elevating the level of acids (such as citrus juice and vinegar) in a dish.

Gild the lily = Improve upon perfection by adding unnecessary-yet-undeniably-enhancing embellishments.

Hero = The best-looking dish or ingredient that exudes star quality, and cries out to be the focus of the photograph.

Hack = A nonconventional fix that makes the task easier or faster, and/or ups the ante. Often eliciting the exclamation, "That was so easy! Why didn't I think of that?"

Fire (as in to "fire a dish") = Professional kitchen speak for "Start cooking it *now*."

Plate (as in to "plate a dish") = Transfer finished food to the plate, ideally in a visually appealing way.

Finish (as in to "finish a dish") = Do a final sprinkle, dusting, or drizzle.

Showtime (as in "it's showtime!") = The time to begin serving.

Proteins = An umbrella term for all meat, poultry, fish, and seafood.

Mise en place = French for *getting your shit together* and doing all of the initial slicing and dicing in advance.

Stage (pronounced *staaahge*) = French for "sweating it out for free in a restaurant kitchen in exchange for avoiding the costs of culinary school."

Toggle (as in to "toggle the heat") = Adjust up or down ever so slightly.

Evergreen = Ingredients that are generally available year-round, as opposed to seasonal specialty items.

Fond = The brown bits that collect on the bottom of a pan. Likely source of origin: I am fond of the fond.

Key Ingredient Defaults
(___ really means ___)

Dairy = full-fat
Salt = kosher
Pepper = freshly ground black pepper
Olive oil = extra virgin
Neutral oil = canola, safflower, sunflower, vegetable, or grapeseed oil
Butter = salted
Eggs = happy and large
Flour = all-purpose
Sugar = granulated cane sugar
Zest = zested with a Microplane after washing and drying the citrus
Makrut lime = the lime formally known as Kaffir
Green onion = use the whole damn thing (white and green parts!)
Freezes for up to six months = I personally would eat it for up to a year.

Eat to the Beat

Music to cook by, dine by, and clean up by

Music is such an integral part of my life that I can't imagine cooking, dining, or washing up without it. In all my previous cookbooks, I recommended an album to cook by for every recipe. Now that audio streaming services have altered the way we consume music, I have created a collection of mixes to accompany your time in the kitchen, as well as at the dinner table and the sink.

These mixes can all be streamed, along with some of the playlists I follow, on my Spotify channel: **bobblumer**

Part 1
A crash course in cranking up the heat, seasoning with wild abandon, and making every bite count

Consider the Margherita pizza. At first blush, it is made up of dough, tomato sauce, and cheese. But if you break it down, there is SO much more going on. Pizza is a textbook example of a food that is composed of individual layers of flavors and textures. A well-made Margherita is built upon a crispy, crunchy, burnished crust. Then it's topped with tomato sauce that screams with bright acidity and natural umami. The sauce is covered in pools of rich, creamy mozzarella cheese. And any proud pizzaiolo finishes their Margherita with a drizzle of vibrant olive oil, a sprinkle of salt and chili flakes, and a few fresh aromatic basil leaves. That, my friend, is a whole lotta layers.

Before that pizza was assembled, a series of choices were made about which ingredients to use, which brands to buy, the source, level, and duration of the heat, and the various techniques involved. The results of these decisions, in combination with all the flavors and textures, come together to make a classic Margherita pizza so much greater than the sum of its parts.

If you use the same strategic approach to every dish you make—thinking it through in advance, choosing the best ingredients, building compounding layers of flavor and texture as you assemble the dish, and adding a finishing flourish at the end—your food will enter a new dimension. Helping you get there is the number one mission of this section—whether you are following the recipes in this book or blazing a trail of your own.

Taste

Flavor Building Blocks

Ingredients are to a cook as notes are to a musician. In both cases they can be served up on their own, but they only realize their true potential when they are integrated in creative combinations.

Teaching yourself about the individual characteristics of your ingredients, learning how to harness their flavors, and getting to know how each category of flavors works in combination with one another, are some of the most empowering steps you can take in your evolution as a cook.

In a perfect world, over time, you should train yourself to be able to identify most of the flavor-building ingredients in your arsenal in a blind tasting. As the flavors of these ingredients are imprinted on your palate, you will create a mental database that you can refer to whenever you need to decipher what *that little something extra* is that a dish needs.

Full disclosure: I am hyper-aware of the benefits of blind tasting because before my wife kissed me for the first time (as I was cooking her dinner on our first date), she surreptitiously chewed on a sprig of oregano. After the kiss, she asked me to identify which herb she had eaten. Had I not guessed correctly, I suspect there would never have been a second date—not to mention any of the "happily ever after" part.

Whatever your motivation, seize every opportunity to taste the ingredients listed on the following pages—be it at a store, a farmers' market, a friend's place, or a restaurant. (For more on becoming a better taster, see pages 38 to 41). Every one of the ingredients has the potential to add to, or alter, the final result of a dish. As a bonus, the ingredients collectively function as a comprehensive pantry list.

Once you are familiar with the individual ingredients, think about the flavor categories in which they are bundled. These categories create the flavor spectrum and anchor almost everything we cook. The ways in which we combine individual ingredients—as well as how we combine and contrast different categories of ingredients—is what builds the compounding layers of flavors that can transform a dish.

Saltiness

No other single ingredient in a chef's arsenal has the ability to draw out and heighten as many flavors as salt does. From savory foods like meat and vegetables to sweet foods like chocolate, caramel, and cookies, salt coaxes and sharpens flavors and brings them to the foreground. (For more on the intensity of salt, see page 34; on the types of salt, see below; on adjusting salt levels, see page 39; and on finishing with salt, see page 42.)

• Kosher (Diamond Crystal, Morton) • Basic sea salts (La Baleine) • Finishing salts (Maldon, *fleur de sel*, *sel gris*, Himalayan pink • Smoked salt • Iodized salt (the much-maligned salt with few to no fans in the chef world)

Heat

Capsicum (the active ingredient found in chilis) and other hot and spicy ingredients add a unique layer of flavor and a distinctive mind-awakening sensation to a dish—not to mention an addictive element that has been clinically proven to cause euphoria. Beyond the tingles and sweats they induce, each source of heat has its own flavor profile that can be harnessed to your advantage once you get to know its personality.

• Fresh chilis (jalapeño, serrano, habanero, poblano, bird's-eye) • Dried whole chilis (chipotle, ancho, chile de árbol) • Dried chili powders (cayenne, chipotle, ancho, New Mexico) • Red chili flakes • Canned chipotles in adobo sauce • Hot sauces (Tabasco, Sriracha, Screaming Sphincter—or your favorite small-batch hot sauce) • Harissa (in a paste, or dried) • Peppercorns (black, white, pink, green) • Szechuan peppercorns (technically not pepper, but used like it—with more zing and citrus overtones) • Brined peppercorns (for more on pepper, see page 20)

Sweetness

In addition to simply sweetening a dish, these ingredients all have the potential to balance saltiness, round out tartness, add luscious mouthfeel, and knock back the heat of chilis and other spicy foods.

• Honey (liquid and whipped) • Maple syrup • Agave syrup • Granulated sugar (white, demerara, brown, coconut, maple) • Molasses • Chocolate (dark, milk, and white—in chip, wafer, and bar form) • Dates • Raisins • Dried fruits • Hoisin sauce • Mirin • Sweet wines

Acidity

Adding acidity to food is like turning up the "treble" dial on your stereo. It adds brightness and zing. It can also be used as a counterpoint to saltiness and fattiness.

• Citrus juices (lemon, lime, orange, grapefruit) • Vinegars (balsamic, wine, rice, sherry, apple cider) • Wine and spirits (red wine, white wine, champagne, beer, sherry) • Yuzu • Ponzu sauce

Citrus

Citrus zest, as the name suggests, adds a vibrant top note to savory and sweet foods. It hums at a very high frequency, adding a fresh, bright aromatic note to food that few other ingredients can duplicate.

• Lemon • Orange • Tangerine • Lime • Makrut lime • Grapefruit • Yuzu

Herbaceousness

Fresh herbs impart herbaceous flavors when added early in the cooking stage. When incorporated at the very end of cooking, they can add brightness and levity to a dish.

• Parsley • Cilantro • Thyme • Mint • Rosemary • Sage • Basil • Dill • Oregano • Tarragon • Chervil • Chives

Dried herbs are the dried, mostly pure, version of fresh herbs. What they lack in brightness, they make up for in earthiness and convenience.

• Thyme • Rosemary • Sage • Basil • Dill • Oregano • Tarragon • Marjoram • Bay leaves

Spice

Fresh spices, like fresh herbs, are more immediate than their dried brethren and can drive the flavor of an entire dish.

• Lemongrass • Ginger • Curry leaves • Wasabi (also dried, or in a tube), horseradish (also jarred in vinegar)

Dried spices can be used to make big, bold statements or to create shading and nuance.

• Cardamom • Coriander • Cumin • Cinnamon • Star anise • Ginger • Nutmeg • Cloves • Saffron • Dry spice blends (India's garam masala, Morocco's ras el hanout) • Dried garlic • Dried onion • Paprika and smoked paprika • Fennel, anise, and celery seeds

Floral

These water-based floral distillations can bring the smell and sensation of fields of flowers to everything from dressings to desserts.

• Rose water • Orange flower water • Elderflower water • Lavender (not water-based or a distillation, but floral nonetheless)

Depth

Sometimes a dish tastes OK but still doesn't feel anchored. In music, this would be the equivalent of a song that lacks bass. There are a wide variety of ingredients that can provide the missing bottom notes.

• Olives • Capers • Homemade stocks • Pig (bacon, pancetta, prosciutto, guanciale) • Mustards (dry, Dijon) • Aged balsamic vinegar • Fortified wines (port, sherry) • Curry pastes • Wine • Spirits (rum, brandy, bourbon, Cointreau, Grand Marnier) • Beer • Beef stock • Chicken stock

Allium

This family of garlic and onions is one with multiple personalities. When used in their fresh form, members of the allium family announce themselves with eye-watering pungency. But when cooked for short periods of time, they add a sweet and savory backbone. And when prepared over low and slow heat, they mellow and concentrate, developing a jammy sweetness. All forms of allium are at their best in their freshest state.

• Garlic • Shallots • Onions • Green onions • Leeks • Chives • Garlic scapes • Ramps

Richness

A rich dish is deeply satisfying on a visceral level. There are many ingredients that can add a pleasing "fattiness," and each of them has the potential to move the needle of the flavor compass in a different direction.

• Olive oil • Vegetable oils • Raw nut oils (peanut) • Toasted nut oils (sesame, pumpkin, hazelnut) • Nuts (almonds, hazelnuts, cashews) • Nut and seed butters (almond, peanut, tahini) • Seeds (pumpkin, sesame, sunflower) • Rendered fat (bacon, duck, chicken) • Dairy (butter, clarified butter, cream, sour cream, cheeses) • Non-dairy milk (coconut milk, nut milks, soy milk)

Umami

Umami is Japanese for "pleasant savory taste." It is also referred to as the fifth taste (after sweet, salty, sour, and bitter). Umami adds a particularly meaty and malty depth of flavor to your food by appealing to different taste receptors. Think of all forms of umami as your stealth weapon. (For textbook uses of umami flavors, check out my Oooh-Mummy Burger, page 158, and Roasted Umami-Glazed Brussels Sprouts, page 207.)

• Anchovies • Mushrooms (fresh and dried) • Parmigiano-Reggiano and other aged dry cheeses (Gouda, Comté) • Soy sauce • Tamari sauce • Worcestershire sauce • Fish sauce • Miso • Bottarga (salted cured mullet or tuna roe) • Olives • Tomato paste • Stewed tomatoes • Vegemite or Marmite

The Flavorbomb15
(The Ingredients that Matter)

Every professional chef and home cook has their favorite go-to ingredients. Here's the highly subjective list of staple ingredients I lean on in this book.

Salt

A chef friend of mine says "food only becomes cuisine with the addition of salt." Salt is a mineral that has been revered throughout the ages for cooking. In ancient Roman times, it was actually used as currency. But these days, it is easy to be skeptical about the ever-expanding salt universe.

All salt is either mined or harvested from the sea. The practical approach is to think of salt with the same mind-set as olive oil and save the fancy sea salts for finishing where you can really taste the subtleties.

Most restaurant kitchens use kosher salt (a mined salt) as their workhorse salt. Kosher salt gets its name from the fact that it was originally used to kosher meats (i.e., draw the blood out of them), not because it is kosher. Chefs like it because it is free of additives, comes in a coarse form, and doesn't cake (stick to itself). They keep a small ramekin of it (*never a shaker*) beside their station, and when they need to season with salt, they pinch a bit between their fingers. The feel of the salt grains is pleasing to the touch, and it allows more control over the amount used. Even if you win the Mega Millions jackpot, don't bother using anything but kosher salt or a basic sea salt for salting water or during any of the initial stages of cooking.

Infinitely more expensive fancy sea salts are generally used to "finish" dishes just before they are served. These salts come in a variety of forms, colors, and prices, and are sourced from all over the globe. To my mind, the craze has gotten a bit out of hand, and the high prices correlate more with the supply and demand than the quality. For that reason, I've chosen Maldon sea salt as my go-to finishing salt. Its delicate flakes are pleasing to the eye and the palate. At about $8 for eight ounces, it is an excellent value. *Sel gris* (also known as *sel de Guérande*) is another great-value salt with unique attributes. The moist, hand-harvested salt from the west coast of France has distinctively grayish, unevenly coarse crystals that don't dissolve immediately when they come into contact with food. This unique characteristic makes it perfect for certain vegetables (especially summer tomatoes and potatoes of any kind), and in any dish where you want to create an intense explosion of salt with every bite. To appreciate the difference, cut a roasted fingerling potato in half, drizzle it with olive oil, then sprinkle one half with your basic salt, and the other half with *sel gris*.

Whole Black and White Peppercorns

I shed a silent tear when I see home cooks go out of their way to buy great produce, then season it with some tired ground pepper from an old spice jar. To get the most out of your pepper, grind it every time you use it with an adjustable grinder. And before grinding, think about what size grind is best for your food. A fine grind will disappear seamlessly into a sauce. A medium grind should be your go-to. And super coarse grains are most appropriate for dishes where you really want the pepper flavors to dominate, like *Steak au Poivre* or a big chop.

Peppercorns can cost anywhere from $10 to $20 a pound, but not all peppercorns are created equal. Given that you are unlikely to grind your way through more than a pound in a year, why not splurge on the best?—especially since whole peppercorns will last for a couple of years.

The two most-available varietals of superior peppercorns are Tellicherry, from India's Malabar coast, and Lampong from Indonesia. You can find them at specialty stores and on Amazon.

White pepper is fermented black peppercorns with the outer skin removed. It's a mainstay of Chinese cooking. White pepper is more floral and understated than black pepper. Use it for delicate proteins like fish, and in light-colored foods like mashed potatoes or eggs if you want to maintain a purity of color.

Get Cracking

Here's a HACK I use when I am cooking large quantities of food: toast a handful of black peppercorns in a dry pan for a minute or so, until you can smell their aroma. Then use a coffee grinder or a mortar and pestle to them grind up. Place the pepper in a small bowl near your workstation for easy access. Store any excess in a tightly sealed jar, and do your best to use it up within a couple of weeks.

Olive Oil

Olive oils are categorized by the way they are created (cold-pressed versus processed or refined), and their level of acidity. Basic mass-produced olive oil is processed, and most of its aroma, flavor, and color are removed intentionally. It's best used for cooking and baking in situations where you don't want any olive oil flavor, and is interchangeable with other neutral-flavored vegetable oils.

Virgin and extra-virgin oils are cold pressed and have a wide range of distinguishing characteristics. Like wine, their personalities are shaped by *terroir* (the sun, soil, and climate), and how lovingly they are produced. They can be "buttery/creamy," "herbal," "spicy," "peppery," or "grassy." Unfiltered oils, which have a cloudy appearance, contain minuscule fruit particles that can enhance the flavor—and texture—of the oil. Unfortunately, these particles will ferment over time, making the bottle less shelf stable. Some of the best oils I've ever tasted are unfiltered. In my kitchen, they get used up quickly—which is why their shortened lifespan never concerns me.

Some olive oils are so full of flavor that I've seen chefs, particularly in Italy, use them in place of a sauce on grilled fish and pasta. Sadly, many of the oils selected and marketed for North American tastes are less flavorful. A good rule of thumb is that deeper-colored olive oils and unfiltered ones are more complex and flavorful, but the only way to be sure is to taste them on a spoon.

Teach yourself When taste-testing oils, try this self-preservation trick I learned when I was a wine judge. It will help you to get all of the information you need from a tiny sip. Place a quarter teaspoon of oil in a spoon. As you tilt the oil into your mouth, suck the air in around it, creating a loud slurping noise. This may sound a bit startling at first, but it serves to splatter the oil over all of the taste receptors in your mouth, thereby creating a big impression from a small sample. Stay focused: that impression (most notably, buttery or peppery), may evolve as the flavors linger in your mouth and trickle down the back of your throat.

High-quality oils from many parts of Europe and California can be exponentially more expensive than everyday oils. To make the most of your oil dollars, keep two grades on hand. Use the inexpensive oil when it's being heated (for example, for sautéing), in marinades, and for all other situations where its subtleties are indistinguishable. And use the best oils where their rich, nutty flavor and peppery finish can be easily distinguished, such as for finishing dishes (page 42), on bread, on delicately flavored pastas, and in simple salad dressings.

All oils—even the so-called "light" oils—contain the same amount of fat. So, if you are trying to cut back on calories, use one that's more robust. A little goes a long way. Always store your oil in a cool, dark place.

Lemon Juice

Lemon juice is the simplest, most available form of acid (followed by vinegar). Virtually every professional kitchen uses fresh-squeezed lemon juice from conventional lemons in their cooking. Lime juice is almost always a perfectly suitable alternative. These days, Meyer lemons (essentially a cross between a lemon and a mandarin orange) are becoming more widely available. Their juice and zest are sweeter and more aromatic than those of conventional lemons. They are fabulous, so grab some whenever they are available at the grocery store. But taste your food as you go, since they don't pack as much of a tart, acidic punch. If you use a lot of citrus juice in your cooking, invest in a hand-held citrus press. They extract every last drop of juice and will pay for themselves over time.

Citrus Zest

There's an old trick I remember from my bartending days that goes like this: take a small piece of citrus rind, hold it a couple inches away from the flame of a candle and twist. As the escaping mist hits the flame, it releases a lovely citrus scent and ignites an explosion of tiny sparks. This is evidence that the natural liquids contained in all citrus peels are true oils. Fortuitously for cooks, those oils are intensely flavored and extremely aromatic. Citrus zest has become my *sparkle pony*, and I find myself using it almost as often as I use citrus juice.

I live in California and I have the good fortune of having citrus trees in my yard, including a Buddha's hand lemon tree and a finger lime tree. The convenience of fresh, exotic citrus encourages me to experiment with it in many of my dishes. But when I am on the road cooking for events, conventional lemons and limes never leave me wanting.

Always thoroughly wash and dry the outer surface of your citrus before zesting it, because the porous skin is a magnet for airborne dirt. Use a Microplane zester (page 57) to shave off the thin, colored outer layer, leaving behind the bitter white pith. Because zest is so delicate, it is generally added in the final phase of cooking. If you need any more motivation to use zest, think of it as the "buy one, get one free" freebie of the citrus world.

Homemade Stock

Full disclosure: I used to laugh at the thought of making homemade stock. I felt that there were so many better uses of my time. But as my skills and palate have evolved, I have come to prize homemade stocks, and now I laugh at the thought of the watery mass-produced varieties that bear more resemblance to oversalted dishwater than stock. With that said, many grocery stores now stock shelf-stable boxes of stock concentrates with the intensity of demi-glazes (a thick sauce that is used as the base for many other sauces). They are your best bet if you are not going to make your own stock.

I tend to make chicken stock over beef stocks because it is easier to make, can be made entirely from rescued ingredients from my own kitchen, and can be used in a wide variety of dishes. To teach yourself how homemade chicken stock can make a difference in your cooking, taste any store-bought chicken stock side-by-side with some you have made. The results will speak for themselves; homemade chicken stock delivers a deeper, purer chicken flavor.

There are a number of other reasons to make your own stock. The two that appeal to me the most are the zero-waste aspects, and the fact that like zest, it's practically free. Once you realize that the carcasses of a few rotisserie chickens (saved in the freezer) and a bag of rescued vegetable cuttings can be turned into $20 worth of high-quality stock, you will be hooked too.

Whether you are making chicken or veggie stock, you can stockpile the building blocks in your freezer, then make the stock on a rainy day. It only takes about 15 minutes to get the stock started and another 15 to lock it down at the end. The rest is like babysitting a kid that's fast asleep. I reduce my stocks to minimize the space they require, then freeze them in 12- and 24-ounce Mason jars, as well as in ice cube trays. This leaves me with options when I need a little for a quick sauce, or enough for a soup, risotto, braised dish, quinoa, or polenta (for a full stock tutorial, see page 251).

Garlic

I have a reoccurring fantasy that I corner the world market on garlic. After limiting its supply, I watch the price skyrocket as home cooks and professional chefs realize how much they are willing to pay for something they had always taken for granted.

Garlic is revered in many cultures. And for good reason. A single raw clove that costs just pennies (at least for now!), can add a tongue-twisting pungency to an entire dish. Garlic comes in many forms, and can be prepared and used in a multitude of ways.

Green garlic and garlic scapes

Green garlic is young, immature garlic, and garlic scapes are the curly flowering stalks. Both are harvested at the beginning of the growing season and are usually limited to farmers' markets, where they are revered by chefs and foodies. Because they are harvested when the plant is in its youth, their flavors are much more delicate than those of mature bulbs. Green garlic and scapes can be used raw, or added as a seasoning to any dish where you would use mature garlic.

Raw garlic

Raw garlic adds a distinctive bite that is very present in any dish it's used in. But when it's added in the cooking stage to something like a tomato sauce, its flavors soften and it melds with the other ingredients, acting more as the backing band than the lead singer. If you want the full band experience, refresh your dish at the very end with one or more freshly minced cloves. When mincing garlic, add a bit of salt to keep it from skidding around on the cutting board (being conscious to use a bit less salt in the dish you are adding it to). When adding raw, minced, or chopped garlic to a pan with other ingredients, be careful not to add it too early, or it may blacken and become bitter before the other ingredients in the pan are fully cooked.

> **HACK:** here's a hack for anyone who likes the taste of garlic but has problems digesting it. It's a trick I observed while touring a restaurant kitchen in Italy: instead of mincing the cloves, add one or two peeled whole cloves while cooking, then fish them out and discard before serving.

Roasted garlic

Roasting garlic magically transforms each clove into a sweet caramelized jewel that has none of the pungency of the raw stuff. Roasted garlic cloves are a great addition to pastas, salads, soups, risottos, and pizzas, or simply schmeared on a toasted slice of rustic bread. If you are going to the trouble of roasting a whole head of garlic, add an extra head or two to have on hand for other uses. Store roasted cloves in oil, in the refrigerator, where they will last for up to three weeks (then use the roasted garlic-infused oil in dressings, on bruschettas, or as a drizzle). It is worth noting that roasted garlic has an odoriferous way of saying "hello" the next morning.

When buying garlic, look for a firm bulb, and only buy as much as you can use up within a couple of weeks. Store your bulbs in a cool, dark place. As the bulbs gets older and move past their prime, they lose their firmness, and green sprouts appear in each clove (although not ideal, both the clove and the sprout can still be used).

Fresh Herbs

Fresh herbs have a more vibrant personality than the dried versions. If you add fresh herbs at the beginning of the cooking process, they will impart their flavors to all of the other ingredients. As a rule, the longer they cook, the more the other ingredients will assimilate their flavors—while at the same time robbing the herbs of their original intensity. If you want a particular herb (especially a delicate one) to stand out in the final mix, add a little more in the last minute of cooking to "refresh" it.

Thyme, rosemary, basil, sage, and mint are the most commonly called for herbs. All of these can be grown at home, indoors or out, which will give you the luxury of adding them to dishes spontaneously. That should be all the encouragement you need to fill a pot with soil and grow a few of them yourself.

Based on its availability, affordability, and versatility, parsley is in a league of its own. I use it daily to brighten countless dishes. Pastas, bean or quinoa salads, sautéed mushrooms, and egg dishes all perk up when a handful of freshly chopped flat or curly leaf parsley is added at the last minute. Because of the amount of parsley I use, I automatically add a fresh bunch to my shopping basket anytime I am at a grocery store or farmers' market.

Creative Uses for Leftover Fresh Herbs

It can be frustrating when a recipe calls for one tablespoon of a fresh herb, but your grocery store only sells it in four-ounce plastic clamshell packages that contain 10 times that amount. More often than not, the leftovers wind up in the back of the fridge, where you eventually discover them wilted and covered in mold. Be realistic and be proactive. If you don't think that you will use up all of the herbs you've bought or picked, repurpose them while they are still in their pristine state.

SPREAD THE LOVE Use up your leftover herbs before they go bad by adding them to soups, stocks, salads (green, bean, quinoa), salsas, marinades, pesto, rubs, tomato sauce, scrambled eggs . . .

FREEZE HERBS IN OIL OR BUTTER Stem the herbs, and if they are large and leafy like basil or sage, chop them finely. Stuff as much as will fit into an individual section of an ice cube tray, then fill the section with olive or vegetable oil, or melted butter. Freeze the tray, then transfer the individual cubes to an airtight plastic bag. When you start a recipe that calls for couple of tablespoons of olive oil or butter and some herbs (for example, scrambled eggs), start by adding a frozen cube to the pan.

DRY HERBS Wrap the stems with a rubber band and hang them upside down. Let them dry for several days, then stem them and store the herbs in an airtight container.

MAKE A COMPOUND BUTTER Stem and chop the herbs, then add them to room-temperature butter along with some citrus zest or seasonings of your choice (pages 245 to 247). Roll the butter in plastic wrap and form into eight-ounce logs. Refrigerate or freeze.

MAKE HERB OIL Stem the herbs and add them to a blender with half a cup of olive oil and any additional herbs, citrus zest, or seasonings of your choice (page 250). Blend for one minute. Keep as is, or let sit for an hour, then use a fine-mesh sieve or cheesecloth to strain out the solids. Or add the herbs to a pan with some olive or vegetable oil and simmer over low heat for 30 minutes. Strain out the herbs. In both cases, store the oil in the refrigerator.

MAKE HERB-INFUSED HONEY Stem the herbs and add them, along with a jar of honey to a large bowl. Place the bowl over a pot of simmering water and let sit, stirring occasionally, for an hour. Strain out the herbs.

MAKE HERB-INFUSED WATER Add the herbs to a large bottle of water and refrigerate overnight. This works best with mint, lemon verbena, and lemongrass.

Parmigiano

Parmigiano-Reggiano is the king of cheeses. No other cheese tastes quite as rich and nutty as authentic Parmigiano-Reggiano, which is made from the milk of specially fed Italian bovine royalty and aged for a minimum of 18 months. And few cheeses contain the high levels of glutamate (a salty amino acid that adds natural umami flavors). In addition to pasta dishes of all kinds, a generous sprinkle of Parmigiano-Reggiano, grated just before serving, can add additional dimension to salads, soups, pizzas, flatbreads, egg dishes, savory baked goods, and so much more. And nugget-size pieces, unadorned or drizzled with aged balsamic or truffled honey, make for quick and explosive little nibbles.

Parmigiano-Reggiano is a commodity. All of the producers in Parma, Italy, are forced to sell to a *consorcio* (essentially a marketing board) that distributes it globally. Consequently, you can't latch on to a producer you prefer. It's the freshness that makes a real difference. Once the giant wheels are cut, time and air become their enemy. Shop at stores that move a lot of it.

At about $20 a pound, Parmigiano-Reggiano is definitely pricey, but an affordable six-ounce wedge goes a long way.

HACK: to get the most cheese for your buck, forage through the pile to look for a center cut "fillet" without any rind. At all costs avoid pieces that have disproportionate amounts of rind. If you can't avoid a big-ass piece of rind, there is a silver lining. Rinds impart richness and umami notes when simmered in sauces, soups, stocks, and stews. (Because the rind never truly dissolves, fish it out before serving). Rinds-in-waiting will last almost indefinitely in the fridge or freezer if well wrapped.

Teach yourself To really appreciate the differences between Parmigiano-Reggiano and mass-produced domestic Parmesan, taste small nuggets of each side by side at room temperature.

Parmigiano-Reggiano Stravecchio is aged for a minimum of 30 months. It is more complex (and not surprisingly, more expensive), with more distinctive crystals than Reggiano. On the other side of the spectrum is Grana Padano, a similar hard Italian DOC (*Denominazione di Origine Controllata*—i.e., government sanctioned and regulated) cheese. Think of it as Parmigiano-Reggiano's younger cousin, with a distinctive, yet less pronounced, personality.

Though Parmigiano-Reggiano is the undisputed king, I would be remiss if I didn't recognize that many other countries produce aged hard cheeses that are similar in their uniqueness, and can be harnessed to equally pleasing results. A few of my favorites are Manchego, aged Gouda, Beemster, and cotija.

BAD PARM (30% RIND)

GOOD PARM (10% RIND)

Bacon and Other Cured Pork Products
(and Judicious Amounts of Their Fats)

At the dawn of my interest in cooking, I walked into the kitchen of a friend's restaurant during afternoon prep and interrupted him as he was frying up a large pan of bacon.

"What's this for?" I asked.

"Our house salad," he responded.

"For the topping?" I guessed naively.

"No. Bacon fat dressing," he answered

With apologies to any vegetarians who thought they were staying the course by ordering my friend's salad, I now fully understand how the unannounced substitution of bacon fat for oil in his salad dressing would have brought his customers to their knees.

Of course bacon on its own is the bomb, but when it comes to cooking, nothing infuses flavor like bacon fat. The fat and meat from just a couple of slices can go a long way. Here's how to get the most bang from your bacon:

1. Slice a couple of pieces crossways into quarter-inch strips.
2. Add the bacon strips to a pan over medium heat, along with a drizzle of oil to jump-start the rendering process.
3. As the bacon begins to cook and the fat melts and starts to sizzle, add a minced garlic clove or two and a finely diced shallot. Cook for about five minutes, or until all the bits are crispy.

By the time the bacon strips, garlic, and shallot have begun to crisp, the fat in the pan is infused with heady flavors and the kitchen air is intoxicating. The resulting two to three tablespoons of liquid gold, along with the bacon bits and golden garlic and shallot shrapnel (think human catnip) will envelop anything you add to the pan. In my day-to-day cooking, I build upon this base to make all forms of egg dishes, pasta sauces, pizza sauces, and sautéed greens. To be clear, this is something I do in the moment, not something that I make in advance and store.

Get Fat

Pork fat isn't just used to flavor foods; it is often used as food itself. I witnessed this firsthand while shooting various episodes of *Glutton for Punishment* and *World's Weirdest Restaurants*. In Ukraine, I ate *salo* (cured pork fat), a national favorite that is slathered on bread in the cold winter months. And when I learned to make *xiao long bao*, Chinese soup dumplings, I discovered that the "soup" in the dumpling is actually created when pig fat and collagen are rendered from the skin and other extremities, then chilled into what I call "pig jello." When the jello is mixed with seasoned minced pork and steamed in a little 18-fold dumpling, it melts and mixes with the pork juices to create the liquid we call soup. That's what explodes in your mouth as you bite into the dumpling.

It should also be noted that duck fat, chicken fat, and beef fat are also revered in many cultures, and can be used in many ways. The prize for the most creative use of fat goes to Republique, a chef-centric restaurant in Los Angeles where they rescue all of the drippings from their wood-burning rotisserie grill and serve them up in small ramekins with their crusty house-made bread—for a $6 surcharge!

Harissa

Harissa is a combination of herbs, spices, and chilis. It's a mainstay of Moroccan and Tunisian cooking, where it is used in everything from couscous to goat dishes. It is so versatile that it can be used in marinades, during cooking, and as a condiment. The garlic, lemon, and spices in harissa round out the flavor, creating a more complex heat than plain chili flakes can deliver. That's why I default to it when I want to add a moderate layer of heat in a way that builds flavor but doesn't steal the show. It can be used in pasta and pizza sauces, egg dishes, and on sandwiches. It will also kick up any ketchup. My homemade harissa (page 240) reflects the best of what I sampled in Morocco. If you don't have the time or the inclination to make it yourself, the inexpensive and widely available brand Dea won't disappoint, and lasts for ages in its handy tube.

Umami

Umami is not an ingredient, per se, so technically it doesn't belong on this list. But all of the ingredients in my umami category (page 17) evoke its characteristics and can be used to infuse additional layers of flavor. Components of umami can be found in a wide range of fresh and packaged ingredients as well as in dried form. The often-demonized MSG (monosodium glutamate—the naturally occurring salt of an amino acid, most commonly associated with Chinese cooking) is the most common source of dried umami, but all-natural versions made with dried mushroom powders and various spices are now available. Like your mommy, umami can be complex and hard to understand at times, but you will grow to love it.

Balsamic Vinegar

Aged balsamic vinegars are my new addiction. The real stuff is made from grape must—a mash of grape juice, skins, seeds, and stems. It is barrel aged, where over time it develops its complex characteristics and viscosity.

Basic $5 workhorse balsamics (sometimes misleadingly labeled "aged") are manipulated with wood chips and caramel coloring. That doesn't mean there isn't a time and a place for them, but they don't compare to the real deal.

True aged balsamics are best used for finishing, where a few drops will add a complex tanginess, and in delicate salads, where a teaspoon will transform a simple vinaigrette into a transcendent dressing (see sidebar). The really old stuff can cost upward of $100 for a precious perfume-size bottle, but a well-chosen $30 bottle, usually aged for around 12 years, delivers eight ounces of richly layered acidity that will last for months if used judiciously.

Three well-distributed, dependable brands are Villa Manodori, Elsa, and Due Vittorie.

Simple Balsamic Vinaigrette

Whisk together two tablespoons of your best olive oil, a teaspoon of authentic aged balsamic, a squeeze of lemon juice, a minced garlic clove, and salt and pepper to taste. Toss with a head of delicate lettuce or a few handfuls of arugula.

Cured Anchovies

We are all born into this world disliking anchovies. The question is not *if* you will come around, but *when*. Be open. You never know when the transformation will happen. In fact you may already like anchovies without knowing it, since they are frequently used to build flavor in olive tapenades, salad dressings, and tomato sauces.

Anchovies have many attributes. They are full of healthy omega-3 fatty acids, they exist at the bottom of the food chain (which minimizes their toxins), and they are one of today's most sustainable fish, because as the predator population dwindles, they thrive. These facts are sure to make doctors and environmentalists happy, but it's their intense salty, fishy, umami flavors that make a chef smile.

Anchovies come in many forms. The familiar version is salted, brined, and boned, then packed in salt or oil. *Boquerones* are a Spanish adaption that are salted, then marinated in vinegar and stored in oil. This curing process gives them a pleasantly subtle, less "fishy" flavor with a firmer mouthfeel. It also maintains the white color of their flesh, which is why they are called "white anchovies" in North America. Both versions can be used on pizzas, in salads, in olive tapenades, on crostini, and in a variety of sauces. When used early in the cooking process, the anchovy's umami flavors will add a deep-yet-unidentifiable backbone to your dish.

Most recipes (for the record, not mine) hold back on the amount of anchovies they use so as not to offend anchovy-phobes. If you love anchovies, double down on them. And if you really, really love them, buy the oversize tins. Store unopened tins in a cool place before opening. The ambient heat of a warm room will "cook" the tin, breaking down your fillets into an unattractive mush (he says, speaking from experience). Refrigerate open tins.

BOQUERONES

Butter

I have intentionally put butter at the end of my list because, unlike many chefs, I don't use it as a weapon of mass destruction. I use it judiciously, and only where it adds noticeable flavor, as opposed to gratuitous richness. When used correctly, butter is a beautiful tool in the ingredient arsenal. A tablespoon of butter combined with a tablespoon of olive oil adds richness to whatever you are frying or sautéing (as long as you don't cook it over too high a heat source). Ditto for adding a couple of tablespoons of butter to a pan along with some fresh herbs at the end stage of pan-searing fish, which coats the fish with a rich layer of buttery herbaceousness. And then there's the steakhouse trick of melting a pat of butter (sometimes a compound butter that includes various herbs and spices) on a hot-off-the-grill steak to coat it with richness.

European and "European-style" butters If you are going to use butter as an accent, European and European-style butters are well worth the extra dollar for a half-pound. They are made from cultured cream, which goes through a fermentation process that adds probiotics and gives it a slight tang. Generally they have a higher fat content and are consequently richer. Even if you don't use much butter in your cooking, these butters are nice to have on hand to butter your morning toast or melt on a fluffy mound of mashed potatoes.

Salted-versus-unsalted I know it is contrarian to say, but when I am cooking, I am happy to use salted *or* unsalted butter, because I can always adjust for salt at the end.

Clarified butter Clarified butter is also known as "ghee." It is conventional butter with the milk solids removed. It is a mainstay of Indian cooking and is used in professional kitchens to sauté foods over high temperatures in situations where conventional butter would burn. It is a nice tool to have—and simple to make from store-bought butter (page 247).

The Importance of Tasting Your Ingredients

Getting into the habit of scrutinizing and tasting the ingredients you cook with will make you more aware—and consequently a better cook.

I was recently in a restaurant kitchen preparing a kale Caesar for a special event. After making the dressing that I have made hundreds of times in my life, tasted it from the blender to see if it needed any adjustments.

To my surprise, the dressing was bitter in a perplexing way I had never encountered. I began running through the list of ingredients in my mind to see which one could possibly have been "off." I started by tasting the anchovies, the Worcestershire, and the Dijon mustard, but they all tasted as they should. The oil? But how could that be? It was the kitchen's go-to oil for everything they cook. Just to be sure, I tasted a few drops on a spoon, directly from the large can. It was so insanely bitter that I nearly gagged. That revelation made me realize that no one in the kitchen had paused to taste it—or apparently any of the dishes it was being used in. My guess is that it wasn't rancid, but that it was either stale, exposed to heat, or simply a poorly made oil.

In your own kitchen, never take anything for granted. Smell and taste all your pantry staples regularly. There are a lot of quality indicators to look for when you taste, but the most basic ones are purity of flavor, depth of flavor, balance of flavor, and viscosity. There's also a trick I've borrowed from my experiences as a wine judge. Wine tasters always pay attention to the "finish" of a wine, which refers to how long the flavor lingers in your mouth after you swallow the wine. For example, the flavors of a cheap merlot you might be served in a bar will likely dissipate in seconds, whereas a well-made, well-structured merlot can keep on giving for up to a minute. In general, a long, pleasing finish is associated with a quality wine. The same is true for quality ingredients.

What follows are some of the specific ingredients to which I pay extra attention.

Salts

Because of the differences in the ways that salts are processed, where they are sourced, and the shape and size of their grains, they can vary greatly in intensity and salinity. A quarter teaspoon of one kind of salt may be twice as "salty" as another. In fact, they can vary greatly within the same category. Of the two major brands of kosher salt, Morton's is actually twice as salty as Diamond Crystal. Consequently, you should always taste any new salt you add to your arsenal side by side with your other salts. And when you cook with these salts, adjust the amount you use—regardless of what a recipe may call for—according to what your taste test reveals.

Hot and Spicy Ingredients

Some hot and spicy products, like chili flakes, harissa, hot sauces, horseradish, or mustard, have wildly different heat and spice levels from brand to brand. Fresh produce, such as jalapeño chilis, can also vary, even from one chili to the next. Before adding heat or spiciness to any dish—be it raw, cooked, pickled, or dried—always take a tiny taste of the ingredient first to assess the levels of heat and spice, and adjust accordingly.

Specialty Herbs and Spices

Have you ever wondered what it is about a bay leaf that causes recipes to call for a single leaf in some stocks, stews, and sauces? Or how much flavor a tiny individual cardamom seed has? Or what makes a Szechuan peppercorn different from a conventional black peppercorn?

To answer these mysteries, put a piece of bay leaf, a single cardamom seed (not to be confused with a whole pod), or a peppercorn in your mouth and suck on it for a minute. They will imprint their flavor profiles on your palate forever. Try this exercise with any herbs or spices you are curious about.

Brands

In the ever-expanding foodiverse, there are a mind-blowing number of options within every category. From olive oil to bacon to marshmallows, there are the basic versions, with many brands to choose from, and there are the boutique or artisanal versions that cost infinitely more. Are there recognizable differences between the basic products? And are the premium products worth it? The short answer is that only *your* palate knows.

You may not even be aware of all the options you have. For example, in the world of soy sauce, most of us are accustomed to buying the same familiar brands. But if you go to a Japanese specialty store, you will discover a dozen artisanal options that take soy sauce to a whole new level.

The best way to compare ingredients is at home without any distractions. You will find that some of the differences are significant and worth the extra cost, while others are *meh*. But if you do this with one or more people, chances are that not everyone will agree on which is which. Ultimately, it's all subjective. The best ways to separate the worthy from the *whaaaat?!* are the following:

- Taste two or more similar products side by side. This will help magnify any differences that do exist.
- Taste products at room temperature (excluding frozen products), to avoid heat or cold masking their subtle characteristics.
- Taste products straight up, without bread or anything else that might interfere with your assessment.

You may have to kiss a lot of frogs to find the products that stand out, but it's a valuable exercise in learning to trust your own palate.

Unfortunately, it's not always possible to taste a product before you have to decide which one to buy. But you can avoid repeating a mistake, or confirm which products are worthy of buying again, by comparing your purchases when you get home with similar products you already have in your pantry (for example, olive oils). Where the price isn't prohibitive, buy two or three brands and taste them side by side to determine which one earns your loyalty. I did this with some $2 cans of coconut milk and discovered that the one recommended to me at a Thai grocery store was infinitely purer in flavor and richer than the familiar national brand I had been in the habit of buying at my neighborhood grocery store.

In the case of more expensive products, we all want to believe that we get what we pay for, but that's not always the case. And even if it is, their flavor profile may not align with your personal taste preferences. Look for opportunities to taste artisanal ingredients at specialty stores, restaurants, and friends' houses.

The Nose Knows

Several years ago, I donated a dinner for four at my house to the Canucks for Kids Fund, a charitable initiative of the Vancouver Canucks. The dinner, along with tickets to a hockey game, a round of golf, and a few other perks, was auctioned off for $20,000.

The four auction winners came straight to my house from their golf game. Out of respect for the money they had donated, I cherry-picked several bottles of my very best wines. After opening the first bottle and pouring them each a generous glass, I watched in horror as all four men unceremoniously knocked back the wine without even momentarily pausing to smell it first. After they repeated the routine with their second glasses, I concluded that they were way more interested in the quantity than the quality, and I surreptitiously swapped out the remaining bottles with my weekday wines.

I don't taste *anything* without smelling it first. All odors—both good and bad—will help you assess what you are tasting. This habit is a self-preservation instinct that can probably be traced back to the Neanderthal days when foods spoiled because of lack of refrigeration and poor sanitary conditions. Smell and taste are intertwined. Just try plugging your nose the next time you taste a ripe strawberry, and you will be reminded of how important your schnoz really is.

Strategic Shopping
Shop like your meal depends on it

Big flavor comes from quality ingredients. And quality ingredients are a result of shrewd, discerning shopping. No matter where you shop, if you buy ingredients at the top of the flavor and freshness chain, they will heighten the flavor quotient of everything you make—and do a lot of the hard work for you.

Farmers' Markets

Many of the vendors at farmers' markets are the actual farmers themselves. If asked politely, they will select the best specimens for your specific needs. And if they detect even a flicker of interest in the fruits (and vegetables) of their labor, they become a fountain of information on everything from storage to recipes.

Grocery Stores

In conventional grocery stores, inspired shopping is half resourcefulness and half sheer determination. Leave your inhibitions behind and scrutinize for freshness by prodding and smelling.

Feather Your Nest

Your ability to knock out spontaneous meals—and your options for adding layers of flavor—are both dependent on a well-stocked arsenal of nonperishables, as well as a cache of canned, jarred, refrigerated, and frozen ingredients. (See pages 18-32 for a master list.)

Quality is paramount—and wildly variable. Every shipment of meat, poultry, or fish, every crate of fresh produce, and many products packaged on premise contain a best and a worst specimen. And even the most pristine specimens deteriorate over time. To be a good cook, you must be a great picker. It may not be your nature to rifle through every package of bacon to find the meatiest one, or ask the fish monger to unpack every fillet on the tray so that you can inspect the perfect one peeking out from the bottom of the pile. But to get the most out of your ingredients (and your money), you have to be prepared to nose out the best available product, and stand your ground with pigheaded determination—leaving what remains for those who are less discriminating and less resolute than you are.

One of the shortcuts to getting the best of everything is to befriend the butchers, fishmongers, and produce people where you shop. Virtually every one I have ever questioned has been incredibly accommodating. Butchers can help you select the best-marbled cuts, point you to lesser-known (and often less-expensive) cuts, repackage portions, and trim meats. Fishmongers can descale, remove pin bones, fillet, and portion fish for you. All of this will reduce your prep work and save you money. And when asked, produce people—who are always under strict orders to blow out their existing stock before replenishing the fruit and veggie displays with the latest shipments—will go to that mystical place behind the swinging doors and get you what you want from the latest shipment. Sure, these guardians of the grocery galaxy may be surly at first, but once they read the determination on your face, they almost always acquiesce. And deep down, they will respect you for appreciating the difference in quality.

When you are in the grocery store aisles, don't hesitate to size up every prepackaged product, poking and prodding when necessary. We all know the trick of reaching to the back of the shelf to pluck out the freshest quart of milk or loaf of bread, but that's kids play. There is so much more to avoid than an expired sell-by date. Some packs of bacon and pancetta have an 80:20 meat-to-fat ratio, while others have the reverse. Every 80-pound wheel of Parmigiano-Reggiano yields a multitude of corner wedges that are 30 percent rind, and a few center-cut "fillets" that

have absolutely no rind at all—yet in each of these cases, you pay the same price per pound, whether or not it is all usable.

Some of the ingredients called for in this book are quite specific, and may not be available in every grocery store. Sometimes you have to venture beyond your neighborhood to get your hands on specialty items and so-called "ethnic" ingredients. When you are in an unfamiliar store, turn your journey into an education by asking for samples and recommendations for products you may be unaware of. If you keep an open and curious mind, the dividends of your trek will manifest themselves in the form of quality ingredients and low prices. If you live in a small town where certain ingredients (such as wonton wrappers) are unavailable, pick some up on your next visit to the big city and freeze them, or march into your local Chinese restaurant and ask to buy a few. When all else fails, order online. With Google, Amazon, and FedEx, the world is literally at your fingertips.

GOOD BACON (25% FAT)

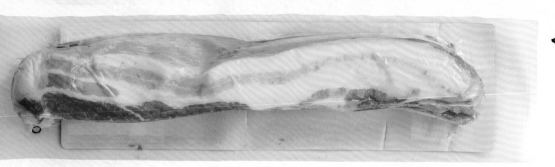

BAD BACON (50% FAT)

Tasting—and Adjusting— *as You Cook*

If you don't taste as you cook, and when you finish cooking, you rob yourself of the opportunity to fine-tune the saltiness, sweetness, spiciness, richness, and acidity of a dish.

Taste. Season. Retaste. It's such a simple mantra, but everyone including professional chefs, home cooks, and yours truly can get distracted while multitasking and forget to taste. Even if you have made a recipe a hundred times, many ingredients, particularly fresh produce and many packaged products, can vary to some degree.

I was pleasantly surprised to find that over the course of writing and testing the recipes for this book, I could sense my own personal skills evolving as I practiced what I am preaching in these pages. Our tongue, like our brain, is a muscle. The more you use it, the stronger it gets. The simple act of focusing on tasting and adjusting more frequently will make you a better taster—and consequently a better cook.

Top Three Rules of Seasoning

1. It's easier to add than subtract.
2. It's easier to add than subtract.
3. It's easier to add than subtract.

Adjusting Salt Levels

Salting is usually a case of too little or too much. Undersalting is more common. I've been in kitchens where I was asked to taste something for its salt level. In some instances, when I thought it was just perfect, the chef added a lot more salt, and when I retasted, it was shockingly better.

To minimize the possibly of oversalting, salt your food judiciously in stages as it cooks. If you are reducing liquids, be extra vigilant since the salt will concentrate. At the end of the cooking process, taste, bring the salt level to its final stage, and retaste. Where possible, step away for a minute to shift your focus, then retaste one last time.

The decision about when to salt proteins is a divisive one, even among professional chefs. Some choose to do it early, which they say seasons the protein more thoroughly. Others feel that salting early leaches out the juices and dries out the flesh. My chef friend Mary Sue Milliken swears by the technique of preseasoning her proteins, then leaving them uncovered in the refrigerator for several hours, or even a day or two, to absorb the salt and air dry the exterior—which helps create a better crust when cooked. Then again, she's a professional to whom salt perfection and time know no bounds.

When combining ingredients, be conscious of the ones that already include salt, are naturally salty, or counterbalance salt. These will all affect the overall salt levels of the dish—yet another reason to taste and season as you go.

Bottom line: salting is a fine line—a fine line that is constantly shifting. Teach yourself how to walk it.

How to Train Your Palate to Adjust Salt Levels

From time to time, isolate a small portion of a finished dish (i.e., one that is already salted to your satisfaction). Then add a pinch more salt, taste it, and decide for yourself whether it has improved or crossed the line. If it has improved, but not crossed the line, keep repeating the process until it does.

What to Do When you Oversalt

- Add acid. Use a squeeze of lemon or a drizzle of vinegar.
- Add sweetness. Use any kind of sugar, honey, maple syrup, or agave syrup.
- Dilute the saltiness by adding more of all the ingredients, but none of the salt.
- Serve oversalted foods on an unsalted starch like potatoes, rice, or polenta.
- For soups and stews, add a raw, peeled potato and simmer for about 30 minutes. Remove the potato before it starts to disintegrate.
- For sauces, add dairy (cream, sour cream, yogurt, condensed milk) and/or an acid.

Adjusting Acidity Levels

All of the experiences I have had working alongside chefs have taught me that the single biggest difference between professional chefs and home cooks is that the professionals are fixated on balancing the acidity of virtually every dish they cook. They use lemon juice and vinegars in the final stages as a tool for two basic functions: to balance salt, and to balance the overall tenor of a dish by adding brightness.

To get into the mind-set of balancing acids, think for a moment about vinaigrettes. Vinaigrettes are a pretty basic combination of fat and acid. If you don't add enough acid (in the form of vinegar or lemon juice) to the oil, the vinaigrette will feel too fatty, and lack zing or "brightness." If you add too much acid, the dish will be mouth-puckeringly tart. And if you nail the proportions, your dressing will taste just right. You know it is right when it doesn't pull in either of the aforementioned directions and has a palate-pleasing taste. Chefs look for that balance in everything they make—even in dishes that you may not think need it.

How to Train Your Palate to Adjust Acidity Levels

The next time you make something like a soup or a stew, put a quarter cup of it in a bowl and add a squirt of lemon. If the lemon juice adds some brightness and balances the dish, add more to the pot. If not, quit while you are ahead, and try the experiment another time, or with another dish.

What to Do When You Add Too Much Acidity

- Add salt.
- Add fat. Use more of whatever fat is already in the dish (oil, cream, or other dairy products).
- Add sweetness. Use any kind of sugar, honey, maple syrup, or agave syrup.
- Add a pinch of baking soda, then stir and taste. Repeat if necessary.

Adjusting Spice and Heat Levels

The heat from chilis and other spicy sources is infinitely easier to add than subtract. Regardless of what amount the recipe calls for, add it in small increments, and taste at each step along the way.

How to Train Your Palate to Adjust Spice and Heat Levels

Spice and heat levels are far more subjective than salt and acid levels. You can isolate a bit of the dish as I suggest for salt and acid levels, and add more spices or heat incrementally, but ultimately the "right" amount of spice and heat is the amount that is right for you and those you are cooking for. One simple solution is to season the dish for the person with the lowest tolerance, then put a selection of the spice and heat sources on the table and allow everyone to adjust their own dish.

What to Do When You Add Too Much Heat or Spiciness

- Add sweetness. Use any kind of sugar, honey, maple syrup, or agave syrup. Or add any sweet ingredient, such as dates or raisins, that is harmonious with the dish (for the full list, see page 15).
- Add creamy ingredients. Use dairy-based products like sour cream, crème fraîche, and yogurt, or coconut milk or cream.
- Add acid. Use a squeeze of lemon or lime, or a splash of vinegar.
- Dilute the heat or spice by adding more of all the ingredients, but none of the heat or spice.
- Serve over something bland and starchy like rice or potatoes.

> **TIP:** After entering several chili-pepper-eating competitions for my TV series *Glutton for Punishment*, I discovered that the most pleasurable way to counteract the mouth-scorching effects of too much heat or spice is to eat ice cream.

Taste *Before* You Waste

During the 2007 recession, I pitched the Food Network on an instructional cooking show called *The Hard Times Hedonist*. It was all about using wartime resourcefulness to create delicious dishes on a budget. The concept and the name were watered down by the network's executives and reinvented as *Cheap Plates* (like "cheap dates," get it?!). Not surprisingly, the show died a miserable death in development. The silver lining from that experience was that I began seeing unloved ingredients and leftovers in a whole new light, and incorporating them routinely into my cooking.

If you are interested in reducing your kitchen waste (and as a bonus, saving money *and* helping the environment), taste the scraps you are in the habit of throwing out. Many of the things we automatically toss are surprisingly tasty on their own—and even better when combined with other ingredients. With minimal effort, most kitchen scraps, including peels, stems, ribs, rinds, and tops can be reconfigured into tasty side dishes or incorporated seamlessly into dishes you are already making, like soups, stews, salads, stir-fries, and frittatas. If you are looking for a place to start, taste any of the following:

- Stems: cauliflower and broccoli (peeled first, then julienned), beet, spinach, parsley, and cilantro

- Ribs: kale, Swiss chard

- Tops: beet, turnip, fennel, radish, and celery

"Sell-by" and "best before" dates can also lead to food waste. These contrivances have been created by food producers as rough guidelines—and ultimately to protect themselves. Just because an item is past its sell-by or use-by date does not mean it is no longer good to eat. Before you automatically toss anything, give it a good smell. If it smells OK, take a teeny taste. If it tastes OK, then use it quickly before it really goes bad.

If you need some motivation to start rescuing ingredients in your own kitchen, pretend that there is a surveillance camera focused on your trash and compost bins. It is so much harder to waste food when the world is watching.

Free Stuff!

The following are free (or come along for the ride when you buy the related product), and can all be repurposed into deliciousness.

- Oil from oil-packed anchovies, sun-dried tomatoes, artichokes, and peppers
- Bacon fat, chicken fat, and duck fat
- Citrus zest
- Fennel fronds, beet tops, celery tops, radish tops, turnip tops
- Pan fonds
- Parmigiano-Reggiano rinds
- Ribs and stems from parsley, cilantro, kale, Swiss chard
- Chicken bones from raw and cooked chickens

Final Flourishes

Just because you have finished cooking the meal doesn't mean your work is done. Virtually anything you make can be taken up to "11" with a little extra attention to detail, or a final touch that delivers the knockout punch. As you finish preparing any dish, ask yourself the rhetorical question: "Is there any additional ingredient I can add, or any additional step I can take, that will enhance the dish? And is there any other way to up the ante?" The answer is inevitably, *yes*. Here is a list of my go-to finishing flourishes (some of which I have referenced elsewhere, but all of which are worth repeating).

Eggs Put an egg on it! If you really want to gild the lily, top your burger, steak, succotash, cassoulet, pizza, pasta, wilted greens, or other savory creation with a poached, sous vided, or fried egg.

Salt and olive oil While doing a *stage* at Craft, Tom Colicchio's original restaurant in New York City, I witnessed a finishing trick that has now become second nature for me. The kitchen at Craft was designed in a *V* formation. As each cook finished preparing their component of a dish, they added it to the plate and passed it down the line to the next station. The fully assembled dishes were funneled to the executive chef who stood tall in his crisp chef's whites at the front of the formation. He inspected every dish closely, tweaking as he saw necessary. Then he finished every component on the plate, regardless of whether it was a protein, a pasta, or a vegetable, with a drizzle of fragrant olive oil and a sprinkle of fancy sea salt. These two final touches served to envelop the customer's first bite with an unrecognizable—yet undeniably rich—layer of flavor and brightness.

Infused olive oils Infused oils add a kick to pizzas, pastas, and many other dishes. The ingredients you use and the uses for the final infusions are only limited by your imagination (see my favorites on pages 248–50).

Spice and herb blends A pinch of a spice or herb blend (your own or store-bought) can add a last burst of flavor to a wide variety of dishes.

Fresh herbs Sure, you may have added some fresh herbs to a dish, but by the time you serve it, they are often indistinguishable to the eye and the palate. Here are several ways to add a last layer of herbalicousness:

- Finish your food with a sprinkle of the same fresh herbs you used in the cooking process. This will goose up their flavors and act as a visual reminder, which in turn stimulates the palate.
- Add some herbs to the butter at the last minute when sautéing.
- Mound a generous amount of fresh herbs like cilantro, basil, or dill on top of proteins (plain, or very lightly dressed).
- Rub the surface of grilled meats with a few sprigs of an appropriate herb (e.g., rosemary on lamb chops) as soon as it comes off the grill. Then leave the spent sprigs on top as the evidence.
- Use a few sprigs of rosemary or thyme as a basting brush for a final flourish of olive oil, or serve a twine-bound bunch of sprigs at the table with a bowl of oil and let your guests do the basting themselves.
- When in doubt, default to a sprinkle of chopped parsley, which adds brightness and color to any dish.

Compound butter Compound butters are conventional butters that are blended with a variety of herbs, spices, and zests. A pad of compound butter placed on top of any cut of steak, chicken, or fish will envelop it as it melts, adding a luxurious mouthfeel to every bite. Ditto for many vegetables (see my favorites on pages 245–47).

Easy pan sauces Pans are a magnet for flavors. As noted in my dissertation on deglazing (page 66), that brown crust that builds up on the bottom of the pan as your food cooks is a pan-sauce-in-waiting. Turn that fond into a tasty sauce with a generous splash of wine, booze, chicken stock, or even water, as well as a few seasonings (fresh herbs or spices), and/or a tablespoon of butter. When this mixture is reduced, the resulting sauce is an excellent finishing flourish for whatever it was you were cooking in the pan.

Aioli A generous dollop of aioli (homemade garlic mayonnaise—often finished with additional flavors to compliment the specific dish), spooned under, over, or alongside certain proteins and vegetables, will add an undeniable layer of lushness to a dish (see page 243 for aioli).

Aged balsamic Aged balsamics can be so intense that as little as one drop of the really good stuff can enhance the flavor of compatible foods. I use it to finish everything from chunks of Parmigiano-Reggiano to ice cream to strawberries. (For more on balsamic, see page 30).

Lemon or lime juice A small squirt, or a DIY wedge of lemon or lime placed on the plate, is an excellent way to finish certain foods like fish, chicken, vegetables, and soups. (For more on lemon juice, see page 23).

Citrus zest Some dishes will benefit from the essence of citrus, but not the acidity. That's where zest works its magic. A quick shaving of lemon, lime, or orange zest just before serving can add some zestiness to anything from fish to yogurt (for more on zest, see page 23).

Breadcrumbs A sprinkle of rustic fried breadcrumbs (page 253) can add a pleasing crunch to pastas, soups, green salads, bean salads, and various vegetables.

Freshly grated cheese A dusting of Parmigiano-Reggiano or another similar hard cheese will add earthiness and depth of flavor to vegetables, flatbreads, pizzas, soups, and salads (not to mention all forms of pasta and risotto).

Climate Control

The serving temperature of any food can affect the overall impression it creates. These tips will help you present everything you serve at its most flattering temperature.

- When serving hot food, preheat your plates. If you serve hot food on a cold plate, you will experience a basic principle of physics: transfer of energy. As the cold plate warms up, the heat you feel in the plate correlates directly to the amount of heat that has been sucked out of the food you are serving on it. The simplest way to keep hot food hot is to serve it on preheated dinner plates, bowls, and serving platters.

  Don't wait until you are just about to dish out the food to discover that your plates are stone cold. Ten minutes before serving, stick your dinnerware in the oven at 200°F. If the oven is full, warm them under hot tap water, then stack them and place a dishtowel overtop to retain the heat. You can also heat your plates by microwaving them for one minute on high (but don't ask me to explain how that works—or guarantee that your heirloom china plate won't explode). For pastas, dip your serving bowls into the pasta water after the pasta is done, adding a half cup of the hot water to each bowl. When you are ready to plate, dump out the water, and the bowls will be nicely warmed.

- When serving cold food that is meant to be served very cold (such as gazpacho, or a crisp salad), chill your plates ahead of time in the fridge or freezer.
- When serving cold food that is not actually meant to be served very cold, let it rise to room temperature.

  Cold temperatures mask subtle flavors. Most foods that are commonly served straight from the fridge are actually at their best when they have been allowed to rise to room temperature (think salmon gravlax, charcuterie, dips, spreads, and cheese). Take the chill out of your food by removing it from the refrigerator 15 to 30 minutes before serving it and allowing it to rise to room temperature. One exception to this rule is cheese, which benefits from sitting at room temperature for even longer—ideally at least two hours.

- When serving frozen foods like ice cream or ice cream cake, make sure it is not rock hard. Take über-frozen foods out of the freezer 15 minutes before serving and let them sit at room temperature, wrapped in a dishtowel.

Visual Flourishes

Think before you plate The first taste is with the eyes (you can quote me on that). Think of your empty plate as a blank canvas, and arrange your food as if it were a painting. If it helps, sketch out your vision on a piece of paper first. Here's how to make the best first impression:

- Choose a plate that works with the food. Size, shape, color, and pattern (or ideally, a lack thereof), should all be considered.
- Designate which part of the plate will sit directly in front of the diner, then plate the food components from the diner's perspective.
- Use color, texture, size, shapes, and schmears to balance your composition. For example, when serving carrots, will they look best sliced length-wise, crosswise, on an angle or left whole?
- Cut foods to expose their attractive interior. Slice meat instead of serving it as a whole dark slab. Cut wraps, roll-ups, etc. in half on the bias, and present them to feature the interior.
- Plate each component to feature it's best side. For example, if you are serving grilled corn, make sure the most caramelized part of the cob is facing up.
- Create symmetric, asymmetric, or circular patterns, according to what satisfies the eye.
- Think like a food stylist and "cheat" the star ingredients to the top. If a beautiful shrimp is buried under a mound of pasta, or at the bottom of a bowl of curry, lift it to the top.

- Garnish with colorful, edible ingredients that pair harmoniously with the components of the dish.
- Take advantage of the wide borders of oversized plates by framing the dish with a dusting of herbs or spices such as ground pepper, paprika, and/or finely chopped parsley or chives. For desserts, use sweet accents such as a dusting of chocolate powder or icing sugar, or drizzles of honey or fruit sauces.

Last Look

Often the finishing touch that has the most impact on a dish is the attention to detail. It's like fluffing your pillow after you have already done the hard work of making the bed. Before you serve any dish, ask yourself the following:

- Has everything been cooked to the appropriate degree of doneness?
- Is the crust crispy?
- Have the individual components been presented in their most flattering light so that their best side is showing (literally and figuratively).
- Have the plates been wiped of any drips or smudges?

If the answer to any of these questions is no, fix the problem—or make a mental note for next time. If the answer is yes, serve it up—it's SHOWTIME!

Technique

KITCHENomics

A rogue cook thinks ahead. The groundwork for any Flavorbomb begins long before you enter the kitchen to start cooking. The following simple kitchen modifications will help you improve the ergonomics, fluidity, and efficiency of your kitchen and reduce the amount of time you spend cooking— making the time you do spend more pleasurable.

Designate Create a permanent, ergonomic prep station that is always in a ready state of alert. The first step is to select the most efficient work area in your kitchen and designate it as the center of your prep universe. Ideally, this will be a space where you can work comfortably and chat with anyone who may be keeping you company. In small kitchens, making room for a permanent prep area often requires some triage and the repositioning of inconsequential objects that take up prime real estate. Secondary appliances like the bread maker you last used six months ago and oversized storage jars are common offenders. Rethink *everything* with fresh eyes. Do you really need that decorative wooden block that houses eight knives, six of which you rarely use? Move the offending items onto overhead shelves, under counters, or into storage. Once you have selected an area to be your prep station, entrench it by installing a solid cutting board as a permanent fixture. HACK: put a thin piece of a anti-slip rubber webbing (the kind used under area carpets), under your cutting board to keep it from sliding around on your countertop.

Luxuriate Make your prep station a foot-friendly zone by putting a foam mat or some other impact-absorbing floor covering at your feet (as they do in restaurant kitchens).

Situate Place your most-used kitchen tools, go-to herbs, spices, and oils, essential knives, and oven mitts within arm's reach of your prep station. Use magnets, hooks, mini-shelves, and empty tomato cans to help situate them. The best five bucks I ever invested in my kitchen was a galvanized steel hook I bought at my local hardware store and the dishtowel that I hang from it. If you install a similar setup in your prep area, you will be able to keep your hands clean without looking down or interrupting the rhythm of your prep work.

Relocate Place your most-used appliances where they are the most accessible. Once I decided to keep my panini maker on my countertop, I found myself using it infinitely more often than my toaster. Move your garbage and compost bins beside your prep station. If you can't reposition them permanently, set an uncovered "feeder" bucket or bag at your feet beside your prep station each time you start cooking.

Illuminate Light your kitchen like a stage. Obviously, your whole kitchen should be lit, but the areas where you perform delicate tasks like wielding a razor-sharp knife require the best available lighting. If you have track lighting, refocus one or more lamps on the workspace, ideally in such a way that your body won't cast a shadow over the cutting surface. HACK: if your head does get in the way of the light, try bouncing the light beam off the wall in front of you. Or, if there is a cabinet over your workspace, stick an easy-to-install LED light underneath it.

Vibrate Find your groove. Music makes a cook happy. And a happy disposition is an ingredient you can really taste (just ask any Buddhist). Instead of upgrading to a new multi-setting 40-horsepower blender, spend your money on a pair of wireless bookshelf speakers.

Mise en Place

Restaurant chefs set up their stations (their designated cooking area) with many of their go-to ingredients for their whole shift already sliced, diced, minced, shredded, shucked, ground, peeled, and prepared in any way that will minimize the work that needs to be done in the moment. The French term for this is *mise en place* (the putting in place). The kitchen shorthand is *mise*. The *mise* gives the chefs the ability to spring into action the moment the order arrives. If you look at the pizza-making station in any restaurant, you will see the entire universe of ingredients the pizza maker may need fanned out in front of their station in small containers. That's *mise en place*.

If you apply the same approach at home, you will avoid becoming flustered when a recipe calls for a particular ingredient to be added at a crucial moment. It will also take the pressure off you, giving you more breathing space to enjoy the pleasures of cooking. To determine what to prep before you dive into the deep end, read the recipe. Most recipes will either include the preparation as part of the ingredient list, or present the information in the instructions section before each ingredient is used. Either way, eyeball the ingredient list and all of the instructions. Then do as much of the prep as possible before the real games begin.

Flavor-Enhancing Gear

Equipment alone will not make you a better cook any more than a fancy camera will turn you into a professional photographer. And there are plenty of gadgets *du jour* that will do nothing more than lighten your pocketbook. But there are a few specific utensils and appliances that in combination with the right ingredients and a deft touch will make a difference you can truly taste. I've listed them roughly in the order of the impact they can have on your cooking.

Chinois (a.k.a. fine mesh sieve)

If you have ever been to a restaurant and tasted a luscious, creamy soup, only to discover that there was no cream in the soup, chances are that a chinois was used to strain out the tiny fibers that can survive even the most powerful blenders.

A chinois (photo opposite) is a large cone-shaped strainer made from a super-fine woven metal mesh (not to be confused with a similarly-shaped metal colander with tiny punched-out holes, which is sometimes called by the same name). If you were to "push" (i.e., use the bottom of a ladle to force the liquids through the mesh) a gallon of soup through a chinois, you might only end up with a half-cup, or even a quarter-cup of fibrous mash caught in the finely knit mesh. But what a difference that makes. The resulting soup will have a velvety mouthfeel that is satisfyingly rich and decadent—even if the soup contains nothing more than stock and vegetables.

A chinois can also be used for filtering stocks, straining fresh cheeses, and in a pinch, straining out wine cork fragments.

Deep Fryer

No other cooking technique adds as much instant gratification as deep-frying. From chicken to potatoes to tofu, deep-frying works a special kind of magic that keeps us begging for more. Sure, you can make delicious, healthy dishes without 350°F of rendered animal fat or bubbling vegetable oil, but when you really want to throw down, one or more deep-fried components are a surefire shortcut to a decadent meal.

Inexpensive consumer deep fryers have two main selling points: they hold about three quarts of oil, and they are designed keep the oil at the desired temperature automatically. The more oil you fry with, the less temperature fluctuation will occur when you add your food to the oil. And the automatic temperature modulation eliminates the need to constantly toggle the heat source to compensate for the spikes and drops in temperature as your food fries.

Convenience aside, you don't need a deep fryer to deep-fry at home. All it takes is a pot or a pan, some oil, and a healthy respect for a combustible liquid that is almost twice the temperature of boiling water. The ideal frying pot is a heavy, tall, four- to five-quart pot. That said, most pots will work. Just be careful not to fill your pot more than one-third full of oil. Otherwise, if your food contains too much moisture, the oil may bubble over when the food is added. Fry baskets and kitchen spiders (wire mesh strainers with a handle) are handy, easy-on-the-pocketbook accessories for getting your food in and out of the bubbling oil, but just about any pair of tongs or slotted spoon will do the job. The easiest way to maintain an ideal frying temperature (other than having a deep fryer) is to monitor the oil with an oil or candy thermometer—a worthy $15 investment.

All-About-the-ASPARAGUS soup
page 115

Deep Fry Basics

- Hot oil is very dangerous. Never leave it unattended on the stove and do not heat it over a high flame for an extended period of time. The best way to put out an oil fire (God forbid) is to smother it with a tightly fitting lid. To avoid flirting with disaster, don't drink and deep-fry.

- Deep fryers are the ideal tool for deep-frying, but it is also easy to deep-fry in a pot. The ideal frying pot is a heavy, tall, 2-quart pot, but most pots will work.

- Peanut oil, with its high smoke point, is perfectly suited for deep frying, but almost any vegetable oil can be used.

- Deep-fry machines hold approximately 3 to 4 quarts. For pots, fill them one-third of the way with oil. The amount of oil required will depend on the size of the pot, but on average, you should expect to use about 1 quart.

- Oil temperature is extremely important. As a general guideline, the ideal frying temperature is 350°F. Any hotter and the exterior burns before the interior is fully cooked. Any lower, and the food will be greasy.

- The best way to monitor oil temperature is to use an oil thermometer. If you do not have one, stick a ½-inch cube of bread on a skewer and dip it in the oil. If the oil bubbles, but the bread doesn't brown, continue heating the oil. If the bread browns instantly, the oil temperature is too high. If the bread turns into a golden crouton in 5 to 10 seconds, you are set to fry.

When food is dropped in 350°F oil, you can expect two things to happen:

- The oil will start to bubble vigorously, due to the water content of the food. As the water evaporates, the bubbling will diminish.

- The oil temperature will quickly spike, then drop below 350°F as the cold food draws the heat out of the hot oil. Deep fryers are designed to maintain a steady temperature (aided by the high volume of oil they hold). When frying in a pot, keep the thermometer in the oil, and toggle the heat source to do your best to maintain 350°F.

You can reuse cooking oil several times. After each use, let the oil cool, strain out the solids, then store it in the original bottle in a cool, dark place. Be sure to mark it as *used* so that you don't confuse it with your other oils.

Food Processor

When I am doing advance reconnaissance for a dinner in an unfamiliar kitchen, the first question I find myself asking is, "Do you have a food processor?" Food processors perform multiple functions, save huge amounts of time, and do things that blenders can't do because they do not require any liquid to perform their tasks. Ideally, choose a processor that comes with a small bowl attachment, which gives you the flexibility to work small batches without having your food settle below the blades.

Grills and Barbecues

In the early days of grilling—as documented in shaky Super 8 footage of spatula-wielding dads in shorts—there was only one type of grill. Typically it was filled with briquettes that were doused in a stream of lighter fluid and then torched with a match.

Now the options are infinite. There are propane and natural gas grills, hardwood charcoal grills, electric grills, ceramic Kamado grills (such as the Big Green Egg), smokers, flattops, not to mention barbecue pits and consumer-friendly wood-burning ovens.

Even the most basic grill will add complex flavors, caramelization, aromas, and a smoky, charred, textural finish to your food that can't be duplicated in an oven or a frying pan.

When it comes to charcoal grilling, it's a common misconception that the "grill flavors" come from the chosen source of fuel. But the true source of most grill flavors is the fats and juices that drip from the food. When these drippings land on the coals with that familiar sizzling sound, they vaporize, sending up a plume of aromatic smoke that envelops the food and delivers the distinctive smell and taste that we associate with charcoal grilling.

Hardwood charcoal briquettes are your best bet for a manageable, even, consistent heat. But all briquettes are not created equal. Look for "natural hardwood briquettes," and at all costs, avoid self-starting briquettes, most of which are full of nasty chemicals that will impart equally nasty flavors to your food. If you can't find pure hardwood briquettes, opt for lump hardwood charcoal. It's a great fuel, but it burns hot and fast—and consequently requires more finesse and vigilance.

In my formative grilling days, I followed in my father's footsteps and grilled on nothing but hardwood charcoal. Then I was introduced to the benefits of gas, and I never looked back. In most cases, a well-designed gas grill will deliver flavors that are just as appealing as those produced by charcoal—with less fuss. Many gas grills, like those built by Weber, have "flavorizer bars" that cover the gas burners at the bottom of the cooking box. These are designed to instantly vaporize the drippings, thereby mimicking the effects of charcoal.

Even in the absence of any drippings, gas grills work their magic in beautiful and mysterious ways by providing a consistent source of even heat that promotes the Maillard reaction—the complex chemical reaction that helps create that pleasing crust on proteins and vegetables (see caramelization, page 62).

These days, grills are getting bigger and flashier, with lots of bells and whistles—many of which will not make a significant difference you can actually taste. The two most important features I look for in a grill are a solid, heavy-duty construction, and an internal drip-pan system designed to channel excess fats and juices out of the cooking box, so that they don't build up and ignite—inevitably at the most inopportune time.

Turn to page 75 to read about grilling techniques over direct and indirect heat.

Uses for a Smartphone

- Recipes
- Timer
- Alarm
- Shopping lists
- Conversions
- Calculator
- Step-by-step photos
- Finished dish photos
- Pizza delivery (for when all else fails)

Knives

A fancy knife is not going to make you a better cook or make your food taste better, but it may make the act of slicing and dicing more pleasurable—which is half the battle when it comes to *wanting* to cook.

Selection Knife sets are for newlyweds. The only three knives you will ever need in your kitchen are a six- or eight-inch chef's knife, a paring knife, and a bread knife. If you really want to expand the artillary, add an inexpensive offset serrated utility knife—the sawzall of kitchen knives. For the chef's knife, I gravitate to the rounded santoku style, rather than straight-edge blades. The curvature of the blade helps harness the weight of the knife when you slice and dice with a rocking motion. For paring knives, I prefer the "bird's beak" shape, which I find very versatile.

Choosing While shooting an episode of my TV series *Glutton for Punishment,* I trained for five days to wield a razor-sharp Japanese knife with wild abandon, then broke a 30-year-old Guinness World Record for the fastest time to peel 50 pounds of onions (2 minutes, 39 seconds—thanks for asking). The bragging rights come in handy at stuffy cocktail parties, but secretly I know that while I may still hold the record, there are hundreds of unsung prep cooks toiling away in kitchens across the country who would bury me in a one-on-one competition on a moment's notice. And I can assure you that every one of them is using a typical restaurant supply chef's knife that cost $15.

So why do we spend so much money on knives? Because they are sexy and they make us feel good. A quality eight-inch chef's knife will set you back anywhere from $50 to $200 dollars. Artisanal, hand-forged works of art with carbon steel blades and handles carved from centuries-old petrified wood can cost many times that amount. I've used all brands of fancy knives, and I can assure you that when they are sharp, they all cut the same. And generally speaking, they all "hold their edge" (stay sharp) for the same duration—which is mostly determined by the way you use and care for them (more on that in a minute). With that said, the more you cook, the more reason there is to invest in a knife that will last, and the more you will appreciate the subtle differences. The right knife for you is the one that feels solid and well-balanced in your hand, and that doesn't intimidate you. Looks should count last, but I know firsthand that knife porn is addictive. If you really want to know, I use Shun knives for all of the above reasons. Shun gave me a few knives years ago, but I'm not on their payroll and report this of my own free will.

Sharpening Many years ago I did a week-long *stage* at Campanile, Mark Peel and Nancy Silverton's legendary (now defunct), quintessentially Californian restaurant. Every morning the chefs would begin their day by sharpening their knives on wet sharpening stones (a.k.a. whetstones). I had a stone at home and was vaguely familiar with how to use it. After a couple of days of quietly observing, I decided to join the ritual. No sooner had I completed my first stroke than one of the chefs leaned over and informed me that the angle of my blade against the stone was incorrect. A few minutes later, another chef commented on the arc of my stroke against the stone. I made both of the suggested changes and continued. The next morning another chef told me the new angle I had adapted was all wrong. Then Mark Peel himself wandered by, watched me for a minute and corrected the new, new angle.

By the end of the week, it seemed as if every single chef in the kitchen had schooled me on their personal sharpening technique—and *every* one of them was different. The moral of the story is that there are many ways to correctly sharpen your knife with a wet stone—and all of them require dexterity, precision, and consistency. At the end of the day, of all your knife-sharpening options, using a whetstone is the most difficult one by a long shot.

Let's back up for a second. There are two stages to sharpening a knife. The first is the grinding stage, and the second is the edging stage. Grinding is either done on a whetstone like the ones used at Campanile, or with some form of electric or manual sharpening wheel. The process takes out the nicks and tapers the blade to a fine point. These days, there are many moderately priced electric sharpeners that do a respectable job of this task. Sure they do grind a wee bit more off your blade than a stone or a professional would, and they require an up-front investment, but I submit that the convenience is worth it. Look for an electric sharpener with angled slots, which eliminates the *angle anxiety* I suffered during my *stage*.

Edging fine-tunes the edge after it has been ground (but it will not sharpen a dull knife). This finishing step is done with a "honing steel," that long rod you've seen chefs and butchers use at a dizzying speed (by the way, I can assure you that they go twice as fast in the presence of onlookers). Using a honing steel regularly between sharpenings realigns the microscopic metal bits on the edge of the blade, keeping it pleasingly sharp. Regardless of what method you choose to sharpen your knives, you should own a honing steel and teach yourself how to use it (better learned from an online video tutorial than a printed page). My favorite kind of honing steel is a diamond grit (about $25). The tactile connection between a diamond-grit steel and the knife blade gives you a better sense of when you are using it correctly. Edge your knives once a week or whenever you feel that the blade is losing its sharpness.

HACK: a simple test for sharpness is to hold a sheet of paper with two fingers. Take your knife in the other hand and try to slice through the edge of the paper. Or try to slice through a tomato horizontally without holding it in place. A well-sharpened knife should slice through both with minimal resistance.

Knife Care

- Don't put knives in the dishwasher.

- Don't store knives in a drawer where the blade will come into contact with other metal utensils.

- Wipe the blade dry after using a knife to cut acidic foods (tomatoes, lemons . . .).

- Don't put knives in a full sink—or you risk cutting yourself. This may sound like common sense, but at the end of the night of food and revelry, it's easy to drop your knives into the sink without contemplating the consequences. This rule was forever imprinted on my mind during my formative years, when I was in the process of shopping for a deal for my third cookbook. As a form of audition, my literary agent set me up to cook for a small dinner party hosted by the acquiring editor of a prominent New York publishing house, in his Manhattan apartment. The stakes were high, but to my relief, the dinner was an unmitigated success. That is, until the editor saw me put a paring knife in a sink full of soapy water—and promptly decided that I lacked the requisite experience to be part of his roster.

- Choose natural wood or restaurant-style plastic cutting boards, not glass, composite, hard plastic, bamboo, or other hard surfaces that will dull the blade.

- Edge your knives frequently.

Mandoline

A mandoline is a versatile manual slicer that is designed to cut vegetables to any desired degree of thickness with speed and accuracy—even in high-volume situations. Its adjustable razor-sharp blade makes it the perfect tool for slicing potatoes for potato chips or cutting cucumbers, which can be sliced crosswise or lengthwise. Most mandolines also come with a couple of additional blades that shred to varying thicknesses. Even the most skilled kitchen prep chef can't come close to cutting uniform paper-thin slices with a knife the way a mandoline can. Paradoxically, you don't need any knife skills to use one.

The first mandolines I recall seeing in restaurant kitchens were made in France from stainless steel, and cost several hundred dollars. Now some of the best ones, like the Japanese Benriner and OXO's various versions, are made from solid plastic and cost about $30.

Even at this price, it's understandable that many people have a phobia about repeatedly running their hand across a sharp blade with nothing but a flimsy vegetable standing between them and the emergency room. Add alcohol to the mix and . . . well, you've seen the movie. If you count yourself among the reluctant, consider buying a $10 cut-resistant glove made from a space-age material that will protect your fingers from the inevitable.

Microplane Zester

Zest and Microplanes are completely intertwined in my mind. A sharp Microplane makes zesting quick and easy. With a Microplane and a bowl of citrus (lemons, limes, oranges . . .) within arm's reach, adding zest to a dish becomes as simple and reflexive as adding a sprinkle of salt.

The Microplane is a recent culinary invention with an unlikely history. It was introduced to the culinary world by baking enthusiast Lorraine Lee, whose husband owned the Lee Valley hardware store in Ottawa. Frustrated by her zester, she picked up a woodworking tool in her husband's store and discovered that it did a perfect job of zesting lemons for her Armenian orange cake. Word of mouth traveled, and soon foodies started mail-ordering it. Once Microplane, the tool's manufacturer, caught wind of this secret life of their product, they added a molded plastic handle, and as they say, the rest is history.

The beauty of the Microplane is that it peels the thin aromatic, oil-filled surface of citrus while leaving behind the bitter white pith. It is also capable of grating ginger and garlic into a paste-like consistency, and transforming hard cheeses into teeny pillowy ribbons that melt instantly when sprinkled over hot foods. The one downside of the Microplane's ability to grate solids into heaps of fluffiness is that it alters the yield of many ingredients. This should be noted when using recipes that list ingredients by volume rather than weight, but don't necessarily specify the tools with which to create that volume. For example, one ounce of Parmigiano-Reggiano grated on a Microplane yields one cup of grated cheese, whereas the same amount grated on the fine side of a conventional box grater will yield half a cup. Be aware, and adjust amounts accordingly.

The teeth of a Microplane tend to lose their bite over time the same way a knife loses its edge. Unfortunately, there is no way to sharpen a Microplane, and it should be replaced once it becomes dull.

Mortar and Pestle

The mortar and pestle is a cooking tool that is as old as civilization itself, yet it can perform certain tasks with ease and simplicity that rival the latest technology-driven kitchen gadgets. Anytime a recipe calls for small amount of spices to be ground, anytime you want to make a quick paste, or anytime you want to crush a few nuts, a mortar and pestle can finish the job faster than you can fish out your spice grinder from the back of your cupboard.

A mortar and pestle also grinds ingredients without heating them in the process (as food processors and blenders can do), which can prematurely release their flavors and aromas. But most importantly, its convenience will encourage you to grind, crush, and bruise your ingredients. This releases their oils and aromas, adding extra juju to your food that you would otherwise miss out on.

A mortar and pestle can be made from a variety of materials, the most common of which are marble, granite, clay, lava rock, and wood. They come in many sizes and vary greatly in price. I use a large, no-fuss, functional granite version, which allows me to crush everything from peppercorns to big chunks of stale bread. They are available at your local Thai or Latino grocery store for a fraction of what they cost at the fancy kitchenware shops.

Panini Maker

Panini makers give bread texture and a visual appeal that screams *this ain't your morning toast*. They make any toasted sandwich look like it just came from an Autogrill on Italy's famous Autostrada. They will also melt grilled cheese sandwiches in a way that integrates the cheese into the bread. And they create the perfect abrasive surface on which to rub a clove of garlic when you are making bruschetta.

The weight of the top half of a panini maker, in combination with the double-sided heat and the ripples of the grooved grill plates, compress whatever you are toasting, creating the signature grill marks and undulating surface. That surface delivers a pleasing mouthfeel and serves to hold any spreadable ingredients you top it with. Bread toasted in a panini maker actually tastes different because the panini plates caramelize the natural sugars in the bread where they come into contact.

Think of the surface of your panini maker like the grates of your backyard grill. The more seasoned it becomes, the more easily it releases the foods you cook on it. Consequently, it is best to clean it gently with a paper towel, allowing any oil residue from your oil-drizzled bread or melting cheeses to stay on the plates. HACK: at home I use a Dustbuster (being careful not to let it touch the surface), to collect the crumbs and other shrapnel from between the crevices so as not to disturb the seasoned surface.

I've used the same single-setting Krups panini maker for more than 20 years. The model I like has been discontinued, so when my first one bit the dust after a dozen years of heavy use, I found another one on eBay. That said, the function of a panini maker is so simple that most brands will do the trick for you.

Pans: Nonstick Pans

You don't see many nonstick pans in restaurant kitchens because chefs use other tricks to achieve the same results, and because the pan's surface scratches quickly in the rock 'em, sock 'em environment of a professional kitchen. But for the home cook, they can act as a gateway pan because they help prevent stickage and burning, and they deliver excellent results with consistency. My first real pan was nonstick, and I remember it like my first kiss.

I still use a nonstick pan for specific applications. They are the perfect vessel for making eggs because . . . wait for it . . . they don't stick. With eggs, stickage usually leads to browning, which is undesirable when your intent is to make creamy, silky scrambled eggs, or perfect sunny-side-up eggs. Beyond eggs, nonstick pans are excellent for cooking crepes, delicate skin-on fish fillets (though you can get better results in a steel or cast-iron pan once you get comfortable with the technique on page 163), and anything else that you want to slide out of a pan with ease. They are also great if you want to cook with less fat. Nonstick pans only function as advertised for as long as their surface remains in pristine condition. To extend their lifespan, use silicone or wooden cooking utensils and place a dish towel or a single sheet of paper towel between them when stacking.

Pans: Cast Iron

Cast-iron pans retain heat longer, and if seasoned religiously will develop a natural nonstick coating. These attributes make them a perfect vessel with which to create a deep dark crust on everything from potatoes to beef. And because they are ovenproof, they are perfect for dishes that start on the stovetop and finish in the oven. There is one notable exception to the positive attributes. Highly acidic foods like tomato sauce will develop a metallic taste if cooked for more than a half hour in a cast-iron pan. But the pans are fine for making quick sauces and deglazing with acids. Relative to other styles of pans, cast iron is inexpensive, practically indestructible, ovenproof, and attractive enough in a rustic kind of way, to serve your food in—while also keeping it warm. It's no wonder Cajun chefs, cowboys, and fried chicken fanatics all swear by it.

Cast Iron Seasoning: Use it or Lose it

Years ago, the art director of my series *Surreal Gourmet* housesat for me over the Christmas holidays. When I returned, I found that she left me an immaculately seasoned cast-iron pan. When I called her to tell her how much I appreciated the gift, she was a bit miffed. As it turns out, it was my pan, but she had used it every day, which had perfectly seasoned it. Moral of the story: the best way to season a pan is to use it frequently.

Sous Vide (the equipment)

Sous vide is a cooking technique and also the name of the equipment used in the process. The technique involves slow-cooking foods in vacuum-sealed plastic bags in a water bath at a precise temperature. Sous vide equipment was once the sole domain of professional chefs. As recently as a decade ago, the equipment consisted of a behemoth circulator machine designed to heat and circulate the water, attached to a large plastic tub. But in the past 10 years, pared-down versions have become more accessible and affordable for the home cook.

Now, instead of the circulator/tub combo, all you need to buy is a user-friendly circulator with Apple-like industrial design that works in any pasta pot. Some brands have digital readouts on them, and the most advanced ones connect wirelessly to your smartphone. Just stick the circulator in a large pot filled with water, add your chosen vacuum-sealed food, and the machine will cook it to your exact desired degree of doneness—each time, every time. With the associated app, you can control the cooking times and temperatures with your phone—while simultaneously taking selfies that document your fabulous sous vide experience. (For when to sous vide, and how, see Techniques That Make a Difference You Can Taste, page 68 to 69.)

Excellent Chef's Tools for Under $15

- Nine-inch tongs (Oxo stainless-steel locking tongs are my hands-down favorites)
- Cooling rack (to keep baked goods, meats, and other foods from getting soggy as they cool)
- Cut-resistant safety gloves (for use with mandolines)
- Egg slicer (good for hard-boiled eggs, mushrooms, and soft cheeses)
- Fat separator (pitcher)
- Fixed-blade, plastic mandoline
- Hand citrus press
- Kitchen scissors
- Kitchen tweezers (for precision plating)
- Meat thermometer (to test doneness)
- Microplane
- Oil or candy thermometer (for deep-frying)
- Pin bone tweezers (for fish)
- "Quarter" sheet pans (9 × 13 inches)
- Restaurant supply stainless-steel mixing bowls (various sizes)
- Salad dressing whisk
- Set of ramekins (for your *mise en place*)
- Sharpie and a roll of masking tape (for labeling jars and dating refrigerated and frozen foods)
- Silicone spatula (for scraping every last bit from a bowl and minimizing waste)
- Silicone basting brush
- Splatter screen
- Squeeze bottles
- Tomato corer

PURE
Maple Syrup
0 ml

PRODUCT OF QUEBEC, CANADA
REFRIGERATE AFTER OPENING
MADE IN CANADA

Techniques That Make a Difference You Can Taste

Each of the following simple-yet-effective techniques has the potential to help you coax more flavor—and deliciousness—from your ingredients. They are all easily learnable skills, and with the exception of sous vide cooking, none of them require special equipment or ingredients. Sure, they involve a little attention to detail, but what they really rely on is courage. Once you understand the fundamentals behind each of these techniques and gain the confidence to execute them without following step-by-step directions, you will feel like you have gained a new superpower.

Caramelizing or High Heat Roasting (a.k.a. the Art of Darkness)

If you put a cup of plain white granulated sugar in a pan over medium-low heat, within a few minutes the sugar will start to melt into a clear liquid. And after another couple of minutes, it will turn golden brown. Pour that liquid gold onto a sheet pan, and it will set into a hard caramel candy.

The same principle of caramelization applies to fruits, vegetables, and proteins. They all contain natural sugars. When a vegetable is steamed, boiled, or cooked over low temperatures, its natural sugars lie dormant in the form of starch(i.e., the sugars remain in their original state, because the heat source isn't high enough to convert them). But when the same vegetable is exposed to any source of high heat (whether via direct contact with a pan or through the heat of an oven or grill), its natural sugars break down and caramelize, browning the surface and transforming the formerly simple vegetable into an addictive candy bomb.

Similarly, when the natural sugars and amino acids in meat, fish, and poultry come face-to-face with the high temperatures of a sauté pan, grill, or oven, a complicated chemical reaction dubbed the Maillard reaction (named after the French chemist, Louis-Camille Maillard, who first described it in 1912) rearranges the molecules on their surface, creating a distinctive brown crust.

The results of both these scientific miracles deliver the flavors and textures that make caramelized food SO appealing. Lucky for us, it's one of the easiest restaurant techniques to duplicate at home. In fact, there are some foods that you can caramelize *better* at home.

Professional chefs usually do a great job of browning their proteins (think well-crusted steaks and crispy fish skin). But they often fail on vegetables, which paradoxically, are easier to get right. It's not that they don't understand the concept ('cause it ain't complicated). It's just that browning takes time, and browning something until it develops a perfect crust can often take more time than a restaurant kitchen can afford as they attempt to knock out tens if not hundreds of similar items during "the rush."

Take hash browns as a case in point. How often have you gone out for brunch and fantasized about a plate of crispy, browned potatoes, only to be disappointed by a mound of snow-white mealy spuds that offer only a teasing hint of the crispiness you yearned for? Ditto for cauliflower steak (page 192), which rarely arrives as advertised.

When you cook at home, you have all the time and surface space required to brown away to your heart's content. Through trial and error you will develop the confidence to take your foods to the edge of darkness. Once you taste the texture and sweetness that caramelization delivers, you will never look back. Simply stated, no other technique can come close to turning everyday vegetables into flavorbombs the way caramelization does.

How to Caramelize

You can caramelize in an oven, a grill, or a frying pan. Using a carrot as an example, here's a quick overview. Cut your carrot into similar-sized one-inch rounds. Or if they are long, thin carrots, leave them whole. With each of the following methods, the goal is to create a crispy, deep golden-brown crust on as much of the surface as possible.

Oven Method

1. Preheat your oven to 425°F. If it has a convection option, use it.
2. Toss the carrots with a generous amount of olive oil and salt.
3. Set the carrots on a sheet pan (ideally lined with parchment paper to minimize cleanup). Be careful not to overcrowd.
4. Turn carrots a quarter rotation every 10 minutes.
5. Roast for a total of 30 to 45 minutes, or until the carrots are nicely browned on all surfaces and cooked through.

Pan Method

1. In a large sauté pan over medium or medium-high heat, add one tablespoon of olive oil and one tablespoon butter.
2. Add the carrots and cook with a lid on for about 10 minutes. Then remove the lid, season with salt, and continue cooking with the lid off.
3. Stir every five minutes.
4. Cook for about 30 minutes, until the carrots are nicely browned and cooked through.

Grill Method

1. Toss the carrots (whole or halved) with a generous amount of olive oil and salt.
2. Place the carrots directly on the grate over medium direct heat, or indirect high heat. Close the lid.
3. Turn the carrots a quarter rotation every 10 minutes.
4. Grill for 30 to 45 minutes, or until the carrots are nicely browned on all surfaces and cooked through.

Learning about caramelizing is easy (you just did!). Learning how to execute it well, and letting your vegetables cook until they are browned to within an inch of their lives takes practice—and courage. As a general rule, color = flavor. But just to clarify, when I say "browned to within an inch of their lives," I mean really, really well browned—*but* not burned, over-charred, or blackened. If you take the browning process too far, your food will become acrid (think about the difference between a really well-browned piece of toast versus one that is burnt).

Teach Yourself To gauge how much roasting time your veggies can withstand, try putting a few of them back in the oven after you think they are done. Let them bake for another 10 minutes. If they are crispier and tastier, you know you can push it next time. If they are overcooked, you have learned a good lesson the *easy* way.

One small detail: if you are caramelizing the surface of a protein like a steak, pork chop, or chicken breast with the goal of creating an appealing crust, rest the finished protein on a wire cooling rack until you are ready to plate it so that the bottom doesn't steam in its own juices.

Toasting, Roasting, and Crusting

Toasting, roasting, and crusting are all forms of caramelization that can enhance a variety of foods. In my late teens, I worked on Cape Cod for a summer. After the bars closed, one diner stayed open and served up a late-night menu. All these years later, I still remember sitting on a stool and watching the cooks slice the leftover blueberry muffins from the breakfast shift, slather a bit of room-temperature butter over each of the cut sides, and set them cut side down on the flattop. After a few minutes, they developed a beautiful golden crust, which gave the day-old muffins a whole new life—one I dare say that was tastier than the original.

Any time you are about to serve any form of bread product, including any type of tortilla, flatbread, naan, etc., ask yourself, Would this taste better if it was toasted and/or crusted? HACK: here's a tip for resuscitating the crust of a "tired" loaf of bread. Baptize it with a generous sprinkle of water and toss it in a preheated 450°F oven for five minutes.

Nuts and seeds also benefit from toasting or roasting, which transforms their flavor and alters their texture. Just think about the difference between a raw hazelnut and a toasted one.

TASTY

TASTIER!

Braising

Braising is the technique of cooking proteins (usually the toughest, most inexpensive cuts of meat that would be difficult to chew if prepared in other ways), in liquids like wine and stock. When simmered at low temperatures for several hours, the muscles and fibers in the proteins break down, and the connective tissues convert to gelatin. The process creates rich, succulent textures. It is also used to achieve similar results with fibrous vegetables like leeks, onions, and fennel.

Today's pressure cookers, Instant Pots, and slow cookers essentially braise at warp speed. But the beauty of oven-braising (beside the fact that you don't need any special equipment) is that you can remove the lid halfway through the cooking time, allowing the foods to brown on top instead of simply gently steaming them throughout, which adds a pleasing crust to the melt-in-your-mouth interior.

Osso buco (veal shank) and lamb shanks, beef short ribs, beef cheeks, pork butts, and duck legs are all good examples of tough Cinderella cuts that become the belle of the ball when braised. In contrast, beef tenderloin, which comes from a part of the cow that doesn't get much of a workout and takes very little time to cook to perfection over a conventional heat source, doesn't benefit from being braised because it is already succulent.

Because of the length of time it takes to braise (two to four hours for many cuts of meat, and more for big pieces like a brisket or a pork butt), the technique is best saved for special occasions. But if you are cooking for a large number of people, or if it's the dead of winter when your kitchen will benefit from the radiating heat of your oven—it's well worth the effort (see page 172 for one-pan chicken and 180 for Chinese-style beef ribs).

BRAISED CHINESE-STYLE BEEF SHORT Ribs page 180

Deglazing

To paraphrase the old expression, one cook's dirty pan is another cook's treasure.

All of the browned bits and reduced drippings (a.k.a. fond) that cling to a pan as you brown proteins and vegetables are full of deep, rich flavors. Leaving those roasty/toasty flavors on the bottom of the pan is like leaving money on the table. But if you add a generous splash of liquid (see sidebar) to the pan—ideally a flavorful one that has some acidity—and stir it, it will liberate all of the flavorful bits and assimilate them into a savory liquid. As a bonus, it will make your cleanup easier. That liquid can either be reintegrated into whatever is in the pan, or become the base for a quick pan sauce or gravy that will add another layer of flavor to your dish. Either way it's a win-win for everything and everyone involved.

If your fond has gone so far as to become burned and blackened, any resulting sauce will be bitter. Toss out the fond and chalk it up to experience. Next time, dial down the heat while cooking, and/or deglaze your pan earlier.

How to Deglaze

- When the pan contents have fully cooked, transfer them (but not the pan juices or the fond that has collected on the bottom), to a plate or bowl. Reserve.
- Add a generous splash of your deglazing liquid (see sidebar). Start with two to three tablespoons.
- As the liquids start to sizzle, turn the heat down, then toggle the heat as necessary to keep the liquids at a brisk simmer. Add more liquid if the pan juices reduce too quickly.
- As the liquid simmers, it will naturally begin to loosen up the fond. Use a wooden spoon (ideally one with a flat head that is designed for scraping) to scrape the bottom of the pan, while at the same time stirring to incorporate the little browned bits that are released.

- As the deglazing liquids reduce, add additional ingredients like butter and herbs to create a rich, flavorful pan sauce. If you want your pan sauce to have a thicker consistency, add a tablespoon each of soft butter and flour to a small bowl and mix it into a paste. Add the paste to the pan in one-teaspoon increments and stir to incorporate it into the pan sauce. It will take a minute or so for the sauce to thicken. Keep adding the flour and butter mixture (allowing it a minute to thicken each time) until the desired degree of thickness is achieved.
- Return your cooked food to the pan, and toss to coat it with the pan sauce. Or if you prefer to use the pan sauce as a sauce, pour it over the contents after plating them.

Whether you are a gourmand trying to get the most flavor from your ingredients, or a frugalista trying to get the most value (or both), deglazing will work its magic for you.

Deglazing Liquids

All of these liquids will help release the fond from the bottom of your pan. With the exception of water, they will all add some flavors of their own as they reduce, concentrate, and meld with the flavors in the pan. In a perfect world, select a liquid that complements the food. Some classic examples include lemon juice or white wine for fish, red wine for steak, apple cider vinegar for pork, and chicken stock for chicken.

- **Lemon juice, or any other citrus juice**
- **Balsamic vinegar, or any other vinegar**
- **Wine (of any kind or color), beer, alcoholic spirits, vermouth, or sake**
- **Chicken, beef, or veggie stock**
- **Tea (I often use the leftovers from a cup or pot)**
- **Water**

Reducing

Reducing cooking liquids concentrates their flavors and gives them more viscosity. It also intensifies your pan sauces, makes your pasta sauce stick to the noodles, helps your glaze coat your food, and thickens your gravy.

Years ago I *staged* for a week at Cordeillan-Bages, the restaurant connected to the famous Bordeaux winery Lynch Bages. The executive chef loved to paint lines of sauce reductions on his plate, which he used as an accent and a visual flourish. The first time I saw the pencil-thin line of sauce on his signature lamb dish, I assumed it was there to delineate the meat from the accompanying vegetables. But then I ran a fork through the reduction, picking up the equivalent of a single drop of water. To my amazement, that micro-dose exploded in my mouth with an insane amount of lamb-flavored intensity. Whaaaa?

The chef explained that it was a reduction of the braising juices the lamb was cooked in. In hindsight, I understand that the "braising juices" he started his reduction with was way more than just a simple liquid. It was a complex combination of the original braising liquids, pan drippings, bone marrow, and rendered (slowly melted) fat. To create the final sauce he painted on the plate, I would guesstimate that he reduced the collective liquids by 90 percent. It tasted like the pure essence of lamb.

To this day, that sauce is the most extreme example I've ever encountered of the powers of reducing. But all forms of reductions (be they from sauces of any kind, braising liquids, or pan drippings—or any combination thereof) burn off some of the water content, thickening the remaining liquid, and deepening the remaining flavors.

How to Reduce

1. When the pan, pot, or Dutch oven contents are fully cooked, transfer them (but not the liquids that have collected on the bottom) to a plate or bowl. Cover with aluminum foil and reserve.
2. Pour the remaining liquids through a strainer into a pot that will comfortably accommodate them. Gently push down on the remaining solids in the strainer with the back of a ladle or spoon to extract the last bits of flavorful liquids.
3. If you have been braising meats or other proteins, let the juices sit for five minutes and allow the fat to rise to the top. Then spoon or ladle off the fat or use a fat separator.
4. Set the pot on the stovetop over medium-high heat, uncovered.
5. The higher the heat, the faster the reduction. But be watchful, stir occasionally, and toggle the heat if necessary so that you don't reduce the liquids so much that you are left with nothing but a burned bottom. Because the original liquids can vary widely in thickness, it's impossible to be specific about how much to reduce them. With that disclaimer noted, a good rule of thumb is to reduce your liquids to a half or a third of their original volume.

A good reduction should be as thick as honey. As a general rule, reduce your liquids until the remaining sauce coats the back of a spoon. Reductions can be used immediately or stored in the fridge (where they may develop a jello-like consistency). Reheat over medium heat to return them to their original consistency.

Emulsifying

Emulsification is the process of binding fat-based liquids such as oil and melted butter with water-based liquids to form a thick, smooth sauce. This scientific miracle only occurs when you add an emulsifying agent to the mix that binds the liquids and prevents them from separating over time. In the culinary world, the most common emulsifying agents are egg yolks and mustard. The process is most frequently used to make aioli (see page 243), mayonnaise, and Hollandaise sauce—all of which have been known to bring diners to their knees.

Vinaigrettes and other salad dressings also harness the magic powers of emulsification.

All it takes to emulsify is a bowl and a whisk, food processor, blender, or immersion blender. But be forewarned, there is a bit of a learning curve at first because the sauce can "break" if the oil is drizzled in too quickly and doesn't bind with the emulsifying agent. You will recognize when this happens because the resulting mixture will settle in a puddle at the bottom of the vessel instead of clinging to the sides like a thick mayonnaise. (I've explained how to avoid this pitfall—and how to remedy it when it does happen—on page 243.) For the mouthfeel alone, emulsifications are totally worth the attention and patience they require.

Sous Vide (the Technique)

Sous vide (French for "under vacuum") cooking is the most foolproof technique available for cooking certain types of food to an exact degree of doneness. It works beautifully on proteins like steak, fish, chicken, and tough cuts of meat that are traditionally braised, or cooked low and slow. It also turbocharges some vegetables like carrots by slow cooking them without allowing any of their flavors to leach into the water they are usually boiled in. And eggs! Sous viding eggs in their shells (which act as nature's own vacuum-sealed bag), poaches them so sublimely that they literally quiver when they are removed from the shell (see potato latke waffles, page 227).

Here is the basic principle and technique of sous vide cooking, using a one-and-a-half-inch thick, one-pound rib eye steak cooked to medium-rare as an example:

The internal temperature of a rosy pink medium-rare steak is approximately 135°F. To get it to that temperature, your basic choices (excluding sous vide), are grilling it, pan-searing it, or oven-roasting it. These methods all use heat sources that range from 325°F to 500°F. That is roughly three to four times as hot as the internal temperature you want the steak to finish at. The problem for all cooks—even seasoned chefs—is in choosing the exact moment to take the steak off the heat source. Testing for doneness requires a lot of imperfect guesswork. Sure, you can use a meat thermometer, or poke, prod, or cut the steak to determine when it is done. But you are still guessing. On top of which, all proteins continue to cook after they have been removed from a heat source that is higher than the desired internal temperature. With sous vide, you set the water bath at the precise temperature you want the internal temperature of your steak to cook to, and the sous vide cooker will do the rest of the work for you.

Once the steak reaches that temperature, it will hold the same degree of doneness—even if you leave it in the water bath for an extra hour—because it can't become any more done unless the temperature of the water is raised.

How to Sous Vide a Steak

1. Season the steak lightly with salt and pepper.
2. Encase the steak in a plastic bag (either vacuum seal it in a heavy-duty plastic bag, or seal it in a conventional resealable freezer bag—which is not sealed under vacuum, but still does the trick). The bag protects the meat from the water and also traps the flavors and moisture inside.
3. Set the water temperature based on your desired degree of doneness. For our medium-rare steak, the magic temperature, as noted, is 135°F (for other degrees of doneness, check out the temperature charts that accompany every sous vide cooker).
4. Set the timer based on the charts that accompany your sous vide cooker. For our one-and-a-half-inch thick, one-pound steak, the cooking time is about two hours.
5. When the water comes to temperature, set the bag in the sous vide bath. The water will gently swaddle the steak. Slowly and gently, the internal temperature of the steak will rise from room or fridge temperature to 135°F (about one to two hours, depending on its thickness).
6. Once the steak is fully cooked, remove it from its water bath. At this point, the exterior has the color of a cadaver. Do not despair.
7. Transfer the steak in its bag to an ice bath until it is fully chilled to the touch.
8. After the steak has chilled, discard the bag and pat down the steak with paper towels to eliminate as much moisture as possible. This will enhance the crusting process.
9. Drizzle the steak with oil and reseason it lightly with salt and pepper.
10. Preheat a heavy pan or grill to high, then pan-sear or grill-sear the steak for about two minutes per side to create the desired crust. Because the steak started this final phase chilled, the exterior will become perfectly crusted before the interior has a chance to rise beyond the 135°F it was originally cooked to—which means the steak will hold its perfect rosy pink color *and* rise to a perfect serving temperature. Visualize the Ruth's Chris ads you see in in-flight magazines and you will get the idea.

Of course it is possible to achieve similar results on a grill or in a pan. But if you are grilling more than a few steaks at the same time, there are a host of variables working against you, including but not limited to small-but-significant variances in the size and thicknesses of each steak and the hot spots on your grill. Sous vide cooking sidesteps these inconsistencies and cooks each steak to perfection—each and every time. You can also sous vide in the afternoon or even a day or two before and refrigerate the steak in its sealed bag. All that is left to do at showtime is sear the steak—another reason that sous vide cooking is perfect for large gatherings.

Taming the Flame (How to Make Varying Levels of Heat Work for You)

One of the most significant differences between professional cooking and home cooking is that professional kitchens have big-ass stovetops—seemingly powered by rocket fuel—that generate insanely high temperatures. Chefs harness this heat to their advantage in a variety of ways by sautéeing, flambéeing, searing, reducing, and caramelizing—all in a fraction of the time it takes most home cooks to achieve the same results. Fortunately, there are many ways to skin a catfish, so if the thought of cooking with high heat fills you with terror, you have plenty of other options.

How to Flambé
(Without Burning Down the House)

- Clear the area of any flammable objects and move your fire extinguisher and a tight-fitting lid to within easy reach.
- Keep your hair out of range.
- Reduce any pan liquids until no more than two to three tablespoons remain before adding the alcohol.
- Move the pan away from the gas burners before adding the alcohol, so that the spattering particles don't ignite the contents before you are ready.
- If the flames burn too high, or for more than 10 seconds, cover the pan with a lid.

If you are willing to crank up the heat, you will be rewarded. Beyond speed, the prime benefits of high-heat cooking are that it can create a deep crust on proteins without overcooking the meat and add a pleasing exterior to greens and other vegetables without causing the interior to turn to mush.

Does this mean you should run out and throw your hard-earned cash dollars at the latest and greatest billion-BTU (British Thermal Unit) restaurant-style oven for your apartment or home? In a word, *no*. For the past 30 years, my home stove has been a 1950s-era O'Keefe and Merritt gas stove—and I don't get too many complaints about the food I knock out with it.

How you modulate the heat you already have is 50 percent of the battle. And having the confidence to stay the course as the food in your pan sizzles, smokes, and threatens to self-combust is the other 50 percent. Some of this can be learned quickly, and some of it takes time to experience and process through trial and error.

Get into the Trenches

I have never worked professionally in a restaurant kitchen, but I have *staged* in many. *Staging* is a French term for volunteering one's time in exchange for the opportunity to learn techniques, tips, and tricks from the prep cooks and chefs. If you love to cook and learn, and you relish the idea of getting into the trenches and experiencing the frenetic highs and lows of a professional kitchen, I highly recommend that you do a *stage* at least once in your life. If you are on the fence, read Bill Buford's *Heat: An Amateur's Adventures as a Kitchen Slave, Line Cook, Pasta-Maker, and Apprentice to a Dante-Quoting Butcher in Tuscany* before you commit.

The easiest way to find a *staging* opportunity is to talk to the owner, chef, or *maître d'* at a restaurant you frequent and ask if you can volunteer your time in the kitchen for a few days that fit both your schedules. Expect to start peeling potatoes, figuratively, if not literally. It's hard, often dull, repetitive work, but it exposes you to everything that goes on behind the curtain. Chefs are respectful of *stagiaires*, and if you demonstrate even a modicum of curiosity and choose your moment wisely, most will be happy to share their knowledge with you, often accompanied by a little taste to illustrate their point.

It's impossible to work in any professional kitchen for a few days without leaving with a few new tricks up your sleeve—and a renewed respect for kitchen workers.

How to Pan-Sear Proteins over High Heat

1. Take the protein out of the fridge and let it rise to room temperature.
2. Pat it dry with a paper towel to remove as much moisture as possible.
3. For large pieces of protein, like a steak or full chicken breast, oil and season the protein generously. For smaller proteins like shrimp or scallops, season the protein and then preheat the pan and add a couple of tablespoons of oil. Avoid overcrowding.
4. Let your heaviest pan heat up on the highest setting for two minutes. You will know it is ready when a few drops of water sprinkled on the surface "dance" and evaporate in a few seconds. (Adding protein to a pan as the pan is heating up will cause the pan's temperature to drop, and the protein will start its cooking process over a temperature that is moderate at best. This will cause the food to slowly steam in its own juices instead of quickly searing the exterior, resulting in a not-so-perfect crust.)
5. Add your proteins to the pan. If you haven't oiled the protein, add the oil to the pan first. Once in the pan, don't move the protein or you will compromise the crust. Cook for about 90 seconds per side, or until the crust is a deep dark brown, but not black and charred. If you are cooking a thick piece of protein, once it is crusted on both sides, reduce the temperature and cover the pan loosely with a lid, or transfer the pan to a preheated oven, until it is cooked to your desired degree of doneness. Seasoned chefs can test for doneness with the poke of a finger. For everyone else, a meat thermometer is a worthwhile investment.

How to Sauté Vegetables and Other Ingredients over High Heat

1. Choose a round-sided pan, if available, to help you toss the contents. Preheat your pan for two minutes, then add a couple tablespoons of oil, half oil/half butter, or clarified butter (see page 74).
2. Add your ingredients when the oil starts to sizzle. Avoid overcrowding.
3. Keep your food moving by flipping it in the pan or stirring it.
4. Continue cooking and turning the pan contents occasionally until they are slightly browned on the outside and cooked throughout. Sautéing times will vary depending on size and density.

Will you occasionally burn things when cooking over high temperatures? Of course you will! Everybody, including yours truly, loses the plot from time to time. But as you get comfortable cooking over higher heats, you will gain the confidence that comes from playing with fire.

Timing

When you add chopped garlic, shallots, and onions to a sauté pan along with other ingredients, be mindful of the timing. Adding them too early in the process will cause them to blacken and become bitter before the rest of the pan's contents have reached their desired degree of browning. Too late, and they end up undercooked and unpleasantly pungent. This is a learned lesson that you will keep adjusting over time.

DUCK SKIN CRACKLIN'S
for PEKING DUCK TACOS page 178

Cooking Fat Options and Their Smoke Points

When it comes to choosing what fat to use in your sauté pan, you have several choices. These are dictated by their smoke points, the flavors they impart, and their cost.

The "smoke point" is the temperature at which liquid fat starts to smoke and vaporize. When fat hits this point, it imparts undesirable flavors, and the molecules break down, creating unhealthful properties. Butter's smoke point is the lowest of all traditional cooking fats. After that, most oils traditionally used for cooking don't start smoking until 370°F. Unless you are blackening something in a pan intentionally, the temperature of a pan will rarely rise above 350°F.

At this temperature threshold, almost all cooking oils, including coconut, sesame, canola, and olive oil, will work. For super-high-temperature cooking, use peanut oil, soybean oil, or clarified butter (ghee).

As a general rule, gravitate to the less expensive versions of unrefined oils for cooking. These oils are expelled through a variety of mechanical processes, unlike their refined cousins, which are expelled with chemicals or heat. As I have noted elsewhere, all oils lose their subtleties when they are exposed to high temperatures. So save your expensive unrefined (and often unfiltered) oils to use at room temperature.

If you use your fancy oils to cook with, you will be burning oil *and* money.

100 percent oil Olive oil, peanut oil, safflower oil, and canola oil are my go-tos. But avocado oil, unrefined nut oils, and sesame oil all have a time and place where their distinctive characteristics can bring additional flavor to a dish.

100 percent butter Cooking in butter imparts a rich, nutty flavor. But when the temperature starts to reach 350°F, those beautiful flavors burn and turn bitter, turning butter from your friend into your frenemy. As a rule of thumb, only cook with straight butter when cooking over moderate heat.

50 percent butter/50 percent olive oil Combining olive oil and butter in the pan gives you the best of both worlds of flavor—at a slightly higher smoke point than for butter alone.

50 percent olive oil/50 percent vegetable oil Many restaurant supply stores sell a blend of olive and vegetable oil. These deliver mild olive flavor at a lower cost than pure olive oil. The advantages are mostly monetary, which is important for high-volume restaurants, but won't have a significant impact on your home shopping budget.

Clarified butter (ghee) If you melt a stick of butter in a pan over low heat, it will separate into a milky froth and a clear liquid. Clarified butter is the pure, clear butterfat with the milk solids and water removed. The resulting liquid (which will harden when chilled), has a nutty, buttery flavor, and burns at a much higher smoke point than regular butter. (See page 247 for how to make clarified butter.)

Harnessing Your Oven

Rack placement can make a big difference in an oven. If you want the top of your food to brown faster, place it on a higher rack. If you want the bottom to cook or brown faster, put it on a lower rack. When in doubt, split the difference and use the middle rack. Some ovens, particularly older ones, do not cook foods evenly. If this is your fate, or if you are cooking foods for a long time, rotate the pan 180° every 20 minutes or so (ideally when you have already opened the oven door to check on the food). If you are cooking on two racks at the same time, chances are that the food on each level will cook at different speeds and brown differently. For uniform results, swap levels and rotate each pan 180° every 20 minutes. Fan-assisted ovens, which have a built-in fan that circulates the heat, are designed to eliminate the need to rotate—but you should always do a visual check to make sure they are doing their job.

Stovetop Solutions

Electric stovetops can be frustrating when you need to toggle the heat quickly. HACK: an easy work-around for the length of time it takes to modulate the temperature is to set one burner at high and another at medium. When you need to knock back or increase the heat quickly, simply move your pot or pan between the two burners.

If you are frustrated by your electric stove, and installing a gas stove is not an option, consider switching to an induction stove top. Induction burners create heat through electromagnetic currents that run through the pan. They are capable of changing temperature in seconds. Because they do not use heat to heat up the pan, they help keep the kitchen cool—which is just one of the reasons they have become so popular in professional kitchens. The downside is that induction burners require pots and pans that are also magnetic, which means that you may need to replace some of your cookware. Cast iron, stainless steel, and carbon steel all work. To see if a particular pot or pan will work on an induction burner, simply hold a magnet to it (fridge magnets, cupboard magnets, etc.). If the magnet sticks, you are good to go.

Grilling: Direct vs. Indirect Heat

When it comes to grilling, you have two methods to choose from: direct and indirect. Choosing which method to use is largely dependent on the size of the protein or vegetable you are grilling.

Direct grilling involves grilling food directly over the heat source. This technique allows the food to develop a crust at the same time that it cooks through. As a rule of thumb, most food that cooks in 20 minutes or less (e.g. burgers, chops, or boneless pieces of chicken) should be grilled using the direct method.

Indirect grilling involves grilling food on a section of the grill that has no heat directly underneath it. This requires your grill to have a lid, which when closed turns the grill into a convection oven. For gas grills, this means keeping off the burners that are directly under the food you are grilling. For charcoal grills, this means either pushing all the coals to one side, or splitting them down the middle and pushing them to the sides of the grill, then placing the food over the section of the grill that is not over the coals. As a rule of thumb, most food that takes longer than 20 minutes to cook (e.g. a whole chicken, a roast, or a rack of ribs) should be grilled by the indirect method, or a combination of direct and indirect methods. When using the combination method, you can sear the food over direct heat, then reconfigure the grill to indirect heat and continuing cooking until the food is cooked through.

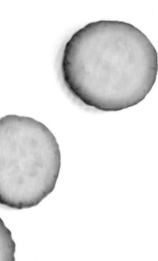

Trust

MENUology

Like any great discipline worth studying, the art of setting a menu requires some meaningful self-inquiry. Be honest about who you are, what you really care about, and what you are confident you can chew off in the available time.

Whether you are cooking a simple weeknight dinner or preparing for a dinner party, a successfully executed meal—like so much else in life—depends on preparation and forethought. Your investment in time and energy will differ according to the stakes, but in every case, a little advance planning before the clock starts ticking will pay big flavor dividends.

Read the Recipe!

How many times have been driving somewhere in your car and run into a huge delay, then kicked yourself for not checking Google Maps before you started? Recipes are like road maps, and reading them in advance can save you untold time and grief. Whether you are cooking a recipe from this cookbook or any other one, make sure you do the advance reconnaissance to avoid any roadblocks. The best time to change up a menu is before you start shopping.

- Cross-check the ingredients list against your ingredients on hand.
- Cross-check the cooking instructions against your kitchen tools.
- Cross-check the active and inactive cooking times against the amount of time you have available.

Be a Minimalist

The biggest mistake I see home cooks make is trying to overachieve. An aspirational menu with too many items exponentially increases the number of steps required—which makes it virtually impossible to give each step the attention it deserves. The win-win solution is simple: make a small number of dishes, but make each one memorable.

Be a Realist

Most fine dining establishments prepare their dishes "*a la minute*" (French for "made to order in the moment"). *A la minute* dishes are fired when ordered, and then served immediately. Cooking in the moment allows every component of a dish to work in concert with each other in their most pristine state—which leads to crispy skin, moist, tender flesh, and al dente toothsomeness. The harmonic convergence of optimally executed ingredients is part of what makes a true Flavorbomb so memorable.

With that noted, you're not running a restaurant, and it's not always possible or practical to prepare everything at the last minute. The most important part of menu planning is to be a realist. If you are still developing your confidence, or are more comfortable preparing everything in advance for any reason, select dishes that fare well if made ahead of time, like soups, stews, and roasts. Cold dishes make great starters since they can be plated ahead of time and won't suffer if your dinner gets off to a late start.

Sometimes a tiny sacrifice in quality (something I rarely champion), can minimize the effort required at showtime. I recently had an epiphany about the timing of my steak preparation. Whereas in the past, I always grilled my steaks just before serving them—which caused me to leave the table and spend 10

minutes at the grill—now I cook them just before my guests arrive. Then I tent them lightly with aluminum foil, and when the time arrives, I serve them warm. The small sacrifice in serving temperature translates into one less thing to worry about at showtime.

If you want to make Flavorbombs that involve a lot of last-minute attention to detail, like the ultimate french fries, or pan-seared fish with crispy skin, be prepared to spend some time in your kitchen after your guests arrive. If you have an open kitchen, it's possible to have it both ways. If not, call an architect or grab a sledgehammer.

Juxtapose Contrasting Flavors

One of the allures of Thai cuisine is that it's composed of sweet, spicy, sour, and salty (and sometimes bitter) ingredients that come together in tongue-twisting ways—often in a single dish like pad thai. Though not all dishes combine as many distinctive taste sensations, the concept of multiple flavor components is always important. It's the same principle behind why a humble cheeseburger, with its fatty beef and gooey, melted cheese, is often served with a slice of sour pickle.

When you plan a meal, walk yourself through all the ingredients in each course, *and* look at the overarching flavor palate of the entire meal. Make sure you are not duplicating too many flavors in any one course—or in the meal as a whole—or you will risk creating *palate fatigue* (just as it sounds). Also consider the balance of richness. If you have an extremely rich main, think about countering it with a simple green salad dressed with a racy, acidic dressing.

Juxtapose Contrasting Textures (e.g., Crunchy/Creamy/Airy)

Textures can add as much pleasing contrast as flavors. Unless you are cooking for a group of toothless toddlers, you don't want every component of your meal to be mushy. And unless you are cooking for a colony of beavers, you don't want all of your food to be crunchy. But a combination of the two textures, along with elements of creamy, crispy, juicy, delicate, and airy will create a palate-pleasing mouthfeel that will lead to a stimulating sensory experience. That's the logic behind the crunchy peanuts in your pad thai, and a juicy piece of pineapple in your *al pastor* taco.

Be Mindful of Portion Size

We all love to eat well, but when we eat too much, our satisfaction meter quickly swings from pleasure to displeasure. My motto is **serve memorable food, not memorable portions**, and I am always amazed at how much people appreciate *less*. The following tips for managing portions will keep everyone in the pleasure zone.

- Keep the pre-dinner appies and nibbles small. Guests usually arrive hungry and will eat whatever is put in front of them. Plan on enough to quell their hunger, but not so much that it spoils their appetite.
- Pace the meal. Leave some breathing space between courses.
- Use garnishes and artful presentation to make less appear like more on the plate.
- Have seconds available upon request.

Remember, you are not being stingy with your food, you are being generous with your concern and mindful of your guests' ultimate state of pleasure.

Think Like an Artist

Creating an artfully presented plate is easier than it may seem—especially if you put on your artist's goggles at the same time that you plan your meal. After you have set the menu, picture the sizes, shapes, and colors of the main food elements on the plate, as well as the plate itself. Does the food presentation have the potential to be visually appealing, or will it look uninspired, unbalanced, or monochromatic? Is each food component being presented in its most visually appealing state? If there is room for improvement, this is the easiest stage at which to make changes to your shopping list.

If you need more color contrast, consider the following additions or substitutions:

- Swap out similar ingredients. If your green pepper will blend in with other greens on the plate, replace it with one that is orange, yellow, or red.
- Add a garnish that connects to the flavors on the plate.
- Add a colorful sauce.
- Add a sprinkle of edible flower petals around the rim of the plate.

Courage and Confidence

"The only real stumbling block is fear of failure. In cooking you've got to have a what-the-hell attitude."

—Julia Child

As noted in my opening manifesto, the key to elevating your game is building your courage and self-confidence. By this, I mean developing the resolve to:

- Season with strength and purpose.
- Suppress your inner voice of restraint.
- Trust yourself to mix, match, and substitute ingredients.
- Taste and adjust flavors on the fly.
- Punt when all else fails.

Developing courage and confidence doesn't happen overnight. As Julia Child also famously said, "No one is born a cook; one learns by doing."

Realistically, the only way to up your game is to learn by failing. If you don't allow yourself to overcook, undercook, drop things (even fully cooked chickens), forget to add ingredients, forget a side dish in the oven, over-season, under-season, cut yourself, burn yourself, and grate your knuckles to the bone—your skills and your confidence will never improve.

Becoming a confident cook also involves developing the instinct to make substitutions when you are missing an ingredient, additions when a dish tastes as if it's lacking a particular dimension, or modifications when you want to adjust a dish to suit your personal tastes.

Familiarizing yourself with the flavor profile and characteristics of the ingredients you cook with will help you think logically about what to add when you realize midway through a recipe that you are missing an ingredient—or when you discover that an ingredeint you have has spoiled. Sometimes an option will be a close fit (peanut butter in place of cashew butter), and other times it will be close enough (romaine lettuce in your ramen noodles in place of bok choy). When all else fails, *wing it*. If there isn't a perfectly suitable solution,

there is always a salvageable one. Remember, it's only rock 'n' roll, and regardless of what happens, the show must go on.

Whether you are testing recipes or making them for the hundredth time, things will inevitably go wrong. Never surrender and never apologize. Just reframe. If your roasted cauliflower comes out a little over-crisped, rename it "blackened cauliflower," put on a zydeco playlist, and call it "Cajun night." And if the soufflé falls, call it a cheesy Dutch pancake.

The outcome of any recipe depends on the sum total of all the tiny decisions you make along the way, and the most important of these are the adjustments you make in the moment (which come from experience and are often influenced by the lessons of previous disasters). As you gain the confidence to make changes on the fly, add your own touches, and take ownership of your successes and failures, you will begin to notice a difference you can taste. That confidence will also help you build quick, satisfying, spontaneous meals with minimal fanfare from whatever is available.

When you get there, you will have arrived at a watershed moment in your evolution as a cook—as well as the beginning of the next phase of your journey.

The Flavorbomb Checklist

Cooking is an art *and* a science. To complicate matters, it's an amorphous art form with constantly changing variables, some of which are based on scientific principles. A lot of what makes or breaks a meal happens in the heat of the moment. Unfortunately, as the flames lap against the bottom of your pan and the contents sizzle, it's hard to concentrate on anything other than trying not to burn the joint down. The following fundamentals are common to almost any dish. Thinking about them before the food starts flying will help you focus on the important stuff.

- ○ Make your workspace work for you.
- ○ Plan a realistic menu.
- ○ Read the recipe.
- ○ Make sure you have the time, ingredients, and gear required.
- ○ Understand the techniques required beforehand.
- ○ Shop like you mean it.
- ○ Set up your mise en place.
- ○ Allez, courage.
- ○ Build layers of flavor and texture.

- ○ Taste as you cook.
- ○ Brown things like you mean it.
- ○ Season with wild abandon.
- ○ Salt carefully and meaningfully.
- ○ Balance your acids.
- ○ Taste, reseason, taste.
- ○ Finish with a flourish.
- ○ Heat (or chill) your plates.
- ○ Plate like an artist.

Part 2
Addictive, bombastic, life-affirming flavorbombs

Now that you have read the first part of this book, you possess a new set of superpowers that make you a formidable threat to the evils of bland food. The tricks, tips, and hacks I have shared with you will help you build layer upon layer of flavor, and up the pleasure quotient of anything you cook. With those tools in your back pocket, the following collection of my favorite flavorbombs is yours to slice, dice, sauté, sear, fry, flambé, caramelize, deglaze, emulsify, braise, roast, toast, and crust. Each dish has been chosen because it echoes my "go big or go home" approach, and screams with flavor, texture, and love.

Life is short. Cook and eat like you mean it.

Pre-show Warm-ups

(Nibbles)

PIRI PIRI PIRI
page 242

CHIMICHURRI
page 244

KETCHUP
page 241

HARISSA
page 240

Spanish-Style Rosemary Almonds

I have a simple criterion for sizing up a restaurant in the first 10 minutes. It goes like this: the quality and attention to detail paid to whatever hits the table first—be it any form of bread and butter, a dip, or a little *amuse-bouche*—is a bellwether for everything else that follows. Rarely does this test fail me. I was served these rosemary-infused almonds many years ago at a winery restaurant in Spain's Alicante region. As soon as a small bowl of the nuts was set down on the table, my expectations were raised. The crunchy roasted almonds, crispy fried rosemary tips, and generous dusting of flaky sea salt did not disappoint. Not surprisingly, the meal that followed was equally inspired, and once again my restaurant litmus test was validated.

Time
< 30 minutes

Yield
Serves 8 to 12

Liquidity
Oloroso sherry (a surprisingly approachable fortified sherry with oxidized aromatics) is a classic tapas bar pairing

Plan-Overs
Keeps for several days at room temperature in an airtight container

10 generous sprigs rosemary
3 Tbsp olive oil
1 pound raw whole almonds
Salt (ideally a flaky sea salt such as Maldon)

Cut the top ½ inch or so off the rosemary sprigs and set aside. Stem the remainder.

Heat the oil in a medium heavy-bottomed pan over low heat (this is an excellent use for a cast-iron pan since you can also use it to serve). When the oil heats up, add all the rosemary, including the tops. Stir for 60 seconds, then add the almonds.

Cook for 20 watchful minutes, stirring frequently, or until the almonds darken slightly in color, but don't overbrown. Let cool and sprinkle generously with salt. Cheat the rosemary tops to the top.

NOTE: when almonds are warm, they are soft and chewy; as they return to room temperature, they regain their familiar pleasing crunch.

SPANISH-
STYLE
ROSEMARY
ALMONDS
page 88

SUGAR AND
SPICE PECANS
page 90

CHAI
CHICKPEAS
page 91

Sugar and Spice Pecans *Photo on page 89*

These curious candied nuts will jump-start any cocktail or dinner party. They are delicious on their own or as an addition to any cheese tray—especially one featuring blue cheese. If you package them in a Mason jar, they make a fabulous host gift for less than the price of a cheap bottle of wine. What separates these candied nuts from all others is a simple hack that employs a beaten egg white to do all the hard work for you. Say what?

Here's how it works: the egg white is whipped until it can stand up on its own. Then it's tossed with the nuts, which are in turn tossed with a mixture of sugar and spice. As the nuts bake at a low temperature, the beaten egg white puffs up and hardens like a meringue (which, not coincidentally, is made from beaten egg whites), and the sugar melts into it. As the nuts cool, so does the sugar. The result is a gloriously roasted nut, swaddled in an airy, crispy, sweet, and savory crust. Baking at its simplest. Candied nuts at their finest. Booyah!

Time
30 minutes

Yield
Serves 8 to 12

Liquidity
A smooth, sipping Bourbon

Plan-Overs
Keeps for a couple of weeks in a tightly sealed container (but only if nobody knows where they are hidden)

½ pound pecan or walnut halves
⅓ cup brown sugar
⅔ cup white sugar
¼ tsp salt
¼ tsp cayenne pepper
1 tsp ground cinnamon
1 egg white, at room temperature

Preheat the oven to 300°F.

Remove any nut *fragments* and save them for a salad, leaving just the full halves. (Fragments will not result in the proper nut-to-coating ratio.)

In a medium bowl, mix together the brown sugar, white sugar, salt, cayenne, and cinnamon. Reserve.

In a large bowl, beat the egg white until stiff. Add the pecans and stir thoroughly so that every nut is completely coated. Sprinkle the nuts with a ¼ cup of the sugar mixture and stir until evenly coated. Add another ¼ cup and stir again, repeating until you have incorporated all of it.

Line a cookie sheet with parchment paper. Add the nuts by the handful, then one by one, turn them flat side down and separate them so that there is at least ¼ inch of breathing space around each nut. Bake for about 20 minutes, or until the nuts are puffed up and a deep golden-brown color. Remove from oven and let cool completely before removing from the tray.

Chai Chickpeas *Photo on page 89*

The secret to these crunchy chickpeas is the combination of chai spices, salt, and sugar. The three components play off each other to create a salty, sweet, spiced treat with a mouthfeel that is reminiscent of a sophisticated corn nut.

Chai spice, much like curry, is a proprietary blend of spices common to the Indian pantry. It changes from chef to chef and region to region. Chai spice blends can include as many as 10 individual spices. (When black tea is added to the spice blend, it becomes chai tea.) As I was developing this recipe and testing various blends, I called Jagdish Gill, the humble chef-owner of Karahi King, an Indian restaurant in Prince George, BC. I developed a love affair with "PG"—which is home to some eccentric personalities, great cycling, and a large population of black bears—after being invited to judge a live, *Chopped*-style cooking competition among the local chefs. Jagdish is the reigning champion. In keeping with her modest approach to everything, Jagdish suggested a thoughtfully chosen mix of just four spices—which, not surprisingly, turned out to be a winning combination.

Time
<15 minutes + soaking (fried method) and <45 minutes (oven method)

Yield
Serves 6 to 8

Chai Spice
1 tsp fennel seeds*
1 tsp cardamom seeds (out of their pods)*
3 whole star anise pods*
1 tsp ground cinnamon*
1 Tbsp sugar
1 tsp salt

Fried Method
1 cup dried chickpeas
Peanut or vegetable oil for frying (before frying see Deep Fry Basics, page 52)

Oven Method
Two 14-ounce cans chickpeas
2 Tbsp neutral oil

In a pan over medium heat, toast the fennel, cardamom, and star anise for about 90 seconds, or until fragrant. Let cool, then transfer to a mortar and pestle or a spice grinder and grind. Transfer the ground spices to a bowl and mix in the cinnamon, sugar, and salt. Reserve.

FRIED METHOD Soak the chickpeas in water for 6 hours. Drain off the water and pat the chickpeas dry on a clean dishtowel.

Preheat a deep fryer, or fill a tall, heavy, medium pot one-third full of oil. Heat the oil to 350°F.

Fry the chickpeas for about 6 minutes, stirring occasionally, or until they are light gold in color and crispy on the outside (they will get a bit crunchier throughout as they cool down). Remove with a kitchen spider or a slotted spoon and transfer to a bowl lined with paper towels. Dredge the excess oil with the paper towel.

OVEN METHOD Preheat the oven to 350°F. Rinse off the packing liquids and pat the chickpeas dry on a clean dishtowel. Transfer to a sheet pan lined with parchment paper and bake for 15 minutes.

Transfer the chickpeas to a large bowl. Add the oil and toss until the chickpeas are evenly coated in oil. Return the chickpeas to the sheet pan and bake for about 15 more minutes, or until crispy/crunchy.

TO SERVE Transfer the chickpeas back to the bowl and sprinkle all of the spice mixture overtop, tossing to incorporate. Transfer to a serving dish.

*NOTE: For a simpler variation-on-the-theme, replace these spices with 1½ tablespoons of garam masala.

Caramelized Cauliflower Florets

There is no better example of caramelization (see page 62) than this simple three-ingredient recipe for roasted cauliflower. Ever since I christened it "cauliflower popcorn" and started serving it in popcorn containers, I have become the Pied Piper of Cauliflower, trailed by a gaggle of devotees. Everywhere I go, I sing its praises. At first, I am met with skepticism. After all, who would think that kids could learn to love a cruciferous vegetable? But it's true. Through the miracle of caramelization, a basic off-the-rack head of cauliflower can miraculously be transformed into sweet, lip-smackin' candybombs that the kids in your world—and you—will devour.

Time
75 minutes

Yield
Serves 4 to 6 as a nibble

Advance Work
Raw cauliflower can be precut and refrigerated for up to 2 days in an airtight bag. With minimal sacrifice, cauliflower can be cooked earlier in the day and reheated in a preheated 450°F oven for 10 minutes

Liquidity
Almost any wine will be attracted to these roasted jewels

Zero Waste
Cauliflower leaves, as well as the trimmed and sliced core and stems, can be used in a Free-ttata (page 236), or in stir-fries

1 head cauliflower
4 Tbsp olive oil
1 Tbsp salt

Set the rack in the top third of the oven and preheat to 435°F.

Cut out the cauliflower's core and thick stems. Trim the remaining cauliflower into florets the size of golf balls.

In a large bowl, add the cauliflower, olive oil, and salt. Toss thoroughly.

Spread the cauliflower on a baking sheet (lined with parchment paper, if available, for easy cleanup).

Roast on the center rack of your oven for 1 hour, turning every 15 minutes, or until most of each floret has become deep golden brown and crispy. (That's the caramelization process converting the dormant natural sugars into sweetness.) Serve immediately.

Fried Baby Artichokes with Aioli

Baby artichokes are conventional artichokes that are picked early in the springtime. They can also be purchased frozen or packed in oil. I'm always inspired to make this crispy, tender appy in the spring when the first baby artichokes show up at farmers' markets, but in any incarnation, it's a special treat.

Time
45 minutes (less if you are starting with frozen or jarred artichoke hearts)

Advance Work
Aioli can be made up to a day in advance

Yield
Serves 4 as an appetizer

Liquidity
The gooseberry notes and lively acidity of a New Zealand sauvignon blanc will play off the richness of the aioli and the deep-fried crust of the artichoke

2 Tbsp lemon juice

12 baby artichokes (if fresh baby artichokes are unavailable, use 12 ounces frozen artichoke hearts, or 16 ounces jarred artichoke hearts—often grilled—packed in olive oil)

6 Tbsp flour

2 Tbsp cornstarch

Olive oil for frying—but not the fancy stuff (before frying see Deep Fry Basics on page 52)

Salt

½ cup aioli (page 243)

FOR FROZEN ARTICHOKES Thaw and quarter them (if they haven't already been quartered.)

FOR ARTICHOKE HEARTS STORED IN OIL Quarter them (if they haven't already been quartered), pat them down on paper towels to remove the excess oil.

FOR FRESH BABY ARTICHOKES Fill a medium bowl halfway with water and add lemon juice. Pull off the tougher outer leaves from the artichoke until all that remains are the pale-green, tender inner leaves. Cut off the top ½ inch of the artichoke. Then use a paring knife to peel off the outer skin of the stem and the shoulder (just below where the leaves start) and the discolored bottom bit of the stem. Quarter the artichoke from the top cut end all the way through the stem. Reserve in water. When you are ready to fry, use a strainer to drain off the water. Shake off as much water as possible.

TO FLOUR AND FRY In a medium bowl, mix together the flour and cornstarch, then add the artichokes. Toss thoroughly, then transfer back to the strainer and shake off the excess flour.

Preheat a deep fryer, or fill a tall, heavy, medium pot one-third full of oil. Heat the oil to 350°F.

When the oil is ready, fry about 12 artichoke quarters at a time for about 3 minutes, or until they are golden brown and the edges are browned. Remove with a slotted spoon and place them on a paper towel to absorb the excess oil.

Skim any wayward flour bits from the oil. Toggle the heat so that it is 350°F again, and repeat with next batch.

Season generously with salt and serve with the aioli.

LAVASH CRACKERS
page 98

AVOCADO AND BUTTER
BEAN HUMMUS
page 99

SMOKED SALMON
LAVASH CRUSTINI
page 98

"Homemade" Lavash Cracker *Photo on page 96*

This simple recipe is straight from the Kitchen Hack Hall of Fame. Lavash is a soft, thin, inexpensive flatbread that can be found in Middle-Eastern stores and many grocery stores. Straight from the package it is soft, malleable, and somewhat confusing to the uninitiated. But when you brush it generously with oil, sprinkle it with a blend of seeds and spices, and bake it for 5 minutes, it becomes so addictive that after your first bite you will immediately contemplate quitting your day job and going into the cracker business. Lavash crackers are at their finest when served alongside Middle-Eastern dips, or as a super-thin and crispy base for any appetizer traditionally served on a crostini.

Time
< 15 minutes

Yield
Makes 1 cracker (enough for 2 people as an accompaniment for a dip); the spice blend makes about 6 tablespoons (enough for 3 lavash)

Plan-Overs
Lavash Spice Blend stores very well, but trust me, you will use it up fast

Lavash Spice Blend
1½ Tbsp white sesame seeds
1½ Tbsp black sesame seeds
1½ tsp poppy seeds
1½ tsp dried minced garlic
1½ tsp dried minced onion
¾ tsp salt

Lavash Cracker
One 10-by-14-inch sheet of lavash (sometimes they are twice this length)
3 Tbsp olive oil

In a small bowl, mix the seeds, spices, and salt.

Set the rack in the middle position in the oven and preheat to 400°F.

Brush lavash generously with the olive oil, then sprinkle with 2 tablespoons of the spice blend (or use your favorite Middle Eastern spice or seed blend (za'atar, baharat, ras el hanout . . .).

Place the lavash directly on rack and bake for 4–5 watchful minutes, or until it is light brown and crispy with a wee bit of charring on the edges. (If you are grilling, you can also grill the lavash over medium direct heat (see page 75) for about 3 minutes.) Remove from the oven and let cool.

Smoked Salmon Lavash Crostini *Photo on page 97*

This is a variation of the smoked salmon pizza from my book *Pizza on the Grill* (co-authored with my pal Elizabeth Karmel). The same toppings on a crispy lavash deliver more crunch for your brunch.

Time
< 15 minutes

Yield
Serves 4 as an appetizer

Liquidity
An unoaked Alsace Pinot Blanc

1 baked lavash (see "Homemade" Lavash Cracker, above)
One 5-ounce package garlic and herb Boursin, or whipped cream cheese, at room temperature
8 ounces cold-smoked salmon, or gravlax, or lox
Zest of 1 lemon
Fresh dill (optional)

Spread the Boursin overtop the whole baked lavash. Top with the salmon and finish with the zest and dill. Cut into 8 squares. (Be forewarned: the lavash will shatter a bit when cut.)

Avocado and Butter Bean Hummus *Photo on page 96*

I adapted this California-influenced hummus recipe from a Los Angeles restaurant that is best left uncredited for its own sake. The main differences between the original recipe and my own interpretation is that I replaced the chickpeas (which can be slightly vegetal when uncooked), with butter beans, and eliminated ¾ cup (not a typo) of olive oil—with virtually no sacrifice! The result is a creamy dip that's naturally rich.

¼ cup olive oil, divided + extra for drizzling

4 garlic cloves, sliced finely

One 14-ounce can butter beans or navy beans, drained

2 tsp Dijon mustard

1 avocado

3 Tbsp tahini

Zest of 1 lemon + ¼ cup lemon juice

Salt and pepper

2 Tbsp crushed pistachios

1 Tbsp finely chopped mint, or, in a pinch, parsley

1 Tbsp pomegranate seeds (*totally* optional)

2 baked lavash, broken into bite-size pieces (see "Homemade" Lavash Crackers, page 98)

In a sauté pan over medium heat, add 2 tablespoons of the olive oil and the garlic. Cook for about 3 minutes, or until the garlic softens. Pull it off the burner before it browns.

In the bowl of a food processor, add the garlic and oil from the pan, beans, mustard, avocado, tahini, and lemon juice. Purée. While puréeing, stream in the remaining 2 tablespoons olive oil. Season to taste with salt and pepper.

Finish with pistachios, mint, pomegranate seeds, lemon zest, salt, pepper, and a generous drizzle of oil. Serve with lavash pieces.

Time
15 minutes

Yield
Serves 6 as an appetizer (about 2 cups)

Liquidity
The Californification of this hummus calls for a big Cali Chardonnay to match its decadence

Just-the-Good-Stuff Guacamole
with House-Made Tortilla Chips

Hass avocados, with their bumpy, reptilian skin, are ubiquitous these days—and for good reason. The oily richness of the fruit requires very little in the way of adornment, as evidenced by the simplicity of avocado toast. When it comes to guacamole, in my humble California-based, avocado-obsessed opinion, too many ingredients can actually hijack it, thereby denying you the pleasurable mouthfeel of the Hass's creamy flesh.

Another thing that can undermine guacamole is bad—or stale—tortilla chips, which in my experience are far more common than good tortilla chips. If you are able to find quality corn tortillas, the chips you can make from them, whether fried or baked, will add a pleasing crunch to your munch.

Guacamole

2 ripe Hass avocados

½ cup fresh cilantro, stems removed, chopped finely

¼–½ tsp ground chipotle, or a pinch of cayenne powder

2 Tbsp freshly squeezed lime or lemon juice

3 scallions, sliced finely

Salt and pepper

Fried Tortilla Chips

Six 6-inch best available corn tortillas (other sizes will work too—always go with the best-quality option)

Peanut or vegetable oil for frying (before frying, see Deep Fry Basics on page 52)

Baked Tortilla Chips

2 Tbsp neutral oil

1 Tbsp freshly squeezed lime juice

Salt, or Tajín Clásico chili lime seasoning (available in many grocery stores)

Six 6-inch best available corn tortillas (other sizes will work too—always go with the best-quality option)

FOR THE GUACAMOLE Slice the avocados in half and discard the skin and pit. In a bowl, add all the ingredients. Blend with a fork, but leave the mixture somewhat chunky. Taste for salt and acid and adjust if desired.

FOR FRIED TORTILLA CHIPS Cut the tortillas as you would slice a pizza, into 6 wedges. Preheat a deep fryer, or fill a tall, heavy, medium pot one-third full of oil. Heat the oil to 350°F.

Drop 12 tortilla wedges into the oil and stir occasionally for about 90 seconds, or until the chips just begin to color and are crispy. Remove the chips with a slotted spoon and drain on paper towels. Sprinkle immediately with salt.

Allow the oil to return to 350°F, then repeat with the next batch.

FOR BAKED TORTILLA CHIPS Preheat the oven to 375°F.

In a small bowl, mix the oil and lime juice. Brush each tortilla on both sides with the oil and lime mixture and sprinkle with salt. Stack the tortillas and cut through them as you would slice a pizza, into 6 wedges.

Line a sheet pan with parchment paper. Spread the tortilla wedges on the sheet pan, without overlapping, and bake for about 8 minutes, or until golden brown. Let cool before serving.

Time
< 30 minutes

Yield
Serves 4 as an appetizer

Advance Work
The guac can be made earlier in the day. Cover it with plastic wrap pressed directly onto the surface. Chips can be made earlier in the day, but are best when served straight out of the fryer or oven

Liquidity
A margarita, made with fresh lime juice and Mescal, will add a bacon-like smokiness to your guacamole experience

Blue Cheese Bruschetta
with Honey and Cracked Black Pepper

Blue cheese is divisive. Those who do like it tend to love its pungent aromas, creamy texture, and veins of blue mold. That cauldron of characteristics, in combination with the sweetness of honey, the odorific pleasures of raw garlic, the bite of freshly cracked black pepper, and the texture of a well-toasted slice of rustic bread make this easy-to-assemble appy a very heady experience.

Time
< 15 minutes

Yield
Serves 4 as an appetizer

Liquidity
Ice cider is an apple-based version of Sauternes, the botrytis-affected dessert wine from France. This sophisticated, adult-friendly apple "juice" is a heavenly pairing with blue cheese

- 4 thick slices rustic country-style or sourdough bread
- 2 garlic cloves
- 4 Tbsp walnut oil, hazelnut oil, or best available olive oil
- 8 ounces Saint Agur, or another creamy blue cheese
- ½ cup best available honey
- Coarsely ground pepper (either adjust your grinder to a coarser grind, or grind a few peppercorns in a mortar and pestle)

Toast your bread in a panini maker, over a grill, in a toaster, or in a toaster oven until it is very brown and crispy.

Immediately after toasting the bread, rub a garlic clove over the entire surface of one side. Each slice should use up about a quarter to a third of a clove. (Be careful: when the garlic meets the toast's hot surface, it will create fumes that will sting your eyes.)

Generously drizzle oil over each slice. Then schmear each slice generously with cheese. Generously drizzle honey over top and finish with the pepper. Slice the bruschetta and serve immediately.

Grilled Oaxacan Shrimp
with Blistered Jalapeño Salsa Verde

Many moons ago, I joined a group of chefs on a culinary excursion through the state of Oaxaca, Mexico, led by Susana Trilling, a respected authority on the region's cuisine. This addictive shrimp dish is an homage to the chilis of Oaxaca. The smoky, spicy shrimp and the brightly flavored blistered jalapeño salsa verde deliver a one-two punch that will have you reaching for an icy beer—and then for seconds.

Time
30 minutes

Yield
Serves 4 to 6 as an appetizer

Advance Work
The dry rub can be made ahead and stored in a sealed jar. Make extra—it lasts almost indefinitely. The shrimp can be peeled and deveined up to a day in advance

Liquidity
These spicy shrimp cry for the light, refreshing crisp carbonated kick of an icy Mexican beer

Dry Rub
½ Tbsp ground chipotle chili
1 Tbsp ancho chili powder
½ Tbsp garlic powder
½ Tbsp dried Mexican oregano
½ Tbsp dried thyme
½ tsp ground cumin
½ tsp ground coriander
2 tsp salt
½ tsp pepper

Shrimp
1½ pounds uncooked 16/20 count shrimp (ideally wild), or whatever size shrimp you prefer, shelled and deveined
2 Tbsp neutral oil + extra 2 Tbsp if pan searing
2 limes for serving, quartered

Blistered Jalapeño Salsa Verde Dipping Sauce
1 Tbsp neutral oil
5 jalapeño chilis, stemmed and seeded
¼ white onion, roughly chopped
3 garlic cloves
1 cup fresh cilantro, lightly packed
½ tsp cumin
½ tsp salt
1 Tbsp white vinegar

FOR THE DRY RUB combine all the ingredients in a small bowl. Reserve.

FOR THE SHRIMP in a medium bowl, add the shrimp, dry rub, and oil. Toss to thoroughly cover the shrimp. Reserve.

FOR THE SALSA VERDE in a large sauté pan over high heat, add the oil. When oil is hot, add the jalapeños, onion, and garlic. Sauté for 5 minutes, tossing frequently, until blistered and toasted on the outside. Let cool. Transfer the pan contents to a blender. Add the cilantro, cumin, salt, vinegar, and ⅓ cup water. Purée until very smooth. Reserve.

GRILL VERSION Preheat the grill to direct high heat. Grill the shrimp for 1 to 2 minutes per side, or until the shrimp are marked and no longer translucent. Serve with the salsa verde and lime quarters.

PAN VERSION Open a window to avoid setting off your smoke alarm. Heat a large sauté pan over high heat. When the pan is smoking hot, add the oil. Wait a beat, then add as many shrimp as the pan will accommodate without overlapping. Cook for about one minute per side, or until the shrimp are no longer translucent. Serve with the salsa verde and lime quarters.

Japanese Fried Chicken
with Soy-Ginger-Wasabi Dipping Sauce

I learned how to make these succulent little chicken bombs at a small, family-run *izakaya* outside of Tokyo, while I was there taping an episode of my TV series *World's Weirdest Restaurants*. Izakayas are casual Japanese pubs that serve snacks designed to entice their patrons to drink more. They are everywhere, and for the most part, they are quite similar. What distinguished this particular izakaya from the rest, and made it of interest to my show, was the fact that it was home to a family of macaque monkeys that served beer to the patrons (yes, real monkeys—and yes, really).

In case beer-serving monkeys weren't enough of a hook, their fried chicken, known as *karaage*, was one of the most memorable dishes I tasted on the whole trip. Karaage is an izakaya staple—and for good reason. As chefs in all parts of the world know, the chicken thigh is the moistest, richest part of the bird. Add the sweet, sake-based marinade, the crunch of the thin, crispy coating, and the nasal-passage-clearing wasabi dip, and you have a Flavorbomb that almost literally explodes in your mouth.

4 boneless chicken thighs, ideally skin on

⅔ cup soy sauce, divided

⅓ cup mirin (a sweet Japanese cooking wine) + 1 Tbsp for dipping sauce

⅓ cup sake

3 Tbsp ginger, freshly grated, ideally on a Microplane, divided

¼ tsp wasabi paste

Peanut or vegetable oil for frying (before frying, see Deep Fry Basics on page 52)

1 cup potato starch (available in Asian stores and health food stores), or cornstarch

Sesame seeds for garnish (optional)

Green onion, sliced, for garnish (optional)

Cut the chicken (skin, fat, and all) into ¾-inch cubes. To a medium bowl or resealable plastic bag, add ⅓ cup each of soy sauce, mirin, and sake, and 2 tablespoons ginger. Add the chicken, toss with the marinade, and refrigerate for a minimum of 1 hour but ideally 3 to 24 hours.

FOR DIPPING SAUCE In a small bowl, mix the remaining soy sauce and mirin, the wasabi, and the remaining ginger. Reserve for dipping.

Preheat a deep fryer, or fill a tall, heavy, medium pot one-third full of oil. Heat the oil to 350°F.

While the oil is heating, drain off the chicken marinade. To a medium bowl, add the potato starch. Add the chicken a few pieces at a time and toss until each piece is well covered. Shake off the excess starch. Transfer the pieces to a drying rack or a plate and let rest for 10 minutes.

Divide the chicken into 2 batches and fry the first batch for 3 minutes, or until golden brown and crispy on the outside, and cooked throughout. Remove the chicken with a slotted spoon and drain on paper towels. Repeat with the second batch.

Sprinkle with sesame seeds and green onion slices, and serve with the dipping sauce.

Time
30 minutes + marinating time

Yield
Serves 4 to 6 as an appetizer, or 2 as a meal

Liquidity
A Japanese draft beer (monkey optional) and/or the rest of that bottle of sake

Papaya-Marinated Grilled Chicken Wings

Most of the chicken wings served in bars are deep fried, then tossed with a mixture of butter and Louisiana hot sauce, or some other flavored concoction that usually comes premixed. I still appreciate them from time to time, but these days my palate craves more complexity.

Time
1 hour + marinating time

Yield
Serves 4 to 6 as an appetizer or 2 as an entrée

Liquidity
The tang of a hoppy, citrusy craft beer will optimize the sweetness of the papaya

Zero Waste
If the wings come attached with a pointy tip section, cut away the tips and save them for stock.

20 chicken wings
2 tsp salt
1 small papaya (about 1 cup when seeded, peeled, and chopped)
6 garlic cloves, minced
6 birds-eye chilis, or 2 jalapeño chilis, or 1 serrano chili
1 tsp ground cinnamon
2 Tbsp honey
¼ cup soy sauce
2 Tbsp toasted sesame oil
2 Tbsp freshly squeezed lime juice

NOTE: These wings are marinated and basted with a sauce made from fresh papaya, a tropical fruit known for its natural tenderizing properties. As the natural enzymes in the papaya tenderize the wing meat, the fruit also imparts a distinctive sweetness, which in combination with honey, balances the heat of the chilis in the marinade. The cinnamon, soy, and sesame oil all add their own characteristics.

Grilling (or baking) the wings instead frying them allows the natural sugars that coat the chicken skin to caramelize, coating the wings with a pleasing layer of sweetness and texture.

Separate the wing at the joint that divides the flat section and the drumette. Using a paring knife, cut around the skinny end of the drumette bone just above the knuckle, slicing through the meat and tendon. Scrape the meat up toward the fat end of the drumette, creating a ball-like shape at that end. (There is no need to be precise; the cooking process will complete your artistry.)

Season the wings generously with salt, then transfer them to a large resealable plastic bag. Reserve.

To a blender, add the papaya, garlic, chilis, cinnamon, honey, soy sauce, sesame oil, and lime juice. Purée. Transfer the purée to the chicken bag, force out the air, and seal. Massage the package, then refrigerate for 2 hours, but not much longer or the chicken will over-tenderize. Massage the package again after one hour.

GRILL METHOD Preheat the grill to medium indirect heat—about 400°F. Place the wings over the section of the grill with no direct heat. Close the lid and cook for about 40 minutes, or until the juices in the fattest section of the wings run clear when poked with a fork. Baste generously with marinade after 15 minutes. Wings come in all sizes, and consequently the cooking times will vary. Keep a watchful eye on them as they grill or cook and adjust the time accordingly.

OVEN METHOD Preheat the oven to 425°F. Set the chicken on a rack over a sheet pan (ideally lined with parchment paper for easy cleanup), or on the pan, and bake for about 35 minutes, until the juices in the fattest section of the wings run clear when poked with a fork. Baste generously with marinade after 15 minutes. Wings come in all sizes, so the cooking times will vary. Keep a watchful eye on them, and adjust time accordingly.

Opening acts

(Soups & Salads)

Thai Coconut Corn Soup
(Rock Star Version)

This cold summertime corn soup is a cinch to make thanks to one of the great time-saving cheats of Thai cooking: fresh, store-bought curry paste. With all of its complex, spicy Thai flavors, this soup is also, as I recently discovered, rock star kryptonite.

While developing the recipe, I was totally fixated on the curry paste and how its unique blend of spices played off the sweet creaminess of the fresh corn and the coconut milk. After some trial and error, I landed on a combination I was extremely pleased with. When I transcribed the recipe and reviewed the ingredients, I realized to my surprise that I had unintentionally created a soup that was vegan. That is, after I discovered a vegan curry paste at my local Thai grocery store.

So as one is wont to do in Hollywood, I decided to invite Moby, the musician and celebrated vegan, for dinner. Fortuitously, because of my formative years in the music business, he was only one degree of separation away from my dinner table. Two weeks later, Moby was in the house—albeit not quite sure why he had been invited. Play is one of my desert island albums, and it was an honor to cook for the man who wrote, produced, and performed such a timeless soundscape. Moby is unassuming and painfully shy—and at the same time as fascinating and eccentric as one could hope for. He said some nice things about the soup, but to be honest, I wasn't sure if he really liked it, or was just being polite in the company of strangers.

The answer took some time to reveal itself . . . Two years ago, Diplo, the DJ/producer/artist/star-maker, moved across the street from me. Not the normal "across the street" that in Los Angeles parlance usually means a few blocks away, but so close that I can see every pixel on his massive HD screen from my living room window. From the daily flurry of activity I witnessed, it was clear to me that Diplo is the hardest-working man in EDM—which explained why he never had time for idle chat. Then one day, out of the blue, he called me over and engaged me in a friendly conversation. At the end of our exchange, he mentioned that he had just been hanging with Moby, who reported that he had come to my place for dinner and loved the soup.

To recap, this Thai coconut corn soup has lots going for it. It's simple to make, can easily be veganized, may be served hot or cold—and is capable of disarming guarded rock stars in a single serving.

(continued)

Time
75 minutes + 2 hours to chill

Yield
Makes 8 servings

Advance Work
Soup can be made up to a couple of days in advance

Plan-Overs
Extra soup will last in the fridge for 3 to 4 days, and in the freezer for up to 6 months

Liquidity
A German Riesling kabinett or Gewürztraminer both have the requisite sweetness (balanced with acidity) to take the edge off the spiciness of the curry paste

7 ears of corn, shucked (or 8 cups frozen corn in a pinch)

1 Tbsp coconut oil (if using the sauté method) + 2 Tbsp coconut oil, or a neutral oil

2 lemongrass stalks

1 medium onion, chopped finely

1-inch piece ginger, peeled, chopped finely

1 large Yukon gold potato, or in a pinch a russet, roughly cut into ½-inch cubes

12 makrut lime leaves (optional)

1 Tbsp red Thai curry paste (see sidebar) + extra, if needed (source a vegan version if serving vegans)

One 14-ounce can best available coconut milk

4 cups vegetable stock or water, or chicken stock if no vegetarians are partaking

2 tsp salt + more, to taste

2 Tbsp fresh makrut lime juice, or conventional lime juice

3 largest available shrimp per person (optional; do not include if Moby is coming over to your house)

1 avocado

2 Tbsp cilantro oil (see page 250), or olive oil, or 2 Tbsp cilantro, chopped finely

Cut the kernels off 6 cobs. Reserve the kernels. One at a time, place the cobs in a large deep bowl. Using the back of a table knife, scrape down the cobs to release the milk from the exposed kernels. Add the milk to the reserved kernels.

On a grill over high direct heat, grill the remaining ear of corn until the kernels are browned. Let cool. Cut the kernels from the cob. Reserve. If you do not have access to a grill, cut the kernels from the cob and sauté over high heat in a tablespoon of the coconut oil until kernels brown.

Use a meat tenderizer or something heavy to bruise the bulb end of the lemongrass (i.e., smash it several times).

In a large pot over medium heat, melt the coconut oil. Add the onion and ginger, and cook, stirring occasionally, for about 8 minutes, or until the onion is translucent.

Add the lemongrass, raw corn kernels, potato, makrut leaves, curry paste, coconut milk, and stock. Bring to a boil over high heat, then reduce to a simmer and cook until the potato is tender, 20 to 25 minutes.

Let the soup cool, discard the large pieces of lemongrass, and then transfer the soup to a blender. Purée until smooth. If you like a more rustic texture, serve it as is. But if you prefer a velvety mouthfeel, pass the puree through a fine-mesh sieve (ideally a chinois).

Add salt, then taste and adjust. Taste for spiciness, and adjust if desired, by adding more curry paste ½ teaspoon at a time.

Chill for at least 2 hours.

Before serving, add ½ tablespoon lime juice. Taste and add more as desired. Retaste for salt and spiciness and adjust if desired. If the soup is too thick (like pancake batter), thin it with a bit of water.

Shell and devein the shrimp, leaving the tails on. Preheat the grill to high. Toss the shrimp with salt and a coconut or neutral oil, and grill over direct high heat until charred on the outside and no longer translucent. If you do not have access to a grill, sauté the shrimp in a pan over high heat.

Serve in prechilled bowls. Top with diced avocado, shrimp, charred corn kernels, and a drizzle of cilantro oil.

Red Thai Curry Paste

Good quality red Thai curry paste usually includes lemongrass, galangal (a cousin of ginger), and makrut lime leaves. I have called for these individually as well to goose up the flavor. If you can source a high-quality red Thai curry paste but can't find the other ingredients, just add a little extra curry. HACK: I freeze my curry paste and cut off small chunks whenever I need it. That way I always have some on hand and don't need to make a special trip to my not-so-local Thai grocery when all I need is a tablespoon.

All-About-the-Asparagus Soup *Photo on page 51*

This is a different kind of Flavorbomb. Instead of hitting you over the head with bombastic flavors—as is my way—this recipe focuses on the unique flavor profile of asparagus to create a deep yet delicate velvety soup. It's a textbook example of how a chinois or fine-mesh sieve can have a significant impact on mouthfeel and consequently alter the overall impression the soup creates. Not surprisingly, this pure expression of asparagus is inspired by Alice Waters, one of the pioneers of California cuisine.

2 pounds asparagus (about 2 large bunches), ideally in season

4 Tbsp butter

1 medium yellow onion, diced

1 leek, white part only, diced

1 large russet potato, peeled and diced into ½-inch pieces

7 cups best available chicken stock (page 251)

1 cup parsley, stemmed (to boost the color)

Salt and pepper

Juice of 1 lemon

Best available olive oil for finishing

Optional additions (see sidebar)

Optional Additions

This asparagus soup is all about purity and simplicity. But if you want to gild the lily or turn it into a more substantial course, there are plenty of additions and garnishes that can add to the pleasure quotient: pan-seared asparagus tips; bacon or pancetta bits; crab meat; grilled shrimp; croutons; crème fraîche.

If the bottom inch or so of the spears are super woody (if your knife barely cuts through them), cut those bits off. Otherwise, you are good to use the whole spear. Cut the top 2 inches off the tip end of each spear and reserve. Roughly chop the rest of the asparagus stalks into ¼-inch pieces.

In a large pot over medium heat, add the butter, onion, and leek, and cook for about 5 minutes, stirring frequently, or until the onion and leek are translucent but not browned.

Add the potato, chopped asparagus bottoms, and stock. Bring to a boil, then lower to a simmer and cook for 30 minutes. Add the asparagus tips and simmer for 5 more minutes.

Let the mixture cool, then purée in a blender along with the parsley. Pass the soup through a fine-mesh strainer (ideally a chinois).

Season to taste with salt, pepper, and lemon juice.

NOTE: If your stock is not already salted, the soup may need lots of salt. This is a great opportunity to do the salt test (page 39) and the lemon juice acid test (page 40).

Serve hot or cold. Top with the optional additions and drizzle with olive oil just before serving.

Time
1 hour

Yield
Makes 8 to 12 servings

Advance Work
The soup can be made up to a couple of days in advance

Plan-Overs
Extra soup will last in the fridge for 3 to 4 days, and in the freezer for up to 6 months

Liquidity
Asparagus is traditionally difficult to pair with wine, but in soup form, it will pair well with a chalky Loire Valley sauvignon blanc. This lean wine acts as a counterpoint to the creamless creaminess of this soup

The Gazpacho Remix

Breaking news: despite a wave of crimes against gazpacho, the traditional cold Spanish soup doesn't have to taste like a bland tomato Slurpee. By remixing the original ingredients and ripping a few samples from another classic, it's easy to create an addictive chilled soup with reverberating layers of flavor.

My spin on the classic recipe starts by emulsifying tomatoes, stale bread, olive oil, and almonds (an ingredient used in Spain's white gazpacho). To this rustic base, I add all the usual suspects, then drop in a few fresh beats: lemon juice, aged balsamic vinegar, and smoky chili powder. When I really want to bring down the house, I finish it with burrata. Gazpacho is always at its best when made in the summer from heirloom tomatoes at their peak of ripeness, but this version has so much going for it that it will play year-round with whatever tomatoes you can get your hands on.

1 poblano chili

4 cups ice for blanching

2 pounds best available tomatoes

⅓ cup roughly chopped stale or rock-hard bread (ideally a rustic sourdough)

¼ cup skinless Marcona almonds (or any other roasted almonds)

2–3 garlic cloves, minced

4 Tbsp best available olive oil + more for drizzling

¼ medium red onion

¼ fennel bulb, trimmed, or 1 celery stalk

½ cucumber, skinned, seeds removed

¼ cup lightly packed basil or cilantro, bigger stems discarded before measuring

2 tsp balsamic vinegar (ideally the good, thick, aged stuff)

1 Tbsp freshly squeezed lemon juice

¼ tsp ground chipotle or New Mexican chili powder

½ tsp salt + more for finishing

¼ tsp pepper + more for finishing

One 8-ounce ball of burrata (optional)

Blacken the poblano chili over a gas burner or barbecue. Put in a paper bag for five minutes, then peel off and discard the skin. Discard the seeds and stem. Reserve.

Bring a large pot of water to a boil.

Set out a large bowl full of ice and 4 cups of water.

Core the tomatoes, then cut a small "X" at the bottom. Drop the tomatoes, 4 at a time, into the boiling water and leave them for 15 seconds. Remove and transfer to the ice bath. Let sit in the bath for a minute, then peel off the tomato skins (which should just pop off into your hands) and discard.

To a food processor, add 2 tomatoes, along with the bread, almonds, and garlic. Run the processor for 30 seconds, then drizzle in the oil in a thin, steady stream until it emulsifies (about 1 minute).

Roughly chop the poblano chili, onion, fennel, cucumber, and basil. Add to the processor along with the remaining tomatoes.

Season with the balsamic vinegar, lemon juice, chili powder, salt, and pepper. Chill in the refrigerator for a minimum of 2 hours. Before serving, retaste for salt, acid, and heat and adjust if desired.

Ladle the soup into chilled bowls and place a quarter ball of burrata, cut side up, in the center of each bowl. Season the burrata with salt and pepper, then drizzle with olive oil.

Time
< 45 minutes

Yield
Serves 4 to 6

Advance Work
Soup can be made up to 2 days in advance.

Zero Waste
In the summer, "rescue" soft and bruised tomatoes from the "scratch and dent" boxes that most farmers' market vendors use to liquidate their damaged fruit.

Plan-Overs
Extra soup will last in the fridge for 3 to 4 days.

Liquidity
Albariño, a dry, racy white wine from northern Spain, bolsters and augments the acidity of the tomatoes.

Classic French Onion Soup

If gazpacho is the most bastardized summer soup, French onion soup au gratin takes the winter prize. Sadly, so many restaurants don't take the time to fully caramelize the onions, make the rich broth, add quality booze, or splurge on the right cheese that wraps its loving arms around this bistro classic in a warm embrace.

   The ooey gooey, deeply flavored French onion soup of your dreams is easily achievable at home, as long as you start with a rich stock (either homemade or store-bought), quality cheese, and the secret ingredient—patience.

Time
90 minutes + extra if you make homemade stock

Yield
Makes 4 generous servings

Liquidity
The backbone of a Loire Valley Cabernet Franc has the strictness and minerality to discipline the rich, gooey, umami-ness of the soup

1½ Tbsp butter + extra for buttering bread

1½ Tbsp olive oil

3 large yellow onions, halved and sliced

8 sprigs thyme, stemmed + more whole sprigs for garnish

1 tsp salt

¾ cup white wine

2 ounces brandy

6 cups intense (undiluted) homemade chicken stock (page 251), or the best available store-bought chicken or beef stock

Salt

Pepper

4 thick slices very stale rustic country loaf or sourdough baguette (if bread isn't stale, place in a 200°F oven for 15 minutes)

1 garlic clove

6 ounces Gruyère or Comté cheese

4 Tbsp freshly grated Parmigiano-Reggiano

To a large pot over medium-high heat, add the butter, olive oil, onions, thyme, and salt. Cover and cook for 15 minutes, stirring every 5 minutes. Remove the lid, reduce the heat to medium, and cook for about 45 minutes, or until the onions are a deep golden brown, stirring and scraping the bottom occasionally—and if necessary, using a splash of water to deglaze the pan and get all the bits off the bottom.

Add the wine and brandy and stir for 1 minute. Add the stock, bring the mixture to a boil, and then reduce the heat and simmer for 15 minutes. Taste and season with salt and pepper.

Preheat the broiler. Trim bread so that it just fits in your serving bowl, then toast it until it is nicely browned. Rub the bread with garlic, then butter lightly.

Transfer the soup to individual ovenproof bowls. Top with the bread, and sprinkle generously with Gruyère, then the Parmigiano. Top with a sprig of thyme. Set under the broiler for 5 watchful minutes, or until the cheese and bread are browned to within an inch of their lives.

Tomato-Bacon Bisque
with a Grilled Cheese Sandwich

There are few things in life that can compete with the nostalgia of cream of tomato soup and a grilled cheese sandwich. But if anything can it's this deeply satisfying, rustic bacon-infused tomato bisque. Add a grilled cheese sandwich with a complex, aromatic cheese and an extra-crispy crust, and you will be flooded with memories of your youth—as channeled through the sophisticated tastes of your adult life.

Time
75 minutes

Yield
Serves 6 to 8

Plan-Overs
Extra soup will last in the fridge for 3 to 4 days and in the freezer for up to 6 months

Liquidity
A well-structured Merlot will play off the bacon that anchors the soup.

Tomato-Bacon Bisque

1 head garlic

12 strips best available bacon, sliced into ¼-inch strips

2 Tbsp butter

1 small yellow onion, diced

½ fennel bulb, cored and chopped, or 3 celery stalks

1 carrot, chopped

3 Tbsp flour

One 28-ounce can tomatoes (whole or chopped), ideally San Marzano

5 cups best available chicken stock

1 bouquet garni with 6 sprigs fresh thyme (or 2 tsp dried thyme) and 2 bay leaves

2 tsp harissa

Salt and pepper

¼–½ cup heavy cream (optional)

Parsley to finish (optional)

Grilled Cheese Sandwich (per sandwich)

2 slices sourdough loaf, brioche, or your favorite bread

2 slices cave-aged Gruyère cheese, or Emmental

2 Tbsp mayonnaise

Preheat a toaster oven or oven to 400°F.

Slice the pointy top off the garlic to expose the cloves. Set on a piece of aluminum foil. Drizzle with olive oil and wrap in the foil. Roast until the cloves are lightly browned and tender, about 50 minutes. Reserve.

In a large pot, cook the bacon until crispy. Remove the bacon and all but roughly 2 tablespoons bacon fat. Reserve the bacon.

In a pot over medium-high heat, add the butter, onion, fennel, and carrot. Cook for about 8 minutes, stirring occasionally, or until the vegetables start to brown. Add the flour and stir constantly for 1 minute, allowing the flour to brown slightly. Add the tomatoes along with all their juices, the stock, all but 2 tablespoons of the bacon, and the bouquet garni. Simmer for 30 minutes.

Let the soup cool, remove bouquet garni, squeezing the juices back into the pot. Squeeze the roasted garlic cloves into the pot and add harissa.

Purée the soup in a blender until smooth. Season to taste with salt and pepper. The soup is plenty rich and creamy as is, but if you really want to go for the gusto, finish with cream or drizzle a bit overtop before serving.

Serve in warmed soup bowls. Crumble or chop the remaining bacon and sprinkle overtop. Finish with the parsley.

Assemble your cheese sandwich, then spread the outside of each side with mayonnaise. Grill in a panini maker, or frying pan until browned and crisped to within an inch of its life.

TRADITIONAL ROMAINE CAESAR
page 125

KALE CAESAR
page 125

GRILLED RADICCHIO CAESAR
page 125

Mediterranean Mash-Up Salad

Classic Greek salads are pleasantly refreshing. But they usually rely on a preordained set of ingredients, with little to no variation, which delivers the familiar, but limits the upside. This Mediterranean mash-up takes the components of a classic Greek salad and punctuates them with the brininess of anchovies, the lusciousness of avocado, and the crispy crunch of torn croutons—all gems of Tuscany's panzanella salad. Enjoy it as an opener or a summertime entrée. Either way, it's a perfect example of how *more is more*.

Time
30 minutes

Yield
Makes 4 substantial salad portions

Advance Work
Croutons may be made up to a couple of days in advance

Liquidity
A citrusy Soave Classico is the perfect party guest at this Meditteranean bacchanal

Fried Garlic Croutons
4 garlic cloves, minced

4 Tbsp olive oil

Salt

2 cups roughly torn sourdough bread pieces, about 1 inch

Salad
2 cups fried garlic croutons (see above)

½ cup kalamata olives, pitted (HACK: to minimize the possibility of a wayward pit sending you to the dentist, cut each olive in half)

1½ cups best available cherry tomatoes, stemmed, or in a pinch, best available tomatoes, quartered

1 Persian cucumber, or ½ English cucumber, peeled and cut into ¼-inch-thick rounds

¼ cup red onion rings cut from the center 2 inches of the onion

1 avocado, peeled, pitted, and cut into ½-inch cubes

4 ounces best available feta cheese, crumbled

3 Tbsp best available olive oil

1 Tbsp sherry vinegar, or red wine vinegar

2 Tbsp stemmed fresh oregano, or in a pinch, 1 Tbsp dried oregano

16 white anchovies or 12 conventional anchovies

Salt and pepper

Preheat the oven to 350°F.

FOR THE CROUTONS set a sauté pan over medium heat. Add the garlic, olive oil, and a couple of pinches of salt. Let the garlic cook for 1 minute, then add the bread, turn off the heat, and toss until the bread absorbs all of the oil.

Transfer the bread along with all of the garlic bits to a sheet pan and bake for about 20 minutes until the croutons are golden brown and crispy. Reserve.

FOR THE SALAD in a large bowl, combine all of the ingredients. Taste and adjust seasonings if desired.

Raw Veggie Slaw
with Peanut-Ginger Dressing

A few years ago, I co-hosted an infomercial for the Ninja Intelli-Sense Kitchen System, a blender that transforms into four high-performance appliances. I've done my fair share of TV, but compared to my experience of winging my way around the world with a motley crew of kindred spirits, this experience was like entering the twilight zone. The infomercial world is a parallel universe that is vertically integrated with agents, writers, directors, and actors who specialize in infomercials. During the 3-day shoot, during which only two of us were on camera, there were a total of 70 people on the set, including three wardrobe stylists, five camera operators (all rolling in sync), and two attorneys—all for what amounted to a sum total of five minutes of screen time.

I've used manual spiralizers before, but the automated version that comes with the Ninja is a real game changer. If it sounds like I drank the Kool-Aid, I did. Without breaking a sweat, you can turn a handful of common veggies into something that looks like a bowlful of colorful party streamers in seconds.

However you choose to slice, dice, or spiralize your veggies, the tangy, peanut-based dressing in this fresh, crunchy slaw adds an extra dimension that will make you forget you are eating a salad. It also makes a great side dish.

Operators are standing by to take your call at 866-826-6941.

Time
30 minutes

Yield
Serves 4

Advance Work
Dressing can be made up to a couple of days in advance. Vegetables can be prepared earlier in the day

Liquidity
Double down on the ginger with a ginger beer—because sometimes you can't get too much of a good thing

Slaw
½ zucchini, skin-on, spiralized or julienned

1 carrot, spiralized or julienned

¼ red bell pepper, julienned

½ cup purple cabbage, sliced finely

½ cup daikon, spiralized or julienned

¼ cup broccoli stems, peeled and julienned (many grocery stores now carry a prepared version)

¼ cup edamame

2 green onions, sliced thinly

¼ cup stemmed, roughly chopped fresh mint + whole sprigs for garnish

½ cup peanut-ginger dressing

½ cup roasted peanuts

Peanut-Ginger Dressing
1 garlic clove, minced

1 Tbsp freshly grated ginger

1–2 birds-eye chilis, minced, or ¼–½ tsp chili flakes

2 Tbsp peanut butter

2 Tbsp freshly squeezed lime juice

1 Tbsp soy sauce

1 Tbsp toasted sesame oil

1 Tbsp neutral vegetable oil

1 Tbsp maple syrup, honey, or palm sugar

FOR THE SLAW Combine the vegetables and mint in a large bowl.

FOR THE DRESSING add all ingredients to a blender and purée. Taste for salt (in the form of soy), acid, and seasonings, and adjust if desired.

Just before serving, add half a cup of the dressing and half of the peanuts and toss thoroughly. Add more dressing if desired. Serve in individual bowls or family style. Top with the remaining peanuts and the mint sprigs.

Headliners

(Main Courses)

Puttanesca Pasta "La Bomba"
with Rustic Fried Breadcrumbs

If you like eating and making pasta, it's hard not to love puttanesca. In a few short minutes, you can transform a can of tomatoes and a handful of pantry staples into a satisfying sauce. But why settle for "satisfying" when "life-affirming" is within your grasp? To get you there, I've used several HACKS and non-traditional additions to up the ante on the classic recipe. The result is a bigger, badder, more bombastic puttanesca.

Time
30 minutes

Yield
Makes 2 generous servings

Advance Work
The sauce can be made earlier in the day, reheated just before showtime, and tossed with the pasta

Liquidity
Nero d'Avola is a simple and approachable—yet streetwise—rustic red from Sicily

1 Tbsp olive oil

8 anchovies, chopped + 1 Tbsp anchovy oil

6 garlic cloves, minced, divided

1 shallot, diced finely

2 Tbsp capers, drained

½ cup pitted and halved olives

¼ tsp pepper

Salt

½ pound spaghetti

One 14-ounce can cherry tomatoes or plum tomatoes

1 Tbsp harissa (or in a pinch, ½ tsp chili flakes)

1 tsp best available aged balsamic vinegar

Zest of 1 lemon

¾ cup grated Parmigiano-Reggiano, divided

½ cup chopped Italian parsley

½ cup fried breadcrumbs (page 253)

In a sauté pan over medium heat, add the olive oil, anchovies, anchovy oil, two-thirds of the garlic, shallot, capers, olives, and pepper. Cook for 3 minutes, stirring frequently, or until the garlic and shallots show the first sign of browning.

Bring a large salted pot of water to a boil and cook the spaghetti according to directions—but keep it al dente.

Add the tomatoes, harissa, and balsamic vinegar to the sauté pan. Bring to a high simmer, then reduce heat and let simmer for 5 to 10 minutes, or until the sauce has thickened slightly. Remove from the heat and add the lemon zest and remaining garlic. Taste for salt and seasonings, and adjust if desired.

When pasta is done, reserve 1 cup of pasta water—which at this point should be starchy. Drain the pasta, then return it to the pot. Add the sauce, ½ cup of the Parmigiano, and half the parsley. Add the pasta water, 2 or 3 tablespoons at a time, incorporating it into the sauce and at the same time coating the pasta with the sauce. You may or may not use up all of the water. The goal is to have your pasta coated by the sauce—but not drowning in it. (Pasta continues to absorb water, even as it is being walked to the table. Learning how much water to add comes through trial and error—and taking note each time you make pasta.)

Transfer to individual pre-warmed bowls and sprinkle breadcrumbs, remaining Parmigiano, and parsley overtop.

The Difference You Can Taste

- Anchovy oil heightens the anchovy flavor

- Dividing the garlic and saving some for the end adds a kick

- Harissa delivers a more complex heat than plain chili flakes

- Aged balsamic vinegar adds richness as well as acidity

- Fried breadcrumbs add an undeniably pleasing crunch

Creamy Carbonara
with Double Pancetta

Many versions of this Italian crowd-pleaser call for gratuitous amounts of heavy cream as a base for the sauce. I prefer to build the sauce with Parmigiano-Reggiano, pecorino, and extra egg yolks. When blended with some of the starchy pasta water, this trio of ingredients creates a sauce that is paradoxically richer and creamier, with more depth of flavor than the cream-based version. To take it over the top, I double down on the pancetta so that you get more crispy nuggets of cured pork belly with every twirl of the fork.

Time
< 30 minutes

Yield
Makes 4 generous servings

Zero Waste
Save your egg whites for Eggs Carbonara (see sidebar)

Liquidity
A Dolcetto from Piedmont has a pleasingly bitter character that will cut through the creaminess of the carbonara

1 Tbsp olive oil

8 ounces thick-sliced pancetta or thick-sliced bacon, cut into ¼-inch pieces

2 garlic cloves, minced

2 tsp pepper

¼ tsp chili flakes

1 cup freshly grated Parmigiano-Reggiano (about 4 ounces) + extra for finishing

½ cup freshly grated pecorino (about 2 ounces)

1 best available egg + 3 egg yolks

Salt

1 pound spaghetti

1 cup chopped parsley

In a large sauté pan over medium-heat, add the olive oil. Add the pancetta and cook for about 7 minutes, stirring occasionally, until the individual pieces are browned and crispy. Turn off the heat and add the garlic, pepper, and chili flakes. Stir for 1 minute to release their flavors. Transfer the whole lot to a large bowl, being sure to include every drop of the rendered fat. Let cool.

Add the Parmigiano, pecorino, egg, and yolks to the pancetta bowl and whisk together thoroughly. Reserve.

Bring a large pot of generously salted water to a boil. Add the pasta and cook until al dente. Reserve 1 cup of the pasta water. Drain the pasta and transfer it to the pancetta bowl.

Add the parsley. Toss, adding pasta water a splash at a time to create a smooth, creamy sauce the consistency of heavy cream. In all likelihood, you will come close to using up all the water.

Serve in individual pre-warmed bowls, or *famiglia* style, and finish with a sprinkle of Parmigiano.

Leftover Eggs Carbonara

Leftovers make amazing morning-after Eggs Carbonara: over medium-high heat, add a tablespoon of butter to a pan. Add a cup of leftover carbonara and stir occasionally for about 4 minutes, or until the pasta begins to brown. Reduce the heat to medium-low. Beat 4 eggs (or 2 eggs and the remaining egg whites from the carbonara) and add to the pan. Stir into the pasta until eggs are fully cooked.

Hope Springs Eternal Risotto

If you believe what most cookbooks tell you, the amount of constant attention required to make risotto rivals the care required by newborn babies. I'm all for being vigilant when vigilance is warranted, but when it comes to making risotto, some occasional stirring between sips of wine and text messaging is all it takes to get the job done.

There was a time when I wasn't a risotto devotee. Although I always enjoyed the first couple of bites, I quickly lost interest after that. Then I had a religious experience. It came to me in the form of an inspired dish that the iconic Italian American chef Lidia Bastianich made for Pope Benedict when he visited New York City. Lidia's recipe calls for fleeting spring vegetables like wild ramps and fresh fava beans. But the risotto's true genius is a brightly flavored pesto, folded into the risotto at the last minute, which adds levity to every bite. My riff draws on ingredients that can be found year-round. It might just make you a convert too.

Pesto

1 leek, white section only (enough for ½ cup when chopped) or 6 green onions

1½ cups (packed) arugula, or baby spinach

½ tsp salt + extra for finishing

½ cup best available olive oil, divided + extra for drizzling

Risotto

1 pound asparagus

7 cups homemade chicken stock (page 251), or vegetable stock (page 252), or best available store-bought stock

3 garlic cloves, minced

1 medium shallot, minced

2 cups Arborio rice (available in many grocery stores and all Italian food stores)

½ cup dryish white wine (as dictated by what's left over in your fridge, or what you are drinking)

1 cup fresh or frozen peas, fava beans, or lima beans

2 Tbsp butter

½ tsp pepper

1 cup freshly grated Parmigiano-Reggiano, divided

Edible flowers (optional)

TO MAKE THE PESTO In a blender or food processor, add the leek, arugula, a couple of pinches of salt, and ⅓ cup olive oil. Purée and reserve pesto.

TO MAKE THE RISOTTO Discard the woodiest sections of each asparagus spear (usually the bottom quarter—unless it has already been trimmed). Use a vegetable peeler to peel the tough outer layer from the lower third of the remaining spear. Cut the asparagus just below the tip. If the asparagus is fat, slice the tip in half from top to bottom. Slice the remainder of the spear on the bias into ⅛-inch rounds. Reserve.

In a medium pot, bring the stock to a boil, then reduce the heat to a gentle simmer.

In a large, heavy pot over medium heat, add 3 tablespoons of the olive oil. Add the garlic and shallot and stir for about 2 minutes, or until the shallot is translucent. Add the rice and stir continuously for 1 minute until all of the rice grains are well coated in oil. Add the wine and stir occasionally for 2 to 3 minutes, until most of the liquid is absorbed.

(continued)

Time

< 45 minutes

Yield

Serves 6

Advance Work

Risotto may be parcooked up to 2 hours in advance. To do so, follow the instructions, then stop after adding the fourth cup of stock, just before adding the peas and asparagus. Just before showtime, reheat the risotto and complete the recipe from where you left off, per the original instructions

Plan-Overs

Leftovers make great arancini. You can also resuscitate leftovers by reheating them with a generous splash of chicken stock or water

Liquidity

The pope may be chaste, but this risotto swings both ways. A promiscuous prosecco, or a polyamorous Nebbiolo will both complete the seduction of this dish.

Use a ladle to add 1 cup of stock to the rice. Stir occasionally. Each time the stock is almost fully absorbed, add another cup. After the fourth cup of stock, add the peas and asparagus. Continue stirring occasionally, adding stock one cup at a time. Risotto, like pasta, should be served slightly al dente. And like pasta, it continues to cook and absorb liquid after it is removed from the heat. So be extra vigilant about the texture of the rice as it cooks. After the first few ladles of stock, taste the grains of rice every couple of minutes to assess their texture. Your risotto is done when the rice is soft but still has a bit of toothiness, and the sauce is creamy and loose. The total time, once the rice has been added, should be 20 to 25 minutes.

When the rice is just shy of the desired degree of doneness, fold in the green pesto, butter, salt, pepper, and three-quarters of the Parmigiano. Stir for one more minute. This will thicken the mixture. To keep the risotto creamy (see photo on page 136) and to avoid the possibility of it thickening up more as it travels to the table, add a last ladleful of stock just before you pull it off the heat.

Taste for salt and adjust if necessary.

Serve in pre-warmed bowls and sprinkle with the remaining Parmigiano and the flowers or flower petals. Finish with a drizzle of olive oil.

Serving Suggestions

At the best of times, risotto is very heavy. The key to keeping every bite pleasurable is to serve it in small portions. I generally serve 1 to 1½ cups per person, or ¾ cup as a first course. A simple green salad, dressed with a racy vinaigrette (i.e., slightly more acidic than usual), serves as a great counterpoint to the richness of risotto.

Rapido Raviloi—Two Ways

Making ravioli at home usually starts with the time-consuming process of kneading, resting, rolling, and cutting the pasta. If you are lucky enough to master that process, on day two you can dedicate yourself to preparing the filling. R-e-a-l-l-y? We're busy people. Luckily, store-bought wonton wrappers are a great time-saving HACK. These ravioli wrappers-in-waiting are made from the same basic ingredients as pasta. And they are about to become your new best friend. The wonton wrappers' perfect size eliminates the need for cutting, and their subtle flavor and texture allows the filling to be the rightful star of the show.

But wait, wait, there's more. "Browned butter" is a fancy name for plain ol' butter that has been simmered in a pan. As it browns, it develops a rich, nutty flavor. On its own, it's not exactly transcendent. However, if you add some fresh herbs, garlic, and nuts or seeds to the butter as it simmers, the garlic and herbs will infuse the butter, and the nuts, garlic, and herbs will all crisp up into little butter-fried nuggets of goodness. The result is a simple yet opulent finishing touch that will give your ravioli the rock star treatment it deserves.

Once you get the hang of making ravioli with wonton wrappers, you'll discover that there are countless combinations of ravioli fillings and browned butters to be imagined. To help kick-start your imagination, I've started you off with a roasted squash ravioli and a wild mushroom version.

Like Beyoncé, both of these raviolis are rich and versatile. You can serve a single overstuffed one as an appetizer, or two as an entrée. So much flavor in so little time. That's no hype.

Wild Mushroom Ravioli
with Hazelnut and Thyme Browned Butter *photo on page 143*

8 Tbsp butter, divided

8 ounces of mushrooms, stemmed and cut into ⅛-inch thick slices

1 shallot

2 Tbsp cognac or brandy

¼ cup fresh goat cheese

2 Tbsp chopped parsley

Salt and pepper

Sixteen 3½-by-3½-inch wonton wrappers (available in many grocery stores and virtually all Asian markets) or 8 if making appetizer portions

4 garlic cloves, sliced thinly

12 sprigs fresh thyme

¼ cup roughly chopped hazelnuts

⅓ cup freshly grated Parmigiano-Reggiano

Olive oil for drizzling

Time
45 minutes

Yield
Serves 4

Advance Work
Ravioli may be made earlier in the day.

Liquidity
An earthy Burgundian pinot is a perfect match for the funk of the mushrooms.

(continued)

FOR THE FILLING Before flambéing, see How to Flambé (page 71).

In a sauté pan over medium-high heat add 2 tablespoons of the butter. Add the mushrooms and stir occasionally for about 4 minutes. Add the shallot and continue cooking for about 3 more minutes, or until the mushrooms begin to brown, soften, and shrink. If necessary, add a tablespoon or so of chicken stock or water to keep the mushrooms from drying out. When the mushrooms are browned, add the cognac to the pan, let it heat up for 5 to 10 seconds, then ignite. The flames should jump about 2 feet high, then burn out after about 10 seconds. Allow the mushrooms to cool, then roughly chop.

To a medium bowl, add the mushrooms, goat cheese and parsley. Season to taste with salt and pepper.

Roll the mixture into eight 1-inch balls (or four 1½-inch balls for appetizer portions). Reserve.

TO PREPARE AND FILL THE WONTON WRAPPERS Set 8 wonton sheets down on a clean surface (4 if you are making appetizer portions).

Fill a small bowl with warm water. Dip your finger in the water and trace the water generously along all four edges of each wonton wrapper. Set a ball of mushroom mixture in the center of each wrapper. Cover each ball of mushroom with a second, perfectly centered wrapper. Use your fingers to press down on all the edges of the top wrapper so that they attach to the outer edges of the bottom wrapper.

Using the tines of a fork, press firmly around the outer edges. Repeat to make the whole package airtight.

Transfer to a sheet pan lined with a damp towel and cover with another damp towel. (At this point, your ravioli may be refrigerated for up to a day.)

Fill your two largest frying pans two-thirds full of water and bring to a boil. Set a clean dishtowel and a slotted spoon within easy reach.

When the water in your pans hits the boiling stage, add your raviolis. Be careful not to stack them or they will stick to each other like mac and cheese. When the water returns to a boil, reduce to a simmer and cook for 3 minutes.

FOR THE HAZELNUT AND THYME BROWNED BUTTER While the water is heating, to a small pot, over medium heat, add the remaining butter, garlic, thyme, and hazelnuts. Bring to the bubbling stage, then reduce to a simmer and continue simmering for about 7 minutes, or until the butter froths and turns a light brown, and the garlic and thyme become crisp.

TO SERVE Remove the raviolis from the pot with the slotted spoon, then serve two per person (one for appetizer portions) in pre-warmed bowls. Spoon the browned butter with thyme sprigs and all the garlic and nut bits overtop. Hit each plate with a smidge of your best salt, sprinkle with Parmigiano, and finish with a drizzle of olive oil.

Roasted Squash Ravioli
with Sage and Pumpkin Seed Browned Butter *Photo on page 142*

1 small kabocha, acorn or
  butternut squash, or
  2 delicata squash (enough for
  1 cup roasted flesh—likely
  with some left over)

4 Tbsp fresh goat cheese

Salt and pepper

Sixteen 3½-by-3½-inch wonton
  wrappers (available in many
  grocery stores and virtually all
  Asian markets) or 8 if making
  appetizer portions

4 Tbsp butter

4 garlic cloves, sliced thinly

12 sage leaves, roughly chopped

¼ cup raw shelled pumpkin
  seeds

⅓ cup freshly grated
  Parmigiano-Reggiano

Pumpkin seed oil or best
  available olive oil for drizzling

FOR THE FILLING Preheat the oven to 425°F.

Cut the squash in half from top to bottom. Scoop out the seeds and discard. Place the squash, cut sides down, on a sheet pan (ideally lined with parchment paper to minimize your cleanup). Roast for 30 minutes. Turn cut sides up and roast for another 20 minutes, or until the flesh begins to brown at the edges (delicata squash will take less time). Remove from the oven, let cool, then scoop out the flesh.

To a medium bowl, add 1 cup of squash and the goat cheese and blend with a fork. Season to taste with salt and pepper.

Roll the mixture into eight 1-inch balls (or four 1½-inch balls for appetizer portions). Reserve. Follow instructions on page 140 for preparing and filling the wonton wrappers.

FOR THE SAGE AND PUMPKIN SEED BROWNED BUTTER While the water is heating, to a small pot, over medium heat, add the butter, garlic, sage, and pumpkin seeds. Bring to the bubbling stage, then reduce to a simmer and continue simmering for about 7 minutes, or until the butter froths and turns a light brown, and the garlic and sage become crisp.

TO SERVE Remove the individual raviolis with the slotted spoon, then serve two per person (one for appetizer portions) in pre-warmed bowls. Spoon the browned butter with sage, garlic bits, and pumpkin seeds overtop. Hit each ravioli with a smidge of your best salt, sprinkle with Parmigiano, and finish with a drizzle of pumpkin seed oil.

Time
30 minutes + 1 hour
roasting

Yield
Serves 4

Advance Work
Ravioli may be made
earlier in the day.

Liquidity
A Marsanne from Côtes du
Rhône region is a lush white
with the confidence to
stand up to the richness of
the buttery squash.

ROASTED SQUASH RAVIOLI
page 141

WILD MUSHROOM RAVIOLI

page 139

GRILLED PROSCIUTTO AND ARUGULA PIZZA
page 149

GRILLED MARGHERITA PIZZA
page 146

GRILLED STEAK PIZZA
page 148

Grilled Pizza—Three Ways

The essence of grilled pizza is its rustic, slightly charred crust. It is, in a word, life-changing. To appreciate the difference between traditional pizza and grilled pizza, consider how the dough cooks. In most pizzerias, the bottom side of the dough browns on the hot oven floor, while the top—which is covered with sauce and toppings—bakes, but remains soggy. When you grill a pizza on your backyard barbecue following the technique outlined in these recipes, you brown the bottom side of the dough first, then flip it and top the browned side with your sauce, toppings, and cheese. As the pizza continues to cook, the new bottom side browns—resulting in a twice-grilled crust that is bolder, crispier, and more textured than its oven-baked counterpart. These characteristics make a grilled pizza crust the perfect foil for a wide range of robust sauces, toppings, and cheeses.

Counterintuitively, even though the crust is the star of the show, it's not necessary to make the dough from scratch. The grill will work its magic on just about any store-bought pizza dough.

I am so addicted to grilled pizza that I cowrote *Pizza on the Grill* with my kindred culinary spirit Elizabeth Karmel. It's now on its second edition and 18th printing. In our book, we shape the dough according to your burner configuration and use a combination of direct and indirect grilling. Here, I've simplified the technique to flatten the learning curve and deliver mouth-pleasing results starting with your very first pizza.

Grilled Margherita Pizza with White Anchovies *Photo on page 144*

The classic Neapolitan Margherita pizza, as noted in my introduction to the first section of this book, is a perfect harmonic convergence of ingredients. With that said, when it's made on a grill, the char adds a layer of texture, and white anchovies will play off the tomato sauce in a way that makes you wonder why the Neapolitans didn't think of them first.

Time
< 1 hour

Yield
Serves 2 to 4

Advance Work
Tomato sauce can be prepared up to a day or two in advance

Liquidity
Valpolicella is a light, friendly red that will never throw shade on a white anchovy

1 ball pizza dough
One 28-ounce can whole peeled tomatoes
5 Tbsp olive oil, divided
4 garlic cloves, minced
1 shallot, diced finely
¼–½ tsp chili flakes
12 basil leaves, stemmed and roughly torn + a few full leaves for finishing
Salt and pepper
¼ cup coarse-ground cornmeal
8 ounces best available fresh mozzarella, sliced into ⅛-inch thick slices
½ cup freshly grated pecorino, grated on the finest part of the grater
16 white anchovies (boquerones), or conventional anchovies
Olive oil for finishing

Remove the pizza dough from the fridge an hour before grilling and allow it to rise to room temperature.

Empty the tomato can into a medium-size bowl and partially crush the tomatoes between your fingers. Reserve along with all the juice.

In a sauté pan over medium heat, add 2 tablespoons of the olive oil, garlic, shallot, and chili flakes. Cook for 2 minutes, stirring frequently, or until the garlic and shallots show the first sign of browning. Add the tomatoes along with all the juice, and the basil. Bring to a high simmer, and cook, uncovered, for about 20 minutes, or until the sauce has reduced by a third and has thickened. Season to taste with salt and pepper. Reserve.

Prepare the grill and roll out the dough

FOR GAS GRILLS Preheat the grill with all the burners on medium for about 10 minutes with the lid down, or until the internal temperature of the grill is approximately 400°F.

FOR CHARCOAL GRILLS Light your charcoal and let it burn until the coals are gray-ashed. Then spread them evenly across the bottom of the grill. Since you can't toggle the heat as you can on a gas grill, it's best to cook the top and bottom over coals that are about 350°F. To test the temperature, hold your hand just over the cooking grate. If you can hold it there for 3 seconds, your grill is good to go. Any shorter and the grill is too hot. Any longer, and it is not hot enough.

TO ROLL THE DOUGH Turn a sheet pan or cookie tin upside down. Sprinkle cornmeal in the center. Roll the dough in the cornmeal to cover it. Drizzle the dough generously with the remaining oil.

Use a rolling pin, wine bottle, or your hands to roll or push out the dough until it is as thin as possible—approximately ³⁄₁₆ to ¼ inch. Embrace the resulting organic shape. Let the dough sit for 10 to 20 minutes to allow it to relax after being rolled.

Transfer the sheet pan with the dough on it, along with your sauce, cheeses, an oven mitt or dishtowel, and a long pair of tongs to the grill area.

TO GRILL THE PIZZA Open the lid. Pick up the sheet pan and reposition your hands so that the pan is resting on the palms of your hands with your fingers facing inward. Lift the pan to chin level and in one motion, flip the sheet pan, landing the dough directly onto the cooking grate with the sheet pan on top. Let the back of the pan rest on the grate, but keep the front an inch or so above the grate so as not to compress the dough. Hold the sheet pan in place for about 10 seconds, or until the dough begins to release. Starting from the front, slowly lift up the sheet pan, allowing gravity to fully release the dough from the sheet pan onto the grate. Immediately close the lid and grill for 3 minutes. Resist peeking. Then open the lid and check the bottom of the crust. If necessary, continue grilling until the bottom is well marked and nicely browned, about 2 more minutes. Quickly rotate the dough 180° before putting the lid down.

When the bottom of the crust is browned to within an inch of its life, use tongs to transfer it from the grill back onto the bottom of the sheet pan. Close the lid to maintain the heat. Flip the crust to reveal the grilled side.

Spread the entire surface of the grilled side with the sauce (you may not need it all) and top with the mozzarella.

TO CONTINUE TO GRILL Return the pizza to the grill and close the lid. If you are grilling on a gas grill, reduce the heat to low. After about 2 minutes, lift the lid ever so slightly and use tongs to peek under the crust to make sure it is browning, not burning. Toggle the heat if necessary. Grill for about 2 more minutes, or until the bottom is the same golden brown color as the original bottom, and the cheese is fully melted. If the cheese is not fully melted after the bottom is fully browned, turn off the gas and leave the pizza on the grill, covered, for another couple of minutes.

Sprinkle pecorino overtop. Finish with the anchovies, a drizzle of olive oil, and some fresh basil leaves.

Grilled Steak Pizza
with Caramelized Onions and Cambozola *Photo on page 145*

The steak dinner of your dreams on a crispy, smoky pizza crust.

Time
90 minutes + time to sous vide steak

Yield
Serves 2 to 4

Advance Work
Caramelized onions and the sous vided steak can be prepared up to a day in advance

Liquidity
This big bold pizza calls for a blustery Aussie Shiraz or a lascivious Napa cab

1 ball pizza dough

Caramelized Onions

2 Tbsp olive oil

1 Tbsp butter

2 large yellow onions, halved and sliced thinly

½ tsp salt

One 16-ounce New York strip steak, tenderloin, or your preferred steak, 1½ inches thick

¼ cup coarse-ground cornmeal

8 ounces Cambozola cheese, cut into 1-inch pieces

Pepper

2 Tbsp finely chopped fresh parsley

Best available olive oil for finishing

Remove the pizza dough from the fridge an hour before grilling and allow it to rise to room temperature.

FOR THE CARAMELIZED ONIONS In a large, heavy sauté pan over medium heat, add the oil and the butter. When the butter bubbles, add the onions and salt. Cover and cook for 20 minutes, stirring occasionally. Remove the lid and cook, stirring occasionally, for about 30 more minutes, or until the onions are a deep golden color. Reserve.

TO SOUS VIDE THE STEAK Sous vide the steak in advance to your desired degree of doneness, then chill it in an ice bath and reserve in the fridge. Just before making the pizza, crust the steak in a pan or on the grill (see page 69). Cover lightly with aluminum foil. Reserve.

TO GRILL THE STEAK Grill the steak to your desired degree of doneness. Cover lightly with aluminum foil. Reserve.

To prepare your gas or charcoal grill, and to roll out your dough, see 147.

Transfer the sheet pan with the dough on it, along with the caramelized onions, cheese, and an oven mitt or dishtowel and a long pair of tongs to the grill area.

TO GRILL THE PIZZA see page 147.

Spread the entire surface of the grilled side with the caramelized onion and top with the Cambozola.

TO CONTINUE TO GRILL see page 147.

Slice the steak into ¼-inch-thick slices.

Top the pizza with steak slices. Finish with salt, pepper, a sprinkle of parsley, and a generous drizzle of olive oil.

Grilled Prosciutto and Arugula Pizza

with Roasted Garlic Purée *Photo on page 144*

This pizza is grilled and then topped with arugula and prosciutto at the last minute. The timing preserves the freshness of the greens and the lush mouthfeel of the prosciutto.

1 ball pizza dough

3 heads garlic

5 Tbsp olive oil, divided + extra for garlic purée

1 tsp best available balsamic vinegar

Salt and pepper

¼ cup coarse-ground cornmeal

2 cups grated Comté, or your favorite aged semi-hard cheese (about 12 ounces)

2 cups arugula

6 ounces sliced prosciutto, ideally the real deal from Italy

Truffle oil or best available olive oil for finishing

Remove the pizza dough from fridge an hour before grilling and allow it to rise to room temperature.

Preheat a toaster oven or oven to 400°F.

Slice the pointy tops off the garlic to expose each of the cloves. Set on a piece of aluminum foil. Drizzle with some olive oil and wrap in the foil. Roast until the cloves are lightly browned and tender, about 50 minutes. Let cool. Squeeze the roasted garlic cloves directly into a small bowl. Use a small whisk or a fork to blend into a purée, then drizzle in a couple of tablespoons of olive oil, chicken stock, or water, and continue whisking to thin out the purée. Reserve.

To a large bowl, add 1 tablespoon olive oil, balsamic vinegar, and a pinch of salt and pepper. Whisk together and reserve.

To prepare your gas or charcoal grill, and to roll out your dough, see 147.

Transfer the sheet pan with the dough on it, along with the roasted garlic purée, cheese, and an oven mitt or dishtowel, a wooden spoon, and a long pair of tongs to the grill area.

TO GRILL THE PIZZA see page 147.

Spread the entire surface of the grilled side with the garlic purée. Sprinkle the cheese overtop.

TO CONTINUE TO GRILL see page 147.

Quickly toss the arugula with the oil and vinegar, then spread the dressed arugula overtop of the pizza. Top with the prosciutto slices and finish with the truffle oil.

Time
< 90 minutes

Yield
Serves 2 to 4

Advance Work
Roasted garlic purée can be prepared up to a day in advance

Liquidity
If prosciutto and roasted garlic could talk, they would order a Rosso di Montalcino, a baby Brunello with great structure and acidity

#Bestsalmonburgerever

The basic rule for salmon burgers is the same as for any well-crafted beef burger: make it thick and juicy. But since salmon is more delicately flavored than beef, there is plenty of room for enhancement. Your burger will benefit from some of the same ingredients traditionally added to fish cakes: herbs and spices will punch up the mild-tasting flesh, sour cream will add a layer of unctuousness, and Dijon mustard will give it some tang. Don't stop there. Bejewel your finished patty with as much luscious bling as you can fit onto the bun.

Time
< 1 hour

Yield
Makes 4 generous burgers

Advance Work
Aioli can be made up to a day in advance. Patties can be made up to a day in advance

Plan-Overs
Patties freeze well and will last in airtight wrapping for up to 6 months

Liquidity
Pinot noir is a classic pairing with salmon. It's hard not to like a Cru Beaujolais—often considered a cheap and cheerful Burgundy—with this burger

- 1 pound skinless salmon fillet , pin bones removed, cut into ½-inch cubes
- 1 poblano chili or 1 jalapeño chili
- ¼ tsp salt
- ¼ tsp pepper
- 1 egg
- 3 green onions, sliced finely
- 2 garlic cloves, minced
- ½ red bell pepper, trimmed and diced
- 2 Tbsp sour cream or mayonnaise
- 1 Tbsp Dijon mustard
- ¼ cup cilantro, roughly stemmed
- ¼ cup breadcrumbs or panko
- Zest of 1 lemon
- 1 Tbsp lemon juice + extra for the avocado topping
- 4 Tbsp homemade aioli (page 243) or store-bought mayonnaise
- 2 Tbsp finely chopped dill
- 1 ripe avocado
- 4 airy burger buns (ideally brioche)
- 3 Tbsp olive oil, divided

Blacken the poblano over a gas burner or barbecue. Put it in a bag for 5 minutes, then peel off and discard the skin along with the seeds and stem. Reserve.

To a food processor, add the salt, pepper, egg, green onion, garlic, poblano, bell pepper, sour cream, mustard, cilantro, breadcrumbs, lemon zest, and 1 tablespoon lemon juice. Pulse. Add the salmon and pulse until it is roughly chopped and blended with the other ingredients—but well before it turns to mush. If you don't have a food processor, chop the salmon into tiny pieces, then blend with all the aforementioned ingredients in a bowl. Form the salmon mixture into 4 patties. Reserve.

In a small bowl, blend the aioli with the dill. Reserve.

In a medium bowl, use a fork to mash the avocado. Add a pinch of salt and a small squirt of lemon juice. Blend and reserve.

If the buns are too thick or too dense, pull a little bread from the center of the top half, or slice a bit off from one or both of the cut sides. While the patties are cooking, brush the buns with olive oil and toast, cut side down, in a pan or on a grill until the cut side is lightly browned.

To a sauté pan over medium-high heat, add 1 tablespoon of olive oil. When the pan is smoking hot, add the patties and cook, loosely covered, for about 4 minutes per side, or until the outsides are crusty and the centers are just cooked (that is, opaque).

Schmear the bottom bun with avocado and the top bun with aioli.

El Diablo Chorizo Burger

In 2018, I was invited by Weber Grills to enter a head-to-head grill-off with a respected Toronto chef for the media launch of their new grill. Our challenge was to use their grill to make 20 portions of anything of our choosing in one hour. First prize, as voted on by the attending media, was a $5,000 donation to the noble cause of the winner's choice.

Quick backstory: I created and hosted a TV series called *Glutton for Punishment*. In every one of the 58 episodes, I had 4 days to train for a daunting food-related competition. Then on the 5th day, I was thrown to the wolves and had to compete against a group of professionals or rise to a challenge. So it should come as no surprise that I am extremely competitive—which tends to manifest itself as pigheaded determination.

On the subject of pig (he says, segueing ever so smoothly), chorizo is made from ground pork seasoned with herbs and spices. In some instances, the seasonings can be as simple as garlic and paprika. But when you are a competitive charlatan like myself and a $5,000 donation is on the line, you pull out all the stops.

The chorizo spices in this burger patty have as much flavor as any patty can possibly handle without exploding in your hands. And the accoutrements are designed to build on those flavors and make the whole package irresistible. That's how one wins competitions—and the hearts and stomachs of one's dinner companions.

Modesty prevents me from divulging who won the Weber throw-down, but suffice to say, this recipe is a sure winner.

¼ red onion

4 Tbsp freshly squeezed lime juice

½ tsp salt + extra for the avocado topping

1 pound ground pork (ideally pork butt, ideally 30% fat)

2 Tbsp Chorizo Seasoning Blend (see page 154)

2 Tbsp apple cider vinegar

1 Tbsp añejo tequila, or any other tequila (optional)

3 garlic cloves, minced

1 avocado

1 lemon

4 airy burger buns (ideally brioche)

2 Tbsp butter or olive oil, at room temperature

4 slices Manchego cheese, or sharp, aged cheddar cheese

4 Tbsp homemade aioli (page 243) or mayo

8 red bird's-eye chilis for presentation (optional)

(continued)

Time
< 90 minutes

Yield
Makes 4 generous burgers

Advance Work
Aioli can be made up to a day in advance. Patties can be made up to a day in advance , and can be frozen for up to 6 months

Liquidity
The big, spicy notes of a Petite Syrah from Baja, California, will pair mischievously with this devilish burger

To make the pickled onions, slice the onion thinly. Add to a bowl with the lime juice and the salt. Let sit for a minimum of 20 minutes. Before serving, drain off the liquids.

Transfer the ground pork to a large bowl. Add the Chorizo Seasoning Blend, vinegar, tequila, and garlic. Mix gently, but do not overmix. Form 4 burger patties. Reserve.

In a medium bowl, use a fork to mash the avocado. Add a pinch of salt and a squeeze of lemon juice. Blend and reserve.

If the buns are too thick or too dense, pull a little bread from the center of the top half, or slice a bit off from one or both of the cut sides. While the patties are cooking, brush the buns with butter or oil and toast, cut side down, in a pan or on a grill until the cut side is lightly browned.

TO PAN COOK Over high heat, heat a cast-iron or other heavy pan until it smokes. Add the burgers, reduce the heat to medium-high, and cook for 4 minutes per side, or until they are almost cooked through. Top the burgers with cheese and cover with a lid for 1 to 2 minutes, or until the cheese is fully melted.

TO GRILL Preheat the grill to direct medium-high heat. Grill the burgers for about 4 minutes per side, or until they are cooked to your desired degree of doneness. Halfway through grilling the second side, top with the cheese and close the lid to help the cheese melt.

Schmear bottom bun with aioli, and top bun with avocado. Add the patty to the bottom bun, and top with pickled onions. Add the top bun, and if the devil makes you do it, poke two bird's eye chilis into each bun (per photo).

Yield
About ½ cup

Plan-Overs
Extra chorizo seasoning blend will last in a tightly sealed jar for a year. Since the seasoning recipe doubles effortlessly, make extra while you are at it. It's perfect for Grilled Heritage Pork Chops (page 185) as well as on grilled shrimp or chicken

Chorizo Seasoning Blend

2 whole star anise pods
5 whole black peppercorns (or ¼ tsp pepper)
1 tsp cumin seeds (or ground cumin)
1 tsp coriander seeds (or ground coriander)
1 Tbsp granulated garlic
¼ tsp ground cinnamon
1 pinch ground cloves

1 tsp dried oregano
1 tsp dried thyme
2 tsp sea salt
1 Tbsp ancho chili powder
1 tsp ground chipotle
1 Tbsp paprika

In a coffee grinder or mortar and pestle, grind the star anise, peppercorns, cumin, and coriander seeds. Add to a bowl and toss with the remaining herbs and spices.

Getting the Most from Your Burger Bun

The bun you wrap your burger in is often an afterthought, but it can have as much impact on the overall taste experience as the burger itself—and deserves the same consideration. The right bun adds just enough bread to every bite without overwhelming the burger and condiments. The wrong bun hijacks the whole experience, or collapses into nothingness.

Ever since Daniel Boulud put foie gras on a burger and charged $50, high-end burgers have established a foothold in the world of fine dining, and "third wave" burger joints have popped up everywhere. Bread makers have risen to the occasion, and now an assortment of artisanal buns designed to complement fancy burgers are available at many grocery stores and bakeries. The most popular options include brioche, ciabatta, potato buns, and pretzel buns.

Although I am grateful for the range of options and the leap in quality, many of the fanciest artisanal buns are still too thick or too dense for my taste. If you feel the same way, slice a thin layer from the center of the bun, or pull out a bit of bread from the inside of the top half. There is no real test other than to size up the bun as Mr. Whipple did the Charmin—with a little squeeze.

Regardless of which bun you choose, toasting it on the cut side only will add another layer of texture to your burger. This technique crisps up the cut side and softens the interior. At the same time, it maintains the integrity of the dome-like top of the bun so that it presents perfectly.

Butter or oil your bun on both of the cut sides, then toast the halves, cut side down, without flipping them. This can be done in a pan, on a grill over low heat, or on an open panini maker.

Bang Bang Thai Chicken Burger

If your favorite Thai restaurant hooked up with your favorite burger joint, this spicy, coconutty, chicken burger would be their love child. If burgers aren't your thing, don't throw out the baby with the bathwater. The vibrant combination of fresh ingredients, spices, and moist thigh meat doubles as an excellent blend for meatballs, as well as being a perfect filling for pot stickers and dumplings. In all likelihood, you will need to trek to a Thai grocery store for some of the ingredients listed below. On the upside, once you've acquired them, they will do all of the hard work for you.

Time
< 45 minutes

Yield
Makes 4 generous burgers

Advance Work
Aioli can be made up to a day in advance. Patties can be made up to 2 days in advance

Plan-Overs
Patties freeze well and will last in airtight wrapping for up to 6 months. They can also be reconfigured into meatballs

Liquidity
A Thai Singha beer, with its street food cred, speaks to the green curry in this delicious burger

NOTE: Many Thai grocery stores stock fresh green curry paste in their refrigerated section.

½ cup aioli (make Three-Clove Aioli, page 243, but note additions below)

Zest of 1 makrut lime, or conventional lime

2 Tbsp of makrut lime or conventional lime juice, divided (about 3 limes)

2 ripe mangos

½ cup mint, stemmed, divided

2 purple cabbage leaves (HACK: if your grocery store sells cabbage by the pound, do as I do and just peel off and buy the 2 leaves you need)

1 egg

3 green onions, chopped

2 garlic cloves, minced

2 Tbsp freshly grated ginger

1 Tbsp Thai green curry paste (see note below)

2 Tbsp coconut cream (not to be confused with coconut milk)

1 pound boneless, skinless chicken thighs, roughly chopped

1 Tbsp panko or breadcrumbs

¼ tsp salt

¼ tsp pepper

4 airy burger buns

3 Tbsp coconut oil, or neutral oil, divided

Make the aioli per instructions but use the makrut lime zest and 1 tablespoon of makrut lime juice in place of the lemon zest and juice. Reserve.

Peel and pit the mango. Cut the remaining flesh into matchstick-size pieces. Finely slice half the mint and the cabbage leaves. Add the ingredients to a bowl along with the remaining 1 tablespoon of lime juice. Toss to mix. Reserve.

To a food processor, add the egg, green onions, garlic, ginger, curry paste, coconut cream, remaining mint, chicken, panko, salt, and pepper, and pulse about 10 times, or until the chicken is well chopped, but not pulverized. If you don't have a food processor, mince the chicken with a knife, then blend it with all the aforementioned ingredients in a bowl. Form the mixture into 4 patties. Reserve.

Set a sauté pan over medium-high heat. Add 1 tablespoon of the oil. When the pan is smoking hot, add the patties and cook, loosely covered, for about 4 minutes per side, or until the outsides are crusty and the centers are fully opaque.

If the buns are too thick or too dense, pull a little bread from the center of the top half, or slice a bit off from one or both of the cut sides. While the patties are cooking, brush the buns with the remaining oil, and set cut side down in a pan over medium heat and toast until browned.

Slather aioli on the bottom bun. Add the patty and top with the mango slaw.

Oooh-Mummy Burger

If you are curious about *umami* (page 17) and want to experience the so-called fifth distinct taste (after sweet, sour, bitter, and salty), in all of its glory, this burger has your name written all over it. The umami factor starts with the beef itself, then is increased exponentially with the addition of umami-rich Worcestershire sauce, dried morel mushrooms, caramelized onions, blue cheese, homemade ketchup, and my special HACK: Vegemite.

If you are committed to making the ultimate umami burger, start by going to a butcher shop and asking the butcher to custom grind a three-part blend of beef for you. Dry-aged rib eye trimmings will add some umami-rich funk, short rib or brisket will contribute richness, and hanger or skirt steak will intensify the "meatiness."

As you take your first bite of the burger and all its fixin's, your taste receptors will be saturated with the pure essence of umami—and the elusive flavor profile will be forever imprinted on your palate.

Time
< 30 minutes + extra for condiments

Yield
Makes 4 generous burgers

Plan-Overs
Patties freeze well and will last in airtight wrapping for up to 6 months

Liquidity
The prince of darkness, Guinness Beer, is the closest a beer can come to matching the umami flavors in this burger

---

1 Tbsp Worcestershire sauce

1 tsp Vegemite or Marmite

1½ pounds ground beef (ideally ⅓ dry aged rib eye, ⅓ boneless short rib, ⅓ hanger steak), or your favorite blend

2 Tbsp ground dried morel mushrooms or any other dried mushrooms (use a mortar and pestle or a coffee grinder)

1 tsp dry mustard

2 tsp salt

1 tsp pepper

4 airy burger buns (ideally brioche)

4 ounces blue cheese or Gruyère, or your favorite burger cheese, crumbled or grated

2 Tbsp garlic butter (page 245) or butter at room temperature

6 Tbsp caramelized onions (page 148)

4 Tbsp homemade ketchup (page 241) (optional)

In a small ramekin, mix Worcestershire and Vegemite. Reserve.

To a large bowl add the ground beef. Add the Worcestershire/Vegemite blend, mushroom powder, and mustard. Mix, but do not overmix. Form 4 beef patties. Season both sides with salt and pepper.

TO GRILL Preheat the grill to direct medium-high heat. Grill the burgers for about 4 minutes per side, or until they are cooked to your desired degree of doneness. Halfway through grilling the second side, top with the cheese and close the lid to help the cheese melt.

TO PAN COOK Over high heat, heat a cast-iron pan or other heavy pan until it smokes. Add the burgers, reduce the heat to medium-high, and cook for 4 minutes per side, or until they are almost at your desired degree of doneness. Top the burgers with cheese and cover with a lid for 1 to 2 minutes, or until the cheese is fully melted.

If the buns are too thick or too dense, pull a little bread from the center of the top half, or slice a bit off from one or both of the cut sides.

While the patties are cooking, brush the buns with butter and toast them, cut side down, in a pan or on a grill until the cut side is lightly browned.

Spread the bottom bun with caramelized onions and the top bun with ketchup.

Bollywood Bean Burger
with Mango Chutney

I'm all about reducing my meat intake and saving the planet. But if I'm going to eat a burger that isn't made from beef, I don't want something that's pretending to be beef; I want a patty that's as succulent and satisfying as a beef burger—but is true to what it is. This juicy bean burger gets its luscious texture from a duo of canned beans, brought to life with a combination of herbs and spices that pay homage to the Indian pantry. It's a simple way to work a plant-friendly burger into your repertoire, because once you dress it up, there is so much going on that it's easy to forget about beef for a while.

Time
45 minutes

Yield
Makes 6 generous burgers, or 12 kid-friendly sliders

Advance Work
Patties can be made up to a day in advance

Zero Waste
Since leftover cans of beans rarely get used, I've made this recipe for 6 burgers. Uncooked patties will last in the refrigerator for 3 days, or the freezer for up to 6 months

Liquidity
A Chenin Blanc has just the right hint of sweetness to balance the dominant flavors of garam masala and the gingery chutney

One 14-ounce can chickpeas, rinsed

One 14-ounce can butter beans or white navy beans, rinsed

4 Tbsp olive or vegetable oil, or butter, divided + extra for the buns

4 garlic cloves, minced

2 Tbsp freshly grated ginger

1 large carrot, peeled and grated on a coarse grater

1 zucchini, coarsely grated

1 medium yellow onion, chopped finely

1 tsp garam masala (an Indian spice blend)

½ cup fresh cilantro, stemmed and chopped finely

½ cup fresh mint, stemmed and chopped finely

2 eggs, beaten

½ cup panko or breadcrumbs

1 tsp salt (will vary depending on the beans)

½ tsp pepper

6 airy burger buns (ideally brioche) or 12 slider buns

½ cup Major Grey's chutney

1 avocado (optional)

1 red onion (optional)

In a large bowl, combine the beans. Reserve.

In a sauté pan over medium heat, add 2 tablespoons of the oil and the garlic. Stir for 1 minute. Then add the ginger, carrot, zucchini, onion, and garam masala. Sauté for 5 minutes, or until the veggies soften.

Transfer the contents of the veggie pan into the bowl of beans. Use a potato masher or fork to mix and slightly mash the mixture, mashing roughly half the beans while leaving the remaining ones whole. Add the cilantro, mint, egg, panko, salt, and pepper. Mix all of the ingredients with a fork, then use your hands to form the mixture into 6 patties (or 12 if making sliders). Reserve.

In a sauté pan over medium-high heat, add the remaining 2 tablespoons of oil. When the oil is hot, add the patties. Cover with a lid and cook for 4 minutes per side, or until cooked through.

If the buns are too thick or too dense, pull a little bread from the center of the top half, or slice a bit off from one or both of the cut sides. While the patties are cooking, brush the buns with oil or butter and toast, cut side down, in a pan until browned.

Top each patty with 1 tablespoon of chutney (or ½ tablespoon if making sliders) and a slice of avocado and onion, if using.

Pan-Seared Arctic Char
with Braised Fennel and Pernod Aioli

This fenneliscious dish doubles down on the flavor of anise (think licorice), which is a natural foil for the delicate nuances of Arctic char. The accompanying Pernod-infused aioli adds a rich component that completes the dish.

Part of the allure of Arctic char is its thin skin, which crisps beautifully in a pan. Cooking skin-on fillets can be a little intimidating, and for good reason. It's one of the learned skills that separate restaurant chefs from home cooks. I have articulated the technique I was taught by Jeremy Charles, Newfoundland's reluctant rock star chef. Jeremy's technique delivers the holy grail of moist flesh and crispy skin.

½ cup aioli (make Three-Clove Aioli, page 243, but note additions below)

1 Tbsp Pernod, or in a pinch, ouzo or sambuca

2 large fennel bulbs plus fronds + 4 fronds for garnishing, divided

2 cups chicken stock + extra if necessary

½ cup white wine

3 Tbsp olive oil, divided

Salt and pepper

6 sprigs fresh thyme (optional)

Four 6-ounce skin on arctic char fillets, or salmon or striped bass

2 Tbsp butter

Preheat the oven to 325°F.

Make the aioli per the instructions, but add Pernod instead of water at the end, and fold in a tablespoon of finely chopped fennel fronds. Reserve.

Trim the fennel arteries just above the bulb, reserving all the fronds, then slice the fennel from top to bottom through the core into ¼-inch-thick slices. Set in a 9-by-14-inch baking dish. Pour the stock and wine overtop, drizzle with 2 tablespoons of the olive oil, and season with a sprinkle with salt and pepper. Top with thyme. Cover tightly with aluminum foil, then bake for 40 minutes, or until the braising juices are simmering and the fennel is tender.

Remove the foil and return to the oven for another 90 minutes, checking every 15 minutes or so to baste the fennel with the pan liquids and make sure the liquid doesn't reduce to nothing. If it is getting close, add extra chicken stock in ½-cup increments. Braise until the fennel has started to brown on top. Reserve in the baking dish.

Check the fish for pin bones and scales, and remove any that you find. (HACK: with your sharpest knife, score the skin side of each fillet 3 times (see photo) about an eighth-inch deep. This keeps the fish from curling when it hits the heat of the pan, which in turn allows the skin to crisp evenly.)

Time
< 30 minutes + 2 hours braising

Yield
Makes 4 servings

Advance Work
Aioli can be prepared up to a day in advance. Fennel and leeks can be braised earlier in the day, refrigerated in the baking dish, and reheated in a 425°F oven for 10 minutes

Liquidity
An Alsatian Riesling is a white wine with sophisticated elegance and structure that will rise to the occasion of this dish

(continued)

Brine

¼ cup salt

¼ cup brown sugar

10 peppercorns

1 cup buttermilk

2 tsp hot sauce (Tabasco, Louisiana, Frank's . . .)

Chicken

2 large boneless, skinless chicken breasts (about 12 ounces each)

Seasoned Flour

2 cups flour

⅔ cup cornstarch

2 tsp baking powder

1½ Tbsp paprika

1½ Tbsp garlic powder

1½ Tbsp onion powder

1 tsp ground cayenne pepper

1 tsp salt

½ tsp white or black pepper

Ingredient List Note

This recipe diverges from the traditional format I have used throughout the book. Instead of listing the total amount of each ingredient required for the entire recipe, I have broken down the ingredients into each of the four main steps and the optional serving methods—which makes each step easier to follow, but means that you notice some duplication. As a separate note, the repetition of spices in the various steps helps to build layers of flavor and heat.

TO MAKE THE BRINE in a small pot, bring ½ cup water to a boil. Add the salt, sugar, and peppercorns, and stir until the salt and sugar dissolve. Let cool to room temperature. Add the buttermilk and hot sauce. Reserve.

TO PREPARE AND BRINE THE CHICKEN cut each breast crosswise into 3 strips. Then cut each strip into 2 or 3 pieces so that each piece is roughly a 1-inch cube. Depending on the size of the breasts, you may end up with a few extra nuggets at the end to snack on.

Transfer the chicken to a medium bowl or resealable plastic bag, add the brine, and refrigerate for 1 hour. Pour off the brine and discard (don't even *think* about reusing it). Pat the chicken down with paper towels.

FOR THE SEASONED FLOUR in a large bowl, whisk together all ingredients.

FOR THE BUTTERMILK WASH add the buttermilk to a separate large bowl.

TO FLOUR THE CHICKEN Set out a wire rack on a sheet pan (or just a sheet pan), within reach. One piece at a time, use your right hand to toss chicken in the seasoned flour, then drop it into the buttermilk wash. Use your left hand to roll it in the wash, then transfer it back to the seasoned flour. Use your right hand to pat the seasoned flour into the chicken. To create extra craggy, extra crispy chicken, dip the balls one more time in the buttermilk and one last time in the flour mixture (*do it!*). Transfer the chicken to a wire rack. Repeat for each piece of chicken. Let the chicken rest on the rack for 15 minutes. (This will help the coating stick to the chicken when fried.)

FOR THE GREAT BALLS OF FIRE SAUCE In a small pot, add all ingredients. Just before you start to fry, over very, very low heat, warm up the sauce until the butter melts. Whisk the ingredients together and turn off the heat.

(continued)

Buttermilk Wash

2 cups buttermilk

Great Balls of Fire Sauce

8 Tbsp butter (1 stick)

1 Tbsp hot sauce (Tabasco, Louisiana, Frank's . . .)

1 Tbsp cayenne powder

3 Tbsp honey

2 tsp garlic powder

1 tsp mustard powder

2 tsp smoked paprika, or paprika

½ tsp pepper

Frying Oil

Peanut or vegetable oil (before frying, see Deep Fry Basics on page 52)

For Sliders

½ cup aioli (page 243), or mayonnaise

8 brioche slider buns, or best available slider buns

½ cup creamy coleslaw (HACK: you've done enough already; just buy it)

8 slices bread and butter pickles

For Waffles

1¼ cups flour

½ tsp baking powder

¼ tsp baking soda

½ tsp salt

1½ Tbsp sugar

2 Tbsp butter

2 eggs

1 cup buttermilk

Maple syrup for topping

TO FRY THE CHICKEN While the chicken rests, preheat a deep fryer, or fill a tall, heavy medium pot one-third full of oil. Heat the oil to 350°F.

Fry the chicken in 2 batches for about 5 minutes, or until super crispy on the outside and cooked through. Drain on paper towels. Transfer the chicken to a large bowl and spoon Great Balls of Fire Sauce overtop. Toss gently to coat the chicken evenly.

TO SERVE AS NUGGETS Serve immediately, and warn your guests that they are hot in every sense of the word.

TO SERVE AS SLIDERS Toast the buns. Schmear the bottom buns with aioli, add one Great Ball of Fire and top with coleslaw and a pickle slice.

TO SERVE WITH WAFFLES Before you fry the chicken, in a large bowl, whisk together the flour, baking powder, baking soda, salt, and sugar. Melt the butter. In a medium bowl, whip the eggs, whisk in the buttermilk, and then whisk in the butter. Add the wet ingredients to the dry ingredients and whisk, but do not overbeat. Let sit for 5 minutes. Preheat the waffle maker, coat with a spray of oil, and cook the waffles until they are extra crispy. Heat the syrup and pour overtop. Top each waffle with one to three Great Balls of Fire.

Piri Piri Chicken

Piri piri chicken is traditionally made with African bird's-eye chilis, hence its name, which is derived from the Swahili word *piri-piri* or "strong pepper." With your first bite, you taste the tomato and bell pepper in the sauce, then the heat of the chilis kicks in, followed by the racy acidity of the lemon juice and cider vinegar. Since piri piri chicken has yet to be appropriated by a major fast food chain, its unique taste profile is a welcome diversion from the more popular styles of chicken.

The beauty of piri piri chicken is that once you have made the sauce, it multitasks as the marinade, the tenderizer, the basting sauce, and the dipping sauce—creating a full 360° piri piri experience.

Time
2 hours + 2 hours
marinating

Yield
Serves 4

Advance Work
Piri Piri Piri! Sauce can be made days in advance

Liquidity
An off-dry cider will offer a hint of sweetness and enough effervescent acidity to compete with the tang the piri piri sauce

1 whole best available
   chicken, or the
   equivalent in boneless
   or bone-in pieces
2 cups Piri Piri Piri! Sauce
   (page 242), divided
¼ cup chopped parsley to
   finish (optional)

If using a whole chicken, butterfly it, or cut it into two halves. To butterfly a chicken, place it on a solid surface, breast side down. Using a pair of kitchen scissors, cut down each side of the backbone from the tail to the neck, and remove it (then freeze it until you are ready to make stock, see page 251). Flip the bird over, splay it out, place your palms on each side of the breast and press down forcefully to crack the breast bone.

Place your chosen cuts of chicken in a large resealable plastic bag and add 1 cup of the sauce. Squeeze out the air and seal the bag. Massage the chicken through the bag until it is thoroughly covered in sauce. Refrigerate for 2 hours.

FOR BUTTERFLIED CHICKEN, CHICKEN HALVES, AND ALL BONE-IN PIECES
Preheat the grill for indirect medium-high heat (see page 75), and place the chicken bone side down over the section of the grill with no direct heat. Close the lid and cook until the internal temperature of the breast is 160°F and the thigh is 165°F, or until the juices in the thigh run clear when poked with a fork—roughly 45 minutes. Baste with extra sauce in the last 10 minutes. If any parts of the skin start to get too dark, lightly tent the darkened section with a small piece of aluminum foil.

FOR BONELESS PIECES Preheat the grill for direct medium heat (see page 75), about 400°F, and place the chicken on to the grate directly over the heat source. Close the lid. Turn once after about 5 minutes; baste with extra sauce before turning. Close the lid again and continue cooking for 5 more minutes, or until the internal temperature of the breast is 160°F and the thigh is 165°F, or until the juices in the thigh run clear when poked with a fork.

Serve with the remaining sauce for dipping. Sprinkle parsley overtop.

Piri Piri Piri! Sauce Safety

The sauce used to marinate the chicken may be reused to baste the chicken, if boiled for 4 minutes. Any marinade that has touched the raw chicken and not been boiled must be discarded after use. Sauce that has not come into contact with raw chicken will last in the refrigerator for 3 to 4 weeks.

One-Pan Braised Chicken Thigh Dinner

This one-pan dish is a classic for many reasons. It's low-fuss, inexpensive, very forgiving, insanely delicious, and it presents beautifully. The dish relies on two separate cooking principles, braising (page 65) and reducing (page 67), to coax a remarkable amount of flavor out of a handful of everyday ingredients. These techniques play off each other like Mick and Keith in their glory years.

For such a simple dish, there is SO much going on. The braising liquids (a combination of wine and chicken stock), tenderize the thighs, and help break down the fibers in the veggies. When the lid is removed midway through the cooking process, these liquids start to reduce, causing their flavors to intensify. At the same time, the garlic cloves and herbs infuse the reducing liquids as they poach in it. The rendering chicken fat and the marrow from the bones add richness, and the flour coating and collagen from the chicken thickens the collective liquids. In 90 minutes, the braising liquids, in concert with everything else in the pan, evolve into a complex sauce that envelopes the melt-in-your-mouth thigh and caramelized veggies.

Time
2 hours

Yield
Serves 4

Liquidity
Languedoc, a sturdy, approachable red wine from the south of France, is a perfect pairing for this rustic braised dish—at a perfect mid-week price point

NOTE: Serve family style in the pan. Pour some of the reduced juices overtop each serving.

4 large chicken thighs, skin-on, bone-in

Salt and pepper

1 tsp smoked paprika

¼ cup flour

2 Tbsp olive oil + extra for drizzling

1 red onion, quartered top to bottom through the core

1 fennel bulb, trimmed above the bulb and quartered top to bottom through the core

4 fat carrots, halved lengthwise

2 fat parsnips, peeled and cut into 1-inch rounds

12 garlic cloves, peeled

2 cups best available chicken stock + a little extra

1 cup white wine

12 sprigs rosemary and/or thyme

1 lemon, sliced thinly

2 cups broccolini, spinach, Swiss chard, or your favorite green

Set the oven rack in the center of the oven and preheat to 325°F.

To a large bowl, add the chicken. Pat generously with salt, pepper, and paprika. Toss with the flour.

In a large heavy, oven proof frying pan (ideally cast-iron, 12 inches or bigger), over medium-high heat, add the oil. Set the thighs skin side down in the pan and sear for about 8 minutes, or until the skin turns golden brown. Flip the thighs.

Add the onion and fennel, cut sides up, and nestle the carrots, parsnips, and garlic in the pan. Everything will shrink as the contents braise. Add the stock and wine, and if necessary extra stock, or water, to bring the liquids roughly three-quarters of the way up the chicken. Top with the herbs and lemon slices, and drizzle with olive oil. Bring to a simmer, then turn off the heat. Cover the pan tightly with a lid or aluminum foil.

Bake for 30 minutes. Remove the foil and bake for another hour, or until the tops of the veggies are browned and the liquid has reduced by about two-thirds. During the last 30 minutes make sure the liquids don't reduce and blacken at the bottom of the pan. If they do, add stock or water ½ cup at a time. In the last 15 minutes, nestle the greens between the pan contents so they simmer.

Rotisserie Chicken Salad—Two Ways
with Pecans and Medjool Dates

If Rotisserie Chicken TV existed, I would watch it all day. I find the golden birds, pirouetting in unison, more mesmerizing than a yule log fire. But when it comes to making rotisserie chicken—especially when it is destined to be one of several components in a dish—I leave it up to the pros. That's because store-bought rotisserie chicken is convenient, fresh, and usually not much more expensive than an uncooked chicken.

With a bird in the hand, this opulent, amped-up version of the perennial American classic is a snap to assemble—and a pleasure to eat.

Time
< 30 minutes

Yield
Serves 4

Advance Work
The aioli may be made up to a day in advance

Liquidity
Viognier is a seductive white with tropical notes that will become BFFs with the nummy nuggets in this salad

1 Tbsp chipotle in adobo sauce, or ½ tsp ground chipotle

½ cup aioli (page 243), or mayonnaise

2 cups rotisserie chicken meat, skin on or off as desired

Zest of 2 oranges

½ cup pitted and quartered Medjool dates

½ cup store-bought candied pecans, or roasted pecan pieces

6 center stalks of celery, tops included, sliced finely

4 green onions, sliced finely

3 Tbsp stemmed, roughly chopped fresh mint

Salt and pepper

1 red cabbage or butter lettuce, or bread or buns for serving

Use a fork to mash the chipotle, then blend it into the aioli. Reserve.

Tear or cut the chicken into ½-inch pieces. In a large bowl, mix the chicken, orange zest, dates, pecans, celery, green onions, and mint. Add enough aioli to coat but not smother the chicken. Season to taste with salt and pepper.

Serve as a salad in the outer leaf of a red cabbage, or in sandwich form.

PURCHASE AT A CHINESE BBQ

EASY PEKING
DUCK RAMEN
page 179

PEKING DUCK
TACOS
page 178

Peking Duck—Two Ways

Making a traditional Peking duck from scratch is very next-level and takes days to prepare if you count the drying time. But if you can get your hands on a precooked duck at a Chinese barbecue, they are a great running start for some Flavorbombs that will expand your repertoire. Talk about a time-saving HACK. Once you've pulled all the meat and skin off the bone for the taco, it takes minimal effort to make the stock and ramen. If you do make both recipes (served together or individually), you will be using every ounce of the bird, thereby hitting the duck trifecta of zero waste.

Peking Duck Tacos
with Duck Skin Cracklings *photo on page 177*

This taco is mash-up of a Peking duck pancake and a very cheffy taco. The tender, moist duck meat is decadent, the crispy duck skin cracklings are the best bacon you will ever taste, and the juicy pomegranate seeds add a tart counterpoint to the richness of the meat and the sweetness of the hoisin sauce.

Time
< 30 minutes

Yield
Serves 4

Liquidity
A Rosé will tame the taco—and still let the duck walk the walk

1 store-bought whole barbecued Peking duck (meat pulled off the bones and skin pulled of the meat; reserve skin and pull meat into ½-inch pieces)

½ cup canned mandarin slices, drained, or ½ cup diced fresh mango

1 avocado, skinned, seeded, and diced

¼ cup chopped mint

2 green onions, sliced thinly on the bias

2 Tbsp pomegranate seeds

8 Szechuan peppercorns or black peppercorns, crushed

Four 6-inch flour tortillas

4 Tbsp hoisin sauce

1 jalapeño pepper, sliced crosswise, paper thin

1 lime, quartered

In a dry, large heavy pan over medium heat, add all of the duck skin, fat side down, and cook for about 10 minutes, turning once, or until the skin is super crispy but not charred. Drain on a paper towel. Reserve. Reserve the pan with the fat.

In a medium bowl, add mandarin slices, avocado, mint, green onions, pomegranate seeds, and peppercorns.

Just before serving, heat the pan used for the duck skin to medium, then add three-quarters of the duck and reserve the rest for the ramen (use it all if you don't plan to make ramen). Cook for 2 minutes.

While the duck is warming up, heat the tortillas. If you have a gas stovetop, use a pair of tongs to grill each tortilla directly over the flames for about 30 seconds per side, turning several times, or until it is burnished on both sides. Otherwise, brown the tortillas in a dry pan over medium-high heat.

Crumble the duck skin. Add, along with the duck, to the bowl of veggies. Spread a tablespoon of hoisin sauce over each tortilla. Spoon a quarter of the duck mixture overtop, and top with a few jalapeño slices. Serve with a lime wedge.

Easy Peking Duck Ramen *photo on page 176*

Traditional ramen is all about the broth, which can take up to two days to make. This rogue version leans on a homemade duck stock (see sidebar) that requires only 10 minutes of active time and 90 minutes of simmering.

Stock

1 duck carcass

½ fennel bulb, roughly chopped

1 carrot, roughly chopped

½ tsp Szechuan peppercorns, or black peppercorns

2 whole star anise pods (optional)

Ramen

2 eggs

4 servings Japanese-style noodles (your choice of ramen, soba, or udon), or in a pinch, conventional spaghetti

4 baby bok choy, halved lengthwise

½ cup pulled duck meat (or whatever you have left from the tacos), or chicken meat, or tofu

2 green onions, finely sliced

TO MAKE THE STOCK in a medium pot, add the duck carcass, fennel, carrot, peppercorns, and star anise, along with 6 cups of water. Bring to a boil, then reduce to a simmer. Simmer for 1½ hours. Strain off the solids. Let cool, then use a fat strainer or a ladle to strain off the fat. Reserve the stock.

TO MAKE THE RAMEN Fill a medium pot half full of water. Bring to a boil and gently add the eggs. Immediately set a timer for 6½ minutes. When the water returns to a boil, reduce to a strong simmer.

Set up an ice bath for the eggs. When the timer goes off, transfer the eggs from the water to the ice bath. Reserve the hot water in the pot for the noodles. After 2 minutes remove and peel the eggs.

Make the noodles according to directions. Strain the noodles out and reserve in a warmed bowl.

In a large pot, bring the stock to a boil. Add the bok choy and reserved duck meat. Reduce to a simmer and cover for 3 minutes.

Set out 4 bowls. Divide the noodles, stock, duck, and bok choy between the bowls. Top with an egg half and a sprinkle of green onion.

Time

2 hours

Yield

Serves 4

Advance Work

Stock can be made a couple of days in advance. Eggs can be cooked earlier in the day

Liquidity

A tiny sipper of dry Fino sherry will bring poise and grace to the aromatics of the duck stock

Peking Duck Stock

Peking duck stock is unlike any other poultry-based stock because it takes on the distinctive, delicately perfumed flavor of the aromatics the duck is infused with. The reward for 10 minutes of minimal effort is huge—and practically free. What's more, by using every part of the duck, you are honoring the duck, the people who raised it, and the people who roasted it. If you don't use the stock to make my simple ramen-style soup, freeze it and use it for soup later, or for a unique risotto or rice dish.

Braised Chinese-Style Beef Short Ribs

This is a *go big or go home* recipe. The ingredient list is long, the bone-on rib is meaty and pricey, and braising takes time. The upside is that the braising process does most of the hard work for you. If you can brave the rest, the payoff for this extravagantly rich cut of meat and its aromatic sauce is HUGE.

Time
< 1 hour + 3 hours braising

Yield
Serves 4

Advance Work
Meat can be braised up to a day in advance, refrigerated in the Dutch oven, and reheated in a 350°F oven for 30 minutes. Root vegetables can be prepared up to a day in advance and reheated

Liquidity
Lambrusco is an everyday sparkling red from Italy's Emilia Romagna region. It's slightly sweet and acidic, which makes it a perfect contrarian pairing for this rich cut of beef

3 pounds bone-in beef short ribs, or bone-out short ribs, beef cheeks, or chuck steak

Salt and pepper

1 Tbsp neutral oil

½ onion, diced

3 garlic cloves, smashed

2 Tbsp minced fresh ginger

2 tsp five spice powder

4 dried chile de árbol chilis or 1 tsp crushed chili flakes

½ cup soy sauce

¼ cup rice wine vinegar

½ cup brown sugar

1 quart beef stock

3 large russet potatoes, peeled

1 celeriac, or turnip, peeled

¼ cup half-and-half

4 Tbsp butter

¼ cup orange juice

2 Tbsp freshly squeezed lemon juice

¼ cup hoisin sauce

Zest of 2 oranges, divided

3 bird's-eye chilis, or another fresh red chili, sliced finely (optional), divided

4 green onions, sliced finely

1 Tbsp sesame seeds (optional)

Preheat the oven to 350°F and generously season the beef with salt and pepper.

In a Dutch oven or large cast-iron pan over medium-high heat, add the oil. Once hot, add the beef ribs and cook for 90 seconds per side until browned. Remove the beef and reserve.

To the Dutch oven, add the onion and stir for 2 minutes. Add the garlic, ginger, five spice powder, and dried chilis, and stir for 2 more minutes. Add the soy sauce, rice wine vinegar, brown sugar, stock, and ribs. When the liquids start to boil, put a lid on the pot and transfer to the oven.

Braise for 2 hours, then remove the lid and continue braising for 1 more hour, or until the meat is tender.

While the meat is braising, chop the potatoes and celeriac. Transfer to a steam basket and steam over boiling water for about 20 minutes, or until tender.

In a large bowl, mash the potatoes and celeriac. Add the half-and-half and butter. Blend and season with salt and pepper. Cover with foil and reserve.

Remove the meat from the braising pot. Reserve. Place a strainer over a large bowl. Pour the juices through the strainer into the bowl. Use the back of a ladle to press out as much juice as possible. Discard the solids.

Transfer the juices to a pot. Let sit for 2 minutes and then spoon off any fat that rises to the top. Add the orange juice, lemon juice, and hoisin sauce. Turn the heat to high and reduce the braising juices by about half. Stir in half the zest and half the fresh chilis.

TO SERVE Reheat the mash over a pot of boiling water. Plate the mash and meat and pour the braising juices overtop. Finish with the remaining zest, chilis, green onion, and sesame seeds.

Melt-in-Your-Mouth Tenderloin
with Succotash and Chermoula Sauce

In my day-to-day life I live by the 80/20 rule. That's 80% plant-based foods, and 20% meat-based. Limiting yourself to a small portion of animal protein gives you an incentive to make every bite count.

Tenderloin fits the bill perfectly. As the name suggests, it is the most tender cut from the cow. When properly cooked, it practically melts in your mouth. The trade-off for such glorious mouthfeel is that it lacks the "meaty" flavor of cuts from the more hardworking sections of the animal. To have your steak and eat it too, season your tenderloin generously. Often this means rubbing the tenderloin with a dry rub, but for this particular recipe, the seasoning comes in the form of garlic and a trio of fresh herbs in the accompanying chermoula sauce, and the ancho chili in the accompanying succotash.

Tenderloin can be cooked quickly and effectively on a grill or in a pan. But if you have a sous vide circulator, the additional time it takes will be rewarded with extra tenderness and picture-perfect rosy-pink slices.

Time
45 minutes + extra to sous vide steak

Yield
Serves 4

Advance Work
Steak can be sous vided up to a day in advance

Liquidity
A Carignan from the south of France has a swaggering braggadocio that allows it to stand its ground alongside the spiciness in the chermoula sauce and succotash

Two 8-ounce center-cut beef tenderloins, 2 inches thick

1 Tbsp butter (if sous viding the steak)

Succotash

1 Tbsp olive oil + extra for drizzling

2 slices smoky bacon, sliced crosswise into ¼-inch-thick strips

8 fat spears asparagus

½ red bell pepper, diced finely

2 garlic cloves, peeled and minced

2 green onions, finely sliced

4 ears corn, kernels cut from cob, or 2 cups frozen corn, thawed

¼–½ tsp ground ancho chili (or any New Mexican ground chili)

⅓ cup stemmed and roughly chopped cilantro

Salt and pepper

½ cup chermoula sauce (page 240) or in a pinch, One-Minute Garlic-Herb Oil (page 250)

If you are sous viding the steak (page 69), start now, then sear it just after the succotash is done. If you are pan-searing or grilling it, start after the succotash is done.

FOR THE SUCCOTASH In a large sauté pan over medium heat, add the olive oil and bacon. Cook for 3 minutes, or until the bacon starts to crisp. Add the asparagus and red bell pepper. Cook for about 3 minutes, stirring occasionally, or until the asparagus starts to brown. Add the garlic and green onion and stir for 30 seconds. Add the corn and ancho chili powder and stir occasionally for 3 minutes, or until the corn begins to brown. Remove from the heat, stir in the cilantro and season to taste with salt and pepper. Reserve.

(continued)

SOUS VIDE METHOD Season the steak lightly with salt and pepper. Seal in a plastic bag with the butter and simmer at 135°F for 3 hours. Transfer to an ice bath. At this point, the steak may be refrigerated for up to 24 hours.

To finish, remove the steak from the bag, pat dry, drizzle with oil, and then season with salt and pepper. Heat a cast-iron or heavy sauté pan over high heat. When the pan is smoking hot, add the steak and sear for 90 seconds per side, or until it develops a deep brown crust. Remove from the heat and cover loosely with aluminum foil to allow the center to warm up while you prepare the plates. Slice just before serving.

PAN METHOD Drizzle the steak with oil, then season with salt and pepper.

Heat a cast-iron or heavy-bottomed pan over medium-high heat. When the pan is hot, add the steak and cook for 5 minutes on the first side. Flip and cook for 3 to 5 more minutes, or until the internal temperature reaches 135°F for medium rare. Remove from the pan and cover loosely with aluminum foil for 10 minutes. Slice just before serving.

GRILL METHOD Preheat the grill to direct medium-high heat. Drizzle the steak with oil, then season with salt and pepper. Grill for 5 minutes on the first side. Flip and cook for 3 to 5 more minutes, or until the internal temperature reaches 135°F for medium rare. Remove from the pan and cover loosely with aluminum foil for 10 minutes. Slice just before serving.

TO SERVE Spoon the succotash in a mound in the center of individual pre-warmed plates. Top with steak slices and serve with chermoula sauce. Drizzle the steak with olive oil and finish with salt.

Grilled Heritage Pork Chop
with Stone Fruit Salsa

When it comes to pork, the loin is my favorite cut. But committing to the loin is just the first step on a long and winding road to Porktopia. Along the way, you will encounter many forks in the road, each of which requires a decision that will either get you closer to your destination or lead you down the path of disappointment. I feel your frustration. After all, who's got time to study the map? And why isn't there an app for that? To go straight to nirvana, while avoiding any unexpected roadblocks or tolls, follow this route planner.

Time
1 hour + 8 hours brining

Yield
Makes 2 to 4 servings (for big eaters, allow 1 full chop per person)

Advance Work
The salsa can be prepared earlier in the day

Liquidity
A floral Torrontes from Argentina will ennoble this little piggy and its peachy salsa dance partner

CHOOSE A BONE-IN LOIN CHOP The bone adds flavor and gives anyone with an oral fixation something pleasing to gnaw on.

ASK YOUR BUTCHER FOR A CHOP THAT IS 1½ INCHES THICK Thicker is better, especially with today's leaner pork. Each chop of this size should yield six ¼-inch-thick slices, enough for one generous portion, or two small-yet-pleasing servings.

BUY HERITAGE PORK If your butcher has a waxed mustache or a bacon tattoo, chances are he or she carries some breed of heritage pork (Berkshire, Kurobuta, Duroc, Tamworth, Hampshire). Pork is still inexpensive compared to other proteins, and the extra few dollars you will spend on a heritage chop will deliver a well-balanced richness you can really taste.

BRINE IT Brining your chop in even the simplest salt and sugar mixture simultaneously seasons and moistens it, which will protect it from drying out when cooked.

RUB IT Pork chops, especially brined heritage pork chops, already have fabulous flavor. But why stop there when you can gild the lily? A well-chosen rub will add another layer of flavor with minimal effort.

GRILL IT Pork chops and grills go together like gin and tonic. The meat, bone, and protective layer of fat on the sides will all benefit from the char of the grill.

CROWN IT A summer stone fruit salsa will add a juiciness and freshness that is a perfect foil for a charred chop.

(continued)

Brine

4 cups water, divided

¼ cup salt

¼ cup brown sugar

6 black peppercorns

1 garlic clove, slightly smashed

1 cinnamon stick (optional)

1 bay leaf (optional)

¼ cup apple cider vinegar (optional)

Pork

Two 1-pound 1½-inch thick heritage pork loin chops, bone-in

1 Tbsp olive oil

2 Tbsp chorizo seasoning blend (page 154), or your favorite dry rub

1 cup stone fruit salsa (see below)

Stone Fruit Salsa

4 fragrant ripe peaches, apricots, nectarines, or plums (depending on which are at their best), pitted and diced into ¼-inch cubes

4 green onions, trimmed then sliced thinly

8 mint leaves, roughly chopped

2 Tbsp freshly squeezed lime juice

4 Tbsp finely chopped red bell pepper (mostly for color)

½–1 jalapeño chili, seeds and membranes removed, minced, or sliced super finely

Salt and pepper

FOR THE BRINE bring 1 cup of the water to a boil.

In a medium bowl, add the salt, brown sugar, peppercorns, garlic, cinnamon stick, and bay leaf. Pour the boiling water overtop and stir until the salt and sugar are dissolved. Add 3 more cups of water and the apple cider vinegar. Let cool. Reserve.

Transfer 1 quart of the brine to a heavy duty resealable plastic bag. Add the pork chops, squeeze out all the air, seal, and refrigerate for 8 hours.

FOR THE SALSA combine the fruit, green onions, mint, lime juice, red bell pepper, and chili in a bowl and mix thoroughly with a fork. Season to taste with salt and pepper. Reserve.

TO GRILL THE PORK When you are ready to grill the pork, preheat the grill to direct medium-high heat—about 400°F.

Remove the chops from the brine and pat dry with paper towels. Brush the chops with the olive oil, then rub with the seasoning blend.

Grill the chops for 5 minutes a side, rotating them 90° halfway through the cooking time to create cross-hatched grill marks. Reconfigure the grill to high indirect heat (see page 75), then transfer the chops to the section of the grill with no direct heat, close the lid, and continue cooking for about 20 minutes, or until the chops reach an internal temperature of 145°F. Remove from the heat, cover loosely with foil, and let rest for 10 minutes.

Cut the meat off the bone, slice, and serve topped with the salsa. Auction the bones off to the highest bidder.

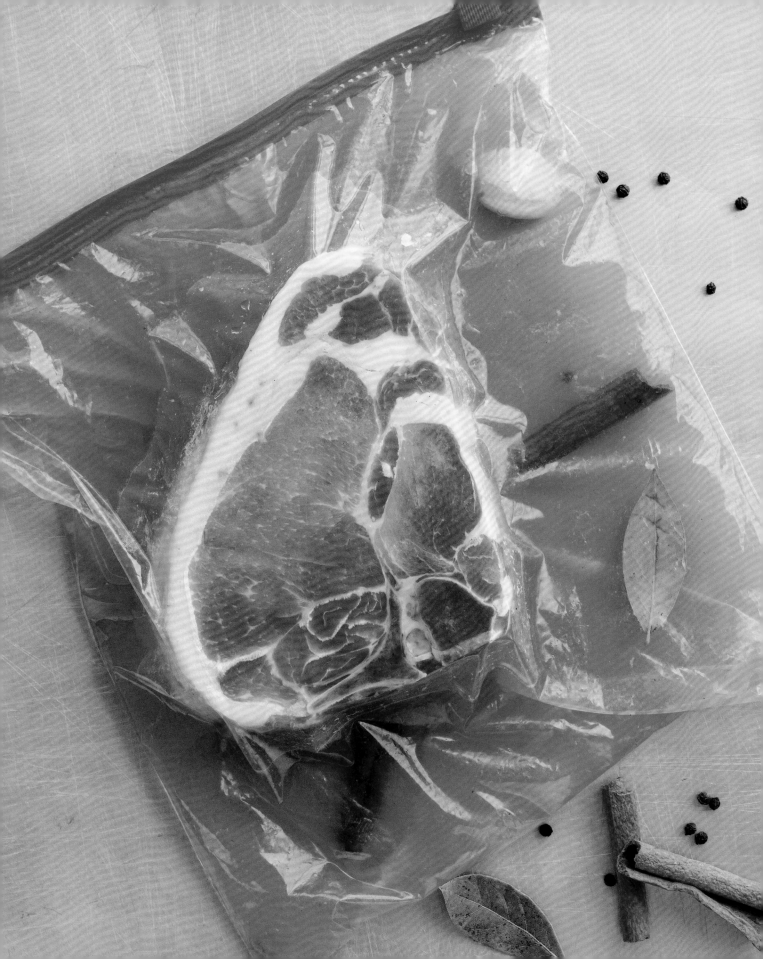

Pineapple and Hoisin–Glazed Pork Ribs

Eating ribs is a quintessential primal experience. To accentuate the tactile nature of the act, I gravitate to St. Louis–style pork ribs, which are from the belly area of the hog. These ribs are larger, meatier, and in my opinion more succulent. The spices in the dry rub and the tangy sweetness of the glaze work in tandem to create a finger-licking, lip-smacking experience that is as satisfying and primal as it gets.

Time
4 hours + chip soaking

Yield
Serves 4

Liquidity
Spanish Cava is a user-friendly sparkling wine with lots of zing

4 cups wood chips (hickory, or your favorite)

Dry Rub
1 Tbsp salt
1 Tbsp pepper
1 Tbsp dry mustard
3 Tbsp Chinese 5-spice powder

Pineapple Hoisin Glaze
2 Tbsp grated ginger
4 garlic cloves, minced
2 Tbsp brown sugar
⅓ cup hoisin sauce
1 cup roughly chopped canned pineapple rings (reserve 3 for garnish)
½ tsp chili flakes

Ribs
1 full rack St. Louis–style ribs (about 3–4 pounds)
3 Tbsp olive oil, divided

Soak the wood chips for an hour.

TO MAKE THE DRY RUB Combine the ingredients in a bowl. Reserve.

TO MAKE THE PINEAPPLE HOISIN GLAZE Blend the ingredients in a blender. Reserve.

FOR THE RIBS Remove the membrane from the ribs if you wish, but it's not necessary. Pat the ribs down with paper towel, then brush with 2 tablespoons of the olive oil. Sprinkle 6 tablespoons of the dry rub generously over the ribs, then rub it in, and let sit for 30 minutes.

Place the chips in an aluminum pan or wrap with foil into a pouch and puncture the foil pouch in a few places with a fork. Place the chips directly over the flames, and preheat the grill to high. After about 20 minutes, the chips should begin to smoke.

Reconfigure the grill to indirect heat (see page 75) and reduce the temperature to 300°F. Move the chip pan to a section of the grill where it is directly over the flames. Set the rack of ribs, bone side down, on the section of the grill with no direct heat. Double check that no part of the ribs is over a live flame. Close the lid and cook for about 2½ hours, or until the ribs have a distinct rosy color and the meat recedes from the edges of the bone.

Divide 1½ cups of the pineapple hoisin glaze into 2 bowls and add a few tablespoons of beer or water to thin out the first bowl. Baste the ribs generously on all sides with the thinned-out glaze and continue cooking for 20 more minutes.

Remove the ribs from the grill, cover lightly with foil, and let rest for 15 minutes before serving.

Lightly brush the reserved pineapple rings with oil. Set them on the grill over direct medium heat, or cook in a pan over medium heat for about 5 minutes, or until nicely browned on both sides.

Flip the ribs upside down (bone side up), and slice into individual ribs. Serve family style, garnished with grilled pineapple slices and serve with the second bowl of sauce.

Spontaneous Sausage Sandwich

Not all Flavorbombs need to be made from scratch, nor do they need to take a lot of time. Sometimes the path to instant gratification is as simple as combining the ingredients you already have on hand in new ways, and eating your *magnum opus* while leaning over the sink. Making spontaneous meals is even easier if you stock your fridge and freezer strategically with a variety of options. Here's an example of one of the go-to meals I make on the fly when I want something quick and satisfying.

Time
15 minutes

Yield
Serves 1

Liquidity
With its bristly effervescence, nothing sashays with a sausage like a German Hefeweizen

1 bagel stick or other flavorful roll

1 big fat fancy sausage

½ avocado

½ tsp of your favorite hot sauce, or a pinch of dried ground chili powder

1 Tbsp olive oil

1 Tbsp honey mustard, or your favorite mustard

1 tsp olive oil

Preheat a toaster oven or oven to 400°F.

Bake the roll for 10 minutes, or until super-crispy on the outside.

Score the sausage with a few shallow knife cuts, or poke it a few times with a fork to keep it from rupturing as it cooks. To a frying pan or grill over medium-high heat, add the sausage and cook for 10 minutes, or until cooked through, turning a quarter rotation every 2 minutes.

While the sausage cooks, mash up the avocado. Add the hot sauce or another option from the Flavorbomb playbook.

Slice the bun lengthwise, being careful not to cut all the way through to the bottom. Splay the bun open and use your fingers or a fork to pull out some of the bread on both sides. Drizzle the inside with oil, then spread mustard on one side and avocado mixture on the other. Add the sausage and enjoy.

Cauliflower Steak
with Lemony Anchovy Sauce

These days, cauliflower is ubiquitous on restaurant menus—but far too often it is disappointing. That's because most busy restaurant kitchens don't dedicate the time required to maximize its true potential.

With enough time and patience, the miracle of caramelization (page 62) works its magic, transforming a thick slice of raw cauliflower into a sweet, lip-smackin' "steak" that is immensely satisfying—whether you are a dedicated vegetarian or a committed carnivore.

To add some complexity to the gloriously crusted veggie steak, I've topped it with a lemon-anchovy sauce that's punctuated with sweet raisins and tangy capers.

Time
< 1 hour

Yield
Makes 2 servings

Zero Waste
Save the exterior section of the cauliflower (which will likely fall apart because there is no stem to hold it together) for salads, crudités, or Caramelized Cauliflower Florets (page 92)

Liquidity
Zibibbo, the zippy Sicilian white, will broaden your wine horizons and pair well with the pan sauce

1 head cauliflower (select a firm head with minimal blemishes)
Salt and pepper
1 Tbsp olive oil
2 Tbsp butter, divided
3 garlic cloves, minced
1 medium shallot, diced
¼–½ tsp chili flakes
6 anchovies, chopped + 1 Tbsp oil from the tin
2 Tbsp capers, drained of brine
¼ cup raisins
3 Tbsp freshly squeezed lemon juice
¼ cup dry white wine (as defined by what's in your fridge, or what you are drinking)
2 Tbsp finely chopped parsley
Zest of 1 lemon

Set the cauliflower on a solid cutting surface, stem side up. Cut the cauliflower in half, vertically, through the center of the stem (it's the stem that will help keep the steak intact). Stand one of the halves up, stem side down. Starting from the cut side, measure in 1 generous inch and slice down vertically to create a 1-inch-thick "steak." Repeat with the other half. Season both halves with salt and pepper.

Preheat the oven to 450°F.

Heat a large cast-iron or other heavy ovenproof pan over medium-high heat. Add the olive oil and 1 tablespoon of the butter. Add the cauliflower steaks, center side down. Cook until the bottom is a nutty brown color, about 15 minutes. Flip the steaks and immediately transfer the pan to oven. Bake for about 25 minutes, or until the cauliflower is tender throughout and the bottom is well browned.

While the cauliflower is baking, heat a medium pan over medium heat. Add the remaining butter, garlic, shallot, chili flakes, anchovies, anchovy oil, capers, raisins, and salt and pepper to taste. Sauté until the garlic and shallots have browned and the anchovies have disintegrated into the butter, about 10 minutes. Add the lemon juice and wine. Turn the heat to medium-high and let the liquids reduce for about 2 minutes, or until reduced by half. Add the parsley. Turn off the heat and reserve. Remove the cauliflower from the oven and set on warmed plates.

Spoon the pan contents over the steaks and finish with the lemon zest.

Sidekicks

(Vegetables)

Mexican Street Corn—Two Ways

Mexican street corn, known as elote, and its cobless cousin, esquites, are street stall favorites that combine the smoky sweetness of charred corn kernels, the richness of fresh cheese and crema, and the heat from two kinds of chilis—all brightened by fresh lime juice. Although the corn is traditionally grilled over natural hardwood, you can get close to the same results on any backyard barbecue. It's an enduring favorite and a great way to make the most of fresh seasonal corn.

6 ears corn

½ cup cotija cheese or queso fresco, crumbled + extra for sprinkling

2 garlic cloves, minced

½ cup finely chopped cilantro + extra for sprinkling

1 tsp ground New Mexican or ancho chili + extra for sprinkling

½ tsp ground chipotle pepper

½ tsp salt

¼ tsp pepper

Elotes (On the Cob)

3 Tbsp mayonnaise

3 Tbsp Mexican crema or sour cream

2 limes, cut into wedges for serving

Esquites (Off the Cob)

2 Tbsp mayonnaise

2 Tbsp Mexican crema or sour cream

1 red bell pepper, stemmed, seeded and diced

4 green onions, sliced finely

2 Tbsp lime juice

Shuck the corn, then cut the cobs in half crosswise. Preheat the grill to direct medium-high heat.

Grill the corn for about 10 minutes, or until the kernels begin to blacken, turning the cobs a quarter rotation every 2 minutes.

ON THE COB In a medium bowl, stir together the mayo, crema, crumbled cheese, garlic, cilantro, chili powders, salt, and pepper.

In a large bowl, toss the corn with the sauce, or use a brush to apply the sauce. Sprinkle the corn with extra cilantro, cotija, and a dusting of chili powder. Serve immediately with lime wedges.

OFF THE COB After grilling the corn, let cool. In a large bowl, stand each ear upright and use a small sharp knife to cut the kernels from the cob.

In a medium bowl, stir together the mayo, crema, crumbled cheese, bell pepper, green onions, garlic, cilantro, chili powders, lime juice, salt, and pepper. Taste for salt and seasonings and adjust if desired.

Add half the sauce to the corn and mix thoroughly. Continue adding sauce until the corn is well dressed but not drowning in the sauce. Finish with a sprinkle of extra cilantro, cotija, and a dusting of ground chili pepper.

Time
30 minutes

Yield
Serves 4 to 6

Zero Waste
For a delicious taco, combine leftover esquites with a little bit of any leftover protein on a tortilla

Smushed Patatas Bravas
with Romesco Sauce

Patatas Bravas are a Spanish fried potato snack traditionally found in tapas bars. When an order arrives at a table, it's not uncommon to see people elbowing their way to the super-browned, extra-crispy bits. My version helps keep the peace with a two-step process that makes *every* bite of every potato the absolute best, crispiest, crunchiest bite. When served with a rustic romesco sauce, the two easily executed components deliver a perfect storm of flavor and texture.

Time
2 hours

Yield
Serves 4 to 6

Advance Work
The potatoes can be boiled earlier in the day. They can also be baked earlier in the day and held on the sheet pan, then reheated at showtime for 10 minutes at 450°F. Romesco, aioli, or ketchup can be made up to a couple of days in advance

3 Tbsp salt

12 tennis-ball-size Yukon gold potatoes

½ cup olive oil

1 cup romesco sauce (page 244), or if you prefer, aioli (page 243), home-made ketchup (page 241), or your favorite store-bought condiment

Bring a large pot of water with the salt to a boil. Add the potatoes and boil for about 40 minutes, or until they are soft to the poke of a fork. Remove from the water and let cool until they can be handled easily.

Set rack in top third of oven and preheat to 450°F.

Set out a large sheet pan ideally covered with 2 sheets of parchment paper. Generously drizzle the surface with olive oil. Space the potatoes evenly across the sheet pan. Using your hand, slowly but firmly smush (I assure you, this is not a typo) the potatoes down on the sheet pan until they are about ¾ inch thick. Use a pastry brush to generously brush the tops with oil.

Bake for about 1 hour, or until the potatoes are browned to within an inch of their lives and super crispy. Serve with romesco sauce.

Fries Fatale

You can keep the foie gras and the truffles. Ditto for the lobster and caviar. And what's with the Wagyu? When my time is up, I want my last meal to be a big bowl of extra-crispy fried potatoes, generously dusted with Parmigiano-Reggiano, fresh herbs, and sea salt crystals that explode in my mouth—all served up with a side of garlicky aioli. Given the option, I'll gladly wash them down with a magnum of '61 Cheval Blanc, but beyond that, I will want nothing more to smooth my transition to the afterlife.

Let it be known that I'll be making these fries at home. When it comes to potatoes, I've lost my faith in restaurants. More often than not, my order arrives sorrowfully under-crisped, or lukewarm and limp. If you have spent any time in a restaurant kitchen, it's easy to understand the problem. It's the sheer volume and a lack of attention to detail that compromise the taste experience. The places that really get it right are usually the ones that have a dedicated fry person, but the vast majority of fried potatoes never live up to their potential. They aren't worth the calories, and they certainly wouldn't make for a fitting end to a life well lived.

As luck would have it, your chances of eating mind-blowing potatoes are far better at home than they are in a fancy restaurant. And it's easier than you think.

Time
45 minutes + extra if you make aioli or ketchup

Yield
Serves 4

Advance Work
Potatoes can be baked hours in advance, then fried at showtime. Aioli or ketchup can be made up to a couple of days in advance

2 pounds fingerling potatoes, halved lengthwise, or in a pinch russets, cut into thick wedges

Peanut or vegetable oil for frying (before frying, see Deep Fry Basics on page 52)

Your best salt (ideally sel gris or Malden)

2 garlic cloves, minced

2 Tbsp stemmed fresh thyme

2 Tbsp stemmed, finely chopped fresh rosemary

Pepper

¼ cup freshly grated Parmigiano-Reggiano

½ cup aioli (page 243), or homemade ketchup (page 241)

Preheat the oven to 425°F.

In a large bowl, toss the potatoes with a tablespoon of oil and a pinch of salt. Reserve the bowl.

Place the potatoes cut side down on a baking sheet (ideally lined with parchment paper to minimize the cleanup). Bake for 25 minutes, or until the potatoes are soft, and their bottom sides begin to brown.

Return the potatoes to the bowl and use a wooden spoon or similar implement to gently smash each potato so that the flesh is exposed.

Preheat a deep fryer, or fill a tall, heavy, medium pot one-third full of oil. Heat the oil to 350°F.

In a second large bowl, mix the garlic, herbs, salt, pepper, and Parmigiano. Reserve.

Fry half the potatoes for about 5 minutes, or until golden brown and über-crispy. Remove with a slotted spoon and drain on paper towels. Allow the oil to return to 350°F, then repeat with the second batch. Transfer the finished potatoes to the bowl with the herb mixture and toss.

Serve immediately with aioli or homemade ketchup.

Sweet Potato Floss
with Chipotle Magic Dust

Years ago, I tried unsuccessfully to convince a potato chip mogul I know to license my Chipotle Magic Dusted Sweet Potato Chips for his line of "celebrity" chef-branded potato chips. Unbeknownst to me, he was in the midst of abandoning his foray into the world of licensing, and my pitch was never considered. From the ashes of that failed attempt, comes this curious sweet potato floss. It is so instantly addictive that it should come with a warning label.

Unlike sweet potato chips or fries, which are both extremely difficult to bake or fry to an even crisp at home, this spiralized floss has a reduced surface area that fries uniformly. As the thin strands fry, they condense and crisp up. The resulting floss is the perfect vehicle for the sweet/salty/smoky/spicy magic dust that plays off the sweet potato to create a multi-sensory rave in your mouth. Serve it on its own as a snack, or as an accompaniment for sandwiches or burgers.

Time
<30 minutes

Advance Work
Sweet potatoes can be spiralized up to a few hours in advance

Yield
Serves 4

Chipotle Magic Dust
½ tsp ground chipotle

1 Tbsp sugar

1 tsp salt

½ tsp ground white pepper, or black pepper in a pinch

Floss
2 large sweet potatoes, skin-on

1 Tbsp Chipotle Magic Dust (see above)

Peanut or vegetable oil for frying (before frying, see Deep Fry Basics on page 52)

TO MAKE THE DUST In a large bowl, mix together the chipotle, sugar, salt, and pepper. If you have a mortar and pestle, grind the spices into a dust, which will help them adhere to the sweet potato. If not, no worries. Reserve.

FOR THE FLOSS Cut the sweet potatoes using a spiralizer on the setting that most closely matches the thickness of spaghetti, or use a mandolin with a comb-like blade attachment (usually designated as "medium").

Preheat a deep fryer, or fill a tall, heavy, medium pot one-third full of oil. Heat the oil to 350°F.

When the oil is ready, fry a handful of the sweet potatoes for about 4 minutes, stirring occasionally, until they are the brownish orange color of a terracotta pot. Remove with a slotted spoon and place on paper towel to absorb the excess oil, then transfer to a large bowl. The floss will crisp up as it cools.

Allow the oil to return to 350°F, then repeat the process with the next batch. As each batch is finished, add it to the bowl. Sprinkle 1 tablespoon of Chipotle Magic Dust overtop, and toss until the floss is evenly covered. Taste and adjust seasoning if desired.

Caramelized Asparagus "Fatties"
with Aioli

In 1999, years ahead of the food truck craze, I toured around North America in an Airstream trailer that I tricked out with a professional kitchen and topped with two 8-foot-long aluminum slices of toast. I dubbed it the Toastermobile. To fund its fabrication and finance my 3-month, 30-city, 30,000-kilometer (18,000 mile) odyssey with a crew of 3, I raised $250,000 from sponsors. One of my anchor sponsors was Weber Grills. The Toastermobile was fitted with a propane grill that could be easily offloaded, and one of my obligations to Weber was that I make and offer samples of grilled asparagus at each of my daily whistle-stop appearances.

Asparagus can taste astringent if it's simply steamed. But when it is grilled over high direct heat, it is one of the best examples of the magic powers of caramelization (page 62). Everyone has their favorite size, but when it comes to grilling, I prefer the fattest stalks available, which deliver the meatiest results. In less than 5 minutes, a thick, raw spear can be transformed into a nutty treat that you can't get enough of—whether you are enjoying it as a finger food with aioli or as a side dish. On the Toastermobile tour, I ate grilled asparagus every day. In addition to confirming that Confucius was correct when he said that "you can't beat [the smell of] asparagus to the bathroom," I can confirm that I never tired of it.

Time
< 15 minutes + extra time if you make aioli or romesco

Yield
Serves 4 as a nibble or a vegetable sidekick

Advance Work
Asparagus can be grilled earlier in the day and served at room temperature. Aioli or romesco can be made up to a couple of days in advance

Zero Waste
Save all the trimmings for asparagus soup (page 115), or a veggie stock (page 252)

- 1 pound fresh asparagus (look for fat, firm stalks with deep green or purplish tips)
- 4 Tbsp olive oil
- 1 tsp salt
- Aioli (page 243), romesco sauce (page 244), or Parmigiano-Reggiano for serving (all optional)

Asparagus Storage
Slice off the very bottoms of the spears and stand your asparagus upright in a small amount of water. Store in the refrigerator.

Preheat the grill to medium-high direct heat.

I used to recommend trimming off the tough bottom end of the spear by grasping each end and bending it gently until it snaps at its natural point of tenderness. But since becoming a zero-waste advocate, I have become aware that there is a lot of great flavor and texture below the snapping point. So just cut off the woody section at the very bottom of the spear. Then use a vegetable peeler to peel off the outer skin of the lower half of the remaining stalk.

Place the asparagus on a plate. Drizzle the olive oil overtop and roll the spears until they are coated. Sprinkle with the salt and roll the spears again.

Grill the asparagus for 5 minutes. Each minute or so, roll each spear a quarter turn. Asparagus should begin to brown in spots (indicating that its natural sugars are caramelizing) but should not be grilled to the point where it can be carbon dated. Dripping oil may cause flare-ups. Keep a glass of water or spray bottle handy to spritz on the coals if necessary. Serve immediately with the aioli.

Moroccan Honey and Harissa–Glazed Carrots

These carrots are inspired by a road trip I took through the Atlas mountains in Morocco, 15 years ago. The flavors still linger on my palate as if it were yesterday. In Fez, I stumbled upon a small stall in a souq, at the center of which was a simmering cauldron of fava bean soup that was the sole offering of the day. The soup was finished with Urfa biber, an earthy, chocolaty chili, and a generous drizzle of local olive oil. I was also blown away by *pastilla*, a savory-sweet crispy phyllo pie stuffed with chicken, pistachios, ginger, and cinnamon amazingness.

Most of my dining experiences on the trip were in small villages and at truck stops that lined the dusty highways. I remember the fragrant fried bread and the omnipresent mint tea. But my fondest memory is of long racks of clay tagines, filled with couscous, lamb, various legumes, and carrots, simmering away in the midday sun. This to me is the essence of what eating is in Morocco.

I've caramelized, glazed, seasoned, spiced, and sauced these carrots in a way that honors the amazing flavors I experienced during the trip.

Time
< 1 hour

Yield
Serves 4 to 6

1½ pounds large whole carrots
1 Tbsp olive oil
¼ tsp salt
2 Tbsp honey
1 tsp harissa
1 Tbsp ginger, grated on a rasp
¼ tsp cumin
⅛ tsp cinnamon
⅓ cup goat-milk yogurt, or plain yogurt
¼ cup stemmed and chopped fresh mint
Zest of 1 lemon
¼ cup shelled pistachios, chopped
¼ cup pomegranate seeds (optional—consider it a bonus if available)

Preheat the oven to 425°F.

Use a wet dishtowel or a clean scouring pad to scrub the carrots clean. Do not peel them. Halve them lengthwise.

In a large bowl, toss the carrots with the olive oil and salt. Reserve the bowl.

Set the carrots cut side down on a sheet pan (ideally lined with parchment paper or foil to minimize cleanup). Roast for 20 minutes, until they begin to brown.

To the original bowl, add the honey, harissa, ginger, cumin, and cinnamon. Whisk the ingredients together, then add the carrots and toss thoroughly to coat. Dump the carrots back onto the sheet pan, spreading them out a bit but basically leaving them as they fall. Roast for another 12 to 15 minutes, or until they are well browned.

Finish the carrots with yogurt, and top with the mint, lemon zest, pistachios, and pomegranate seeds.

Roasted Umami-Glazed Brussels Sprouts

When it comes to preparing Brussels sprouts, many restaurants employ a sneaky little technique that is the worst-kept secret since Lance Armstrong's doping habit. Here is the simple test to detect if the sprouts you are eating have been *jacked*: if you hear yourself thinking "these are SO delicious, I never knew that I liked Brussels sprouts so much," I can assure you that your sprouts have been deep-fried. Deep-frying crisps the outer leaves while the inner leaves trap the deep-frying oil, which contributes to a super-flavorful—albeit highly caloric and often one-dimensional—sprout.

Don't get me wrong, I am all about deep-frying (as evidenced by the many deep-frying recipes in this book), when it's the best way to create flavor and texture. But often there is a better way to get there from here. This recipe, with its combination of sweet, tang, acid, and umami, delivers complex layers of flavor without any cheating.

1½ pounds Brussels sprouts (if you have a choice, choose the largest ones)

2 Tbsp neutral oil

1 Tbsp fish sauce

1 Tbsp freshly squeezed lime juice

1 Tbsp soy sauce

2 Tbsp maple syrup

1 tsp Dijon

½ tsp freshly ground Szechuan or black peppercorns

Bonito flakes or sesame seeds (optional)

Set rack on the top third of the oven and preheat the oven to 425°F.

If necessary, trim the bases of the Brussels sprouts. Then cut them in half from top to bottom. Add the halves to a medium bowl with the oil and toss thoroughly. Set the sprouts out on a sheet pan (ideally lined with parchment paper or foil to minimize cleanup), cut side down. Reserve the bowl. Roast for 20 to 30 minutes, or until the sprouts are well browned on the bottom.

While the sprouts are roasting, add the fish sauce, lime juice, soy sauce, maple syrup, mustard, and peppercorns to the bowl and whisk to combine.

When the sprouts are browned on the bottom, remove them from the oven, toss thoroughly with the fish sauce mixture and dump them back onto the sheet pan, spreading them out a bit but leaving them as they fall. Roast for another 15 to 20 minutes, turning once, or until they are browned to within an inch of their lives but not blackened.

Finish with a sprinkle of bonito flakes.

Time
1 hour

Yield
Serves 4 to 6

207

Sweet little thangs

(Desserts)

Pancake Beignets

If a blueberry pancake and a doughnut both swiped right on Tinder, and the stars aligned, it's likely that the result of their comingling would be as sweet and sexy as this dessert.

   The true origin of these beignets was somewhat more utilitarian. As someone who is always a couple of meals ahead of himself, I found myself contemplating what to make for the night's dessert at the same time that I was looking for a zero-waste solution for the leftover batter from my blueberry cornmeal pancake breakfast. A few slices of candied ginger and one zested orange later, these beignets were born. If you follow the same meal plan, it's like getting two courses for the price—and effort—of one.

Time
< 30 minutes

Yield
Serves 4

Advance Work
Pancake batter can be made hours in advance

3 heaping Tbsp finely chopped candied ginger (optional)

½ batch pancake batter—ideally leftover from a pancake breakfast (see page 225)

Peanut or vegetable oil for frying (before frying, see Deep Fry Basics on page 52)

4 scoops vanilla ice cream

4 Tbsp maple syrup, or if you prefer something a bit less sweet, orange marmalade, at room temperature

Powdered sugar for dusting (optional)

Gently fold the ginger into the pancake batter.

Preheat a deep fryer, or fill a tall, heavy, medium pot one-third full of oil. Heat the oil to 350°F.

When the oil is ready, drop in 1-tablespoon dollops of pancake batter (any bigger and the interior will not cook before the exterior browns), 4 at a time. Fry for about 90 seconds, or until well browned and cooked throughout. Roll the dough balls over midway through frying. Remove with a slotted spoon and place on a paper towel to absorb excess oil. Repeat until you have 2 beignets per person.

Place 1 scoop of ice cream in each bowl. Add two beignets and top with a tablespoon of syrup.

Finish with a dusting of powdered sugar.

Chocolate, Caramel, Peanut Butter, and Banana Wontons

If you give a professional pastry chef all the time and money they need to make *any* dessert they want for a dinner party, and you counter with this insanely easy, four-ingredient dessert wonton, I *guarantee* you that as long as there is alcohol involved, your dessert will win :).

Time
15 minutes

Yield
Makes 8 wontons (they are sweet, so 2 per person usually suffices)

Advance Work
Wontons can be assembled earlier in the day. Cover with a damp dishtowel and refrigerate. Do not let the wontons touch. To minimize stickage, dust the surface of the storage plate and the wontons themselves with cornstarch. They can also be made well in advance and frozen.

Multiplicity
Additional wontons do not require extra frying oil

Plan-Overs
Extra wontons may be frozen for up to 3 months

Eight 3½-by-3½-inch wonton wrappers (available in the refrigerated or frozen section of many grocery stores and in all Asian grocery stores)

¼ cup peanut butter (smooth or crunchy—your choice)

1 banana, peeled and sliced into ¼-inch-thick slices

8 Rolo or Caramilk bar segments—HACK: chocolate and caramel, in one package!

Powdered sugar for dusting (optional)

Peanut or vegetable oil for frying (before frying, see Deep Fry Basics on page 52)

Place a small bowl of warm water beside the wonton wrappers. Put a single wonton wrapper on a clean, dry surface in front of you. Schmear 1 teaspoon of peanut butter onto the center. Press a banana slice on top of the peanut butter and top with a Rolo segment. Dip your finger in the water and generously wet the outer edges of the wonton wrapper (water is the glue of wonton wrappers). Pinch and seal the wrapper around the ingredients. Be sure that seams are tightly sealed to keep the frying oil from seeping in. If you are not frying immediately, place a damp towel overtop, or store in the freezer where they will last for days (months if sealed in an airtight container) after they are frozen. Wontons can be fried straight from the freezer.

Preheat a deep fryer, or fill a tall, heavy, medium pot one-third full of oil. Heat the oil to 350°F.

When the oil is ready, fry the wontons for about 1 minute, or until the wonton wrappers are golden brown. If making multiple batches, fry no more than 8 wontons at a time. Remove with a slotted spoon and place on a paper towel to absorb excess oil. Dust with the powdered sugar. Let cool for 1 minute before serving.

Molten Nutella Chocolate Cake

My *Pizza on the Grill* coauthor Elizabeth Karmel recently released a brilliant cookbook called *Steak and Cake*. In it, she included my recipe for Steak au Poivre. To return the favor, Elizabeth gifted me with this genius spin on the timeless molten chocolate cake.

   I've tweaked Elizabeth's recipe a bit to make it even simpler, and now it's one of my go-to desserts for dinner parties. It's a snap to whip together, and versatile enough that it pairs with a variety of foils. Sometimes I make smaller versions in mini muffin tins, and other times I mix up the sauces I serve it on. When the mood strikes, I serve it with ice cream. In any configuration, this warm, chocolatey crowd-pleaser with hazelnut overtones is a new classic.

Time
30 minutes + extra time for Nutella to freeze

Yield
Serves 4

Advance Work
Batter can be made earlier in the day and baked just before serving

5 Tbsp (about 6 ounces) Nutella

4 Tbsp (½ stick) unsalted butter + extra for greasing ramekins

2 Tbsp flour + extra for dusting ramekins

4 ounces best available semi-sweet chocolate (55% cacao, or a close percentage)

2 large eggs

¼ cup granulated white sugar

Pinch of salt

Powdered sugar (optional)

Serving Options (per Serving)

- 1 scoop ice cream
- 1 tablespoon raspberry coulis or jam (as pictured)
- 1 tablespoon fig jam
- 2 tablespoons canned or jarred sour cherries
- 1 fresh passionfruit, pulp and seeds

Spoon the Nutella onto a sheet of waxed paper or parchment paper and roll into a log form, about ¾-inch in diameter. Freeze for 30 minutes.

Preheat the oven to 400°F.

Butter 4 individual 4-ounce ramekins or small coffee cups. Dust each ramekin with flour and tap out the excess. Set the ramekins on a sheet pan.

In a small pot over the lowest heat, melt the chocolate and the butter. Stir until smooth.

In a medium bowl, whisk the eggs. Add the sugar and whisk until the mixture is light in color. Add the flour and salt. Whisk until smooth.

Pour the melted chocolate mixture in a slow, thin stream into the egg mixture, beating the entire time to prevent the eggs from cooking. Let the batter cool.

Unwrap the Nutella and slice into ¾-inch pieces. Fill each ramekin three-quarters full of batter. Gently press a Nutella round into the center of each ramekin, allowing the batter to flow over it.

Bake for 12 minutes, or until the edges are firm. Cooking time will be affected by the size of the ramekin, so check the edges. If they are a wee bit under, or overcooked, they will still be delicious.

Let the cakes cool for 2 minutes. Serve immediately in their ramekins (the safe route), or remove and serve on plates. Finish with powdered sugar.

Maple, Bourbon, and Miso Tart

This sweet and savory tart is my homage to a maple tart I tasted at the Inn at Shelburne Farms, a historic property perched on the shore of Vermont's Lake Champlain. The tart I enjoyed at the Inn oozed with the essence of maple—a flavor that is the soul of Vermont. It was perfect in every way, but it also made me curious to see what other directions I could take it in.

In this incarnation, the miso adds a savory bass note, the black pepper counters the sugar, and the bourbon . . . well, as we all know, everything's better with bourbon. I topped it with a sesame brûlée, and (HACK alert!) eliminated a big step by using a store-bought graham cracker shell in place of the house-made pastry crust. The graham cracker shell absorbs some of the custard as it cooks, and by the time it comes out of the oven, it tastes homemade.

Time
30 minutes

Yield
Makes 8 tarts

Advance Work
Tarts can be made earlier in the day

Eight 3-inch-diameter store-bought graham cracker tart shells
4 Tbsp unsalted butter
½ cup brown sugar
¼ cup maple syrup
¼ cup buttermilk
2 eggs
1 Tbsp flour
2 Tbsp bourbon
2 tsp miso
¼ tsp pepper
1 Tbsp sesame seeds for finishing (or a combination of black and white sesame seeds)
3 Tbsp sugar

Preheat the oven to 350°F.

Set the empty tart shells on a sheet pan and bake for 5 minutes. Reserve on the sheet pan.

While the shells are baking, melt the butter over low heat. To a large bowl, add the melted butter, brown sugar, maple syrup, buttermilk, eggs, flour, bourbon, miso, and pepper. Whisk the ingredients together until smooth. Fill the tart shells almost to the top.

Bake for about 15 minutes, or until the tarts are set (soft and puffed up, but not runny). Let cool, then sprinkle with 1 teaspoon sugar each and a smattering of sesame seeds.

If you are a fan of TV cooking competitions and asked for a blowtorch for Christmas, use it to caramelize the sugar. Otherwise, place the tarts under a broiler for 3 watchful minutes, or until the sugar bubbles and browns. Let cool, then serve.

Caramelized Pineapple Rings
with Coconut Ice Cream and Homemade Salted Dulce de Leche

This old-school dessert with a contemporary twist is refreshingly decadent. The juicy acidity of the caramelized pineapple plays off the richness of the dulce de leche, and the sea salt balances the sweetness.

As if that isn't enough, the recipe employs the greatest culinary HACK since JC turned water into wine. By simply simmering an unopened can of sweetened condensed milk in a pot of water for two hours, you can transform it into a glorious, caramel-y dulce de leche. No fuss, no muss—and no mythical healing powers required.

Time
2+ hours

Yield
Serves 4

Advance Work
Pineapple can easily be cooked in advance and held at room temp, or in the fridge. The dulce de leche can also be made a couple of days in advance

Dulce de Leche
1 14-ounce can sweetened condensed milk

1 fresh pineapple, or in a pinch, 1 can of pineapple slices

1 Tbsp butter

1 pint coconut or vanilla ice cream or sorbet

Maldon sea salt or any sea salt or salt

TO MAKE THE DULCE DE LECHE Place the unopened can of condensed milk in a medium pot and fill the pot with water, covering the can completely. Cover the pot tightly with a lid. Bring the water to a boil, then reduce to a low simmer for two hours. IMPORTANT: Check the water level every 30 minutes to ensure that the can is fully covered and then some. Add more water if necessary. If the water level gets too low, the can could overheat and explode—in which case you will definitely need a bona fide miracle. Let the water cool slightly, then remove the can and reserve.

FOR THE CARAMELIZED PINEAPPLE Use a chef knife to cut the top and bottom off the pineapple. Cut off the thick outer skin, slicing from top to bottom following its curvature, then turn the pineapple on its side and slice it into ¾-inch-thick slices. Use a paring knife, pop out the core. HACK: Since you may not need all the slices, start with the ones at the bottom of the pineapple as they are always the sweetest.

In a heavy-bottomed pan over medium or medium-high heat, add the butter. When it sizzles, add four fresh pineapple rings (or eight of the thinner, canned rings). Cook for about five minutes per side, until nicely browned, rotating each ring 90° every minute or so, so that they brown evenly. Reserve.

To serve, set a pineapple ring on each plate (or two per for the canned rings). Top with a scoop of ice cream, then spoon a couple tablespoons of dulce de leche over the top. Finish with a sprinkle of salt.

Morning glories

(Breakfast & Brunch)

Cinnabon French Toast
with Grand Marnier

If it's a weekend morning when the early warning app announces that Rocket Man (or the latest villain *du jour*) has just pushed the nuclear button, this is the brunch I will make.

Time
15 minutes

Yield
Serves 2 big eaters, or 4 light eaters

2 Cinnabon cinnamon rolls, or the best, gooiest, cinnamon rolls available. (Day-olds are perfectly acceptable). If you feel you can improve on Cinnabon's rolls, don't hesitate to bake your own.

2 Tbsp orange marmalade

2 eggs

¼ cup milk

2 Tbsp Grand Marnier or Cointreau (optional)

Salt

1 Tbsp butter

Maple syrup for serving

Zest of one orange

Slice the cinnamon rolls horizontally through the middle. Lift up the top, iced half of each roll and place it cut side down beside the bottom half. Spread the marmalade over the icing. Take the bottom half of each roll and put it on top of the iced half so that the sticky bottom sits over the icing and marmalade, and the cut side is facing up. (At this point, the top and the bottom should both be the cut sides, and all the gooeyness should be in the center of the "sandwich.")

In a medium bowl, add the eggs, milk, Grand Marnier, and a pinch of salt. Whisk everything together. Reserve.

In a deep pan (one that you have a lid for), over medium heat, add the butter.

Set out a large plate.

As the butter melts, take one of your cinnamon roll sandwiches and place it in the egg mixture. Press down lightly to help it absorb the egg mixture. Flip it and press lightly again. Repeat this once more on each side so that the whole sandwich is thoroughly soaked in the egg mixture. Set it on the plate. Repeat with the second cinnamon roll.

Transfer both cinnamon rolls to the pan and cover with a lid.

Cook for about 4 minutes per side, or until egg has set throughout, and the top and bottom are nicely browned.

As the cinnamon rolls are cooking, in a small pot over low heat, warm the maple syrup.

Top the cinnamon rolls with a generous drizzle of maple syrup and finish with the orange zest.

Blueberry Cornmeal Pancakes
with Rosemary Balsamic Maple Syrup

Most pancakes are sugar bombs made with granulated sugar, topped with syrup—and often finished with powdered sugar for that final knockout punch. One moment you are enjoying a heady sugar rush, and the next you are crashing hard. These pancakes were inspired by a transcendent dinner I had at Fäviken, Magnus Nilsson's now-closed 16-seat restaurant that was nestled in the middle of Jämtland, Sweden. Magnus is at the vanguard of new Nordic cuisine (along with Noma's René Redzepi). His cooking honors local ingredients that sometimes appear to be foraged by wood fairies. This recipe doesn't require you to make your own birch syrup, but it does honor the Scandinavian sensibility of incorporating savory, herbaceous ingredients in places North Americans would least expect them. The result is a pancake that's sweet enough for breakfast, but savory enough to keep you from bouncing off the walls.

½ cup coarse ground cornmeal

¾ cup flour

1 Tbsp sugar

¾ tsp baking soda

¾ tsp baking powder

½ tsp salt

4 Tbsp butter, divided

1¼ cups buttermilk (see sidebar for buttermilk replacement HACKS, page 226)

1 egg

1 cup blueberries, divided

Zest of 1 orange

½ cup maple syrup

1 tsp best available aged balsamic vinegar

2 sprigs fresh rosemary

10 black peppercorns

In a large bowl, mix the cornmeal, flour, sugar, baking soda, baking powder, and salt.

In the large sauté pan you plan to make the pancakes in, melt 1½ tablespoons of the butter.

Add the melted butter to a second bowl along with the buttermilk and egg. Reserve the pan. Use a whisk to mix.

Slowly pour the wet ingredients into the dry ingredient bowl, using a rubber spatula to incorporate. Do not overmix. The batter should be thick and airy at the same time—but not too thick. The proportions of the flour and cornmeal to buttermilk in this recipe should get the batter very close to the desired thickness, but it may be necessary to add one or two additional tablespoons of flour or buttermilk. Use your instincts. Gently fold in two-thirds of the blueberries, and the zest. Let rest for 15 minutes. Bubbles should form in the batter.

Just before you start making the pancakes, in a small pot over medium heat, add the maple syrup, balsamic vinegar, rosemary, remaining blueberries, and peppercorns. Bring to a high simmer, then reduce to a low simmer for about 5 minutes. Reserve.

(continued)

Time
< 45 minutes

Yield
Makes 2 servings (about eight 3-inch pancakes)

Plan-Overs
Make a double batch and save half for Pancake Beignets (page 210)

In the pan you used to melt the butter, over medium/medium-high heat, add 1 tablespoon of butter. If you have a second pan, set it up in the same way so that you can work both pans at the same time to cook all the pancakes at once. When the butter is sizzling, drop in ¼-cup dollops of batter. Cook until bubbles form on top (after 2 minutes, sneak a peek under the pancakes and toggle the heat if the pancakes are blackening before bubbles start to form. Flip and continue cooking for about 90 seconds, or until browned on the bottom and cooked through. Repeat with the remaining batter if necessary.

Top the pancakes with the warm syrup (leaving the peppercorns behind in the pot).

Buttermilk Replacements

The reason pancakes often call for buttermilk is that the acid in the buttermilk activates the baking soda, which helps make your pancakes fluffy. If you don't have buttermilk on hand (and really, who does?), any one of these 3 HACKS will save you a trip to the grocery store. Each hack yields the equivalent of the 1¼ cups of buttermilk required for the pancakes:

1. Mix 1 cup and 3 tablespoons milk with 1 tablespoon lemon juice or white vinegar. Let sit for 5 minutes.
2. Mix 1 cup plain yogurt with ¼ cup water.
3. Mix ¾ cup sour cream and ½ cup water.

Waffle Latke
with Smoked Salmon and a Poached Egg

This dish has it all: the crunch of a crispy fried potato-celeriac-parsnip waffle, the silkiness of smoked salmon, the salty pop of salmon roe, and the unctuousness of a perfectly poached egg. It's a decadent combination that's perfect for a special breakfast or brunch, and equally suitable for dinner.

Making the latke waffle is easy, but it does involve a two-step process that requires a waffle maker and some deep-frying. If that seems like too much trouble, feel free to reconfigure the waffle into a conventional pan-fried latke fritter, or quit while you are ahead after cooking the latkes on a waffle iron. But let it be known, deep-frying the latke waffle is the shizzle that turns this dish into a Flavorbomb.

6 eggs, divided

1 large russet potato, peel on

1 large parsnip (may be replaced with a second russet potato)

½ celeriac (may be replaced with a second parsnip or a second potato), trimmed

2 Tbsp flour

1 Tbsp coarse cornmeal, or another grind of cornmeal, or one additional Tbsp of flour

1 shallot, minced

¼ cup fresh dill, stemmed + the nicest tops reserved

1 tsp dill seeds or fennel seeds (optional)

½ tsp baking powder

1 tsp salt

½ tsp pepper

Vegetable oil, or olive oil spray

Peanut or vegetable oil for frying (before frying, see Deep Fry Basics on page 52)

½ cup sour cream

8 ounces best available cold-smoked salmon, lox, or gravlax

1 lemon

1 ounce salmon roe (optional)

2 Tbsp white vinegar or lemon juice

If you plan to poach the eggs, do so as the final step before serving. If you plan to sous vide the eggs, set the sous vide maker to 147°. When the water comes to temperature, gently add 4 of the eggs in their shells and cook for 60 minutes. To serve: crack the eggs one at a time into a bowl. Some watery white will separate from the rest of the cooked white and yolk. Use a slotted spoon to lift out the egg, leaving the watery bit in the bowl. Repeat with the remaining eggs.

FOR THE LATKE WAFFLES Grate the potato on the large side of a grater. Cup the grated potato in your hands, stand over a bowl or the sink, and squeeze out every last drop of water your gym-toned muscles can extract. Reserve the potato. Grate the parsnip and celeriac. Reserve.

In a large bowl, beat 2 eggs. Add the potato, parsnip, celeriac, flour, cornmeal, shallot, dill, dill seeds, baking powder, salt, and pepper. Mix thoroughly with a fork.

Preheat a waffle iron. When the iron is smoking hot, spray with oil.

Spoon ½ cup of the potato mixture onto each segment of the waffle iron. Close the top and cook until browned and crispy. Remove the waffles and reserve. (At this point, the waffles can be refrigerated for up to a day.)

(continued)

Time
45 minutes + extra time if you sous vide the eggs

Yield
Serves 4

Advance Work
The waffles can be made earlier in the day, then deep-fried just before serving

Preheat a deep fryer, or fill a tall, heavy, medium pot one-third full of oil. Heat the oil to 350°F. When the oil is ready, fry the waffles for about 4 minutes, or until golden brown and crispy. Remove with a slotted spoon and place on a paper towel to absorb excess oil.

If you are poaching the eggs: while waffles are frying, fill a medium-size pan with 3 inches of water and add the vinegar or lemon juice. Over high heat, bring the water to a boil. HACK: to help your eggs "set up" in the water, crack them into a small, not-so-fine strainer and let the thin liquid that surrounds the egg white drip through the strainer. Tip the strainer into the water to release the eggs. When the water returns to a boil, reduce the heat to a simmer and cook for 90 seconds, or until the egg whites are no longer translucent. Transfer with the same strainer to a clean dishtowel.

TO SERVE: Schmear a couple of tablespoons of sour cream over the center of each waffle. Top with salmon and squeeze a bit of lemon juice overtop. Top the salmon with a poached or sous vided egg and finish with a teaspoon of salmon roe, a dill sprig, and some black pepper.

Smokin' Trout Schmear

Sure, you can top a bagel by adding all of the traditional ingredients one at a time. But sometimes it's easier to combine the best of everything into a simple schmear.

For this schmear, I've chosen smoked trout, a fish that is inexpensive and readily available. Alternately, you can create your own version by using smoked or cured salmon, mackerel, or whitefish. As a rule of thumb, the higher the ratio of rich, oily fish to the other ingredients, the more decadent the spread. And the more fresh herbs you add, the merrier. Don't stop there. Add your own touches and create your own schmear campaign (sorry, I couldn't help myself).

Time
< 15 minutes

Yield
Makes 4 to 6 servings (about 1½ cups)

Advance Work
Can be made a couple of days in advance

Zero Waste
This is a great use for smoked fish trimmings

Plan-Overs
Remaining schmear will last in the fridge for about a week in a tightly sealed container

---

1 cup (about 8 ounces) labneh (a strained yogurt, often made from sheep's milk, found in many grocery stores and most eastern European markets), or cream cheese

1 Tbsp fresh thyme, stemmed + extra sprigs for garnish

2 Tbsp stemmed, chopped parsley

2 green onions, trimmed and roughly chopped

1 lemon, zested and sliced paper-thin on a mandoline or with a sharp knife

Zest of one orange

2 Tbsp capers, drained

1 tsp brined green peppercorns, or ½ tsp pepper

8 ounces smoked trout

Salt

Bagels or your favorite toasted bread or crackers for serving

---

In a food processor, add the labneh, thyme, parsley, green onions, lemon and orange zest, capers, and peppercorns.

Pulse several times until ingredients are well incorporated but not pulverized.

If you are using skin-on trout, peel away the skin. If you are using tinned trout, drain off the liquids. Break the trout into 1-inch pieces, add to the processor and pulse several more times until the trout is well distributed. If you do not have a food processor, mince the thyme, green onions, capers, and trout together, then use a fork to blend with the labneh. Season to taste with salt (which may not be needed at all depending on the saltiness of the trout).

Taste for seasonings and adjust if desired.

Toast and lightly butter the bagels. Schmear with schmear, and top with lemon slices and a thyme sprig.

OIL: rescued oil from the
dregs of a sun dried
tomato jar, jarred
artichoke hearts, canned
fish, or from anything else
stored in olive or vegetable
oil—or any mix thereof

ALLIUM: sprouting garlic
or a handful of the
neglected teeny center
cloves, the unloved middle
section of a leek, or that
last bit of an onion—or any
mix thereof

PROTEIN: leftover bits
of cooked ham, sausage
ends, sandwich meats,
smoked or cured fish—or
any mix thereof

GREENS: beet tops,
radish tops, turnip tops,
celery leaves, fennel
fronds, or any tired wilted
greens such as spinach,
kale, or swiss chard—or any
mix thereof

FRESH HERBS:
Whatever you've got that
pairs appropriately with
your chosen ingredients

VEGGIES: Cherry
tomatoes, bell peppers,
broccoli, mushrooms,
potatoes . . .

CHEESE: (about 1 cup,
chopped) leftover ends of
stale cheese from your
fridge, or the last grating
of a Parmiggino Reggiano
rind—or any mix thereof

Weekend Free-ttata™

Nothing tastes better than free! My Weekend Free-ttatas™ are an effective way to rescue your tired veggies, cuttings, and miscellaneous bits that lurk in the crevices of your fridge, and turn them into a hearty zero-waste breakfast that is gratifying on many levels. Flexibility, creativity, and resourcefulness are the hallmarks of a well-made Free-ttata™. No two are ever the same—which is part of what makes Free-ttatas™ the Stone Soup of egg dishes. Once you discover how rewarding they are to make, you will instinctively become more proactive about repurposing your unloved ingredients and scraps, instead of automatically tossing them.

2 Tbsp oil
Palmful allium, chopped
Handful protein, chopped
2 to 4 cups greens, chopped
2 to 4 Tbsp chopped fresh herbs
1 cup chopped veggies
8 eggs
2 tsp harissa (optional) or an appropriate amount of your favorite hot sauce—or nothing
Salt and black pepper
¼ to ½ cup grated or chopped cheese

Time
< 45 minutes

Yield
Serves 4–6

Set rack in center position and preheat oven to 425°F.

In a cast iron or ovenproof sauté pan over medium-high heat, add the oil, and your chosen allium. Cook for 3 minutes, stirring occasionally, or until it browns. Add a handful of chopped protein and stir for a couple of minutes. Add the greens, a cup or so of veggies, stemmed herbs, and a splash of water. Cover with a lid and let steam for 3 minutes. Remove lid and continue cooking, stirring occasionally for another few minutes until greens reduce in volume by about half.

While greens are cooking, in a large bowl, whisk together eggs, harissa, salt, pepper, and cheese.

Pour egg mixture overtop and poke around the pan contents with a wooden spoon so that the egg mixture is spread out evenly and sinks between the pan contents. If you have any extra grated hard cheese leftover, sprinkle some of it overtop.

Transfer immediately to oven and bake for about 12 minutes, or until eggs are cooked throughout. If eggs seem cooked throughout, but still loose on top, finish under a broiler for 2 minutes, or until top is fully cooked and nicely browned.

Scrambled Egg Sandwiches
on Cheddar, Chive, and Bacon Biscuits

This recipe employs two ingredient HACKS and one shopping HACK to help fast-track the already fast prep of this breakfast sandwich. Self-rising flour, which is made with baking powder, eliminates the need for baking powder—and the worry that what you have on hand may be past its stale date. Heavy cream eliminates the tricky step of "cutting" butter into the flour with a pastry cutter (hands up, who's got one?).

With these two shortcuts, the only step that takes any real time is cooking the bacon. That's where my shopping hack comes in. When I only need a few slices of cooked bacon, I buy them from the ready-to-eat breakfast buffet section of my grocery store. In addition to streamlining the recipe, cooked bacon is the ultimate grocery store bargain because it is super light, and functions as a loss leader to entice you to load up on scrambled eggs and potatoes—which add up when you are paying for them by the pound.

These hacks will save you time, money, and labor, but the real biscuit secret is also the simplest: serve 'em hot out of the oven, and they will taste like a million dollars.

Time
30 minutes

Yield
Makes 4 biscuit sandwiches

Cheddar, Chive, and Bacon Biscuits

6 strips bacon, ideally precooked

1 cup self-rising flour, or 1 cup all-purpose flour + 1 tsp baking powder + ¼ tsp salt

1 tsp sugar

⅔ cup sharp white cheddar cheese, or any other cheddar cheese, roughly grated

2 Tbsp chives, sliced finely

1 cup (8 ounces) whipping cream + extra for brushing tops

4 eggs

Salt and pepper

Butter for buttering biscuits and greasing egg pan

FOR THE BISCUITS Preheat the oven to 450°F.

If the bacon is not already cooked, cook it until it is crispy. Let cool, then chop into small pieces. Reserve.

In a medium bowl, combine the flour and sugar. Stir in the bacon, cheese, and chives. Add the cream and stir until the dough comes together. If the dough is still dry, add more cream, or water, 1 tablespoon at a time until the dough is slightly sticky. If dough is too wet, add more flour.

When the dough forms a ball in the bowl, turn it out onto a floured surface. Roll and knead it a few times until smooth. Transfer the dough to an ungreased cookie sheet. Pat the dough down until it is ¾ inch thick, and form it into a 6-by-6-inch square. Use a sharp knife to divide it into 4 squares, then separate each square by at least an inch. Brush the tops with cream (or a bit of soft butter) and bake for about 17 minutes, or until the tops are golden brown and biscuits are cooked through. Let rest for 5 minutes.

In a small bowl, beat the eggs and season with salt and pepper. In a sauté pan over low-medium heat, add the eggs and cook, stirring constantly to keep from browning. Halve the biscuits with a serrated knife, butter both sides and fill with egg.

Maple-Sweetened Granola
with Crystallized Ginger

On weekday mornings, I am all about granola. It's a quick, convenient, and satisfying breakfast on the fly. But sadly, I find most store-bought brands, even the "gourmet" varieties, uninspiring. The majority of them are unnecessarily high in fat and cloyingly sweet. Most are also chewy rather than crunchy—which is my preference. That's why I developed this recipe over a decade ago, and since then I've never looked back.

The three ingredients that contribute to the distinctive flavor profile of this granola are: the maple syrup it's sweetened with, the rye flakes that add a subtle-but-pleasing depth of flavor when combined with the rolled oats, and a generous amount of candied ginger.

Baking granola is more like cooking than baking, so you don't need instinctive baking skills to make it. And once you grasp the basics, you can customize the mix of dried fruit and nuts to suit your own personal taste.

Time
1 hour

Yield
Makes 7 cups, about 20 servings

Plan-Overs
Store in an airtight container at room temperature. In hot climates, store in the fridge, where it will last for up to 2 months.

*NOTE : Roasted nuts may be used instead of raw. Simply add them at the end instead of during the baking process. I usually make a double batch on 2 sheet pans. If you do this, rotate the pans (both top to bottom and front to back) every time you remove the pans from the oven to stir the contents.

2½ cups "old fashioned" rolled oats (not the instant variety)

1½ cups rye flakes

¼ cup coconut oil (or grapeseed, canola, or safflower oil)

4–6 Tbsp maple syrup

½ cup raw hazelnuts, roughly chopped (or pecans, walnuts, almonds . . .)*

¼ cup raw shelled pumpkin seeds (or sunflower seeds)

½ cup crystallized ginger, sliced

⅓ cup dried blueberries (and/or raisins or apricots)

⅓ cup toasted unsweetened coconut chips or flakes

2 Tbsp ground flax seeds (optional)

HACK: to add a brightness that can't be baked into the granola, add the zest from half an orange to your granola just before serving.

Preheat the oven to 325°F.

Mix the oats and rye flakes. Spread evenly in a large sheet pan, and toast in the oven for 12 minutes, turning once midway. (HACK: A large roasting pan with tall sides will make the job of stirring the toasted oats easier—and there will be infinitely less spillage. After making hundreds of batches of granola, I can assure you that a tall-sided pan is a game changer.)

To a small pot, over medium heat, add the coconut oil and maple syrup. Bring to a simmer. Reserve.

Transfer the oats and rye flakes to a large bowl. Add the oil and maple syrup mixture and stir until it is evenly absorbed. (If you are using a deep roasting pan, you can skip the bowl step and simply pour the oil and maple syrup overtop, then stir until it is evenly absorbed.)

Transfer the oats and rye flakes back to the pan and bake for 7 minutes. Remove the pan from the oven, stir the contents, rotate the pan, and return it to the oven. Repeat the process every 7 minutes until the granola is a deep golden brown (about 30 minutes in total after the syrup and oil mixture has been added—depending on how browned you like your granola). Before the last round of baking, spread the raw nuts and pumpkin seeds overtop.

Let granola cool, then mix in the ginger, dried fruit, coconut and flax.

ROMESCO
page 243

Love Potions

(Sauces, Condiments , Compound Butters & Stocks)

CHERMOULA
page 240

AIOLI
page 243

Sauces

Each one of these sauces will deliver an enviable return on your ingredient/time/energy investment.

Hair-Raising Harissa *photo on page 238*

I find myself using harissa more and more frequently, as both a condiment and in my cooking. Unfortunately, not all store-bought harissas are the same—and some leave much to be desired. If you discover one you like, by all means stick with it, but if you can't find the love, it's worth the effort to make your own.

Time
< 30 minutes

Yield
About 1 cup

Plan-Overs
Will keep in the refrigerator for about 2 weeks when stored in a jar with a drizzle of olive oil overtop to seal it. Will keep in the freezer for up to 6 months. For easy access, freeze in log form and cut off slices as needed.

3 dried ancho chilis, stemmed and seeded
3 dried guajillo chilis, stemmed and seeded
1 Tbsp caraway seeds
1½ tsp coriander seeds
1 tsp cumin seeds
4 garlic cloves, minced
¼ cup fresh mint leaves
1 Tbsp freshly squeezed lemon juice
1 Tbsp white vinegar
2 Tbsp olive oil
¾ tsp salt
¾ tsp cayenne pepper

Preheat the oven to 300°F.

On a sheet pan, place the chilis, caraway seeds, coriander seeds, and cumin seeds. Toast for 3 minutes. Transfer the pan contents to a small bowl and pour ½ cup boiling water overtop. Let sit for 10 minutes, covered.

Transfer the contents of the bowl to a mini food processor or a mortar and pestle. Add the garlic, mint, lemon juice, vinegar, olive oil, salt, and cayenne. Purée into a smooth paste. Taste for salt and seasonings, and adjust if desired.

Chermoula Sauce *photo on page 238*

Chermoula sauce from North Africa is my new chimichurri. In fact it has every ingredient that chimichurri has (with the exception of vinegar), *plus* a handful of additional fresh herbs, and spices that add extra layers of dimension and vibrancy. It's fabulous on most proteins and grilled vegetables.

Time
< 15 minutes

Yield
About 1 cup

Plan-Overs
Will keep in the refrigerator for about 5 days

½ tsp cumin seeds, or in a pinch, ground cumin
½ tsp coriander seeds, or in a pinch, ground coriander
½ tsp salt
1 cup chopped fresh coriander
1 cup chopped fresh parsley
½ cup fresh mint leaves
2 tsp paprika
2 garlic cloves, chopped
1 shallot, chopped
½ tsp chili flakes
Zest of 1 lemon
4 Tbsp lime juice
½ cup olive oil

Place the cumin and coriander seeds in a pan over medium heat for about 60 seconds, or until fragrant. Crush them in a mortar and pestle—or leave them whole, as I do, to create tiny flavor explosions in the sauce.

To a food processor, add the toasted seeds along with the rest of the ingredients. Pulse until well chopped, but not puréed. Taste for salt and acid balance and adjust if desired.

Real Ketchup *photo on page 238*

I spent the first half of my working life backstage at concerts, and the second half taking backstage tours of production facilities ranging from wineries to lobster processing plants. Sometimes I'm invited to these facilities, and sometimes I request the visit. A few years ago, I found myself traveling through Leamington, Ontario, which bills itself as the "tomato capital of Canada." At the time, Leamington was also home to the Heinz ketchup factory (now shuttered). While I was there I thought, "when in Leamington . . ." So I made a call, expecting the Heinz PR folks to throw open their arms once they discovered who I thought I was. To my surprise, they unceremoniously shut me down. I up-dialed and was shut down again. For love or money, I could not get a tour of the plant. It was the first time in my professional culinary life that I could not talk my way into a production facility.

Perhaps the gatekeepers at Heinz were right to keep me out, because as curious as I was to see the operation, I am not a fan of traditional ketchup. I find it cloyingly sweet (not surprising since the third ingredient listed is sugar) and bland. Blasphemous, I know. Sorry, did I just lose you?

If you are going to go to the trouble of making a great burger or hand-cut fries, why not let your ketchup rise to the occasion? This ketchup is closer to the true origins of ketchup. It is spicier, more savory, and far more complex than any of the popular brands. Taste it side by side with that bottle in your fridge and judge for yourself.

1 Tbsp olive oil

½ onion, diced

2 garlic cloves, chopped

3 Tbsp apple cider vinegar

1 Tbsp best available balsamic vinegar

2 Tbsp brown sugar

½ tsp salt

¼ tsp pepper

¾ tsp ground allspice

½ tsp mustard powder

¼ tsp ground cloves

2 whole star anise pods, ground up in a mortar and pestle or a coffee grinder

¾ tsp harissa

One 14-ounce can whole, crushed, or diced plum tomatoes (fire-roasted if available)

2 Tbsp raisins

In a medium-size pot over medium heat, add the oil, onion, and garlic and cook for about 5 minutes, or until translucent, stirring occasionally. Add the cider vinegar, balsamic vinegar, and brown sugar. Increase the heat and reduce the liquids for 2 minutes.

Add the salt, pepper, allspice, mustard, cloves, star anise, harissa, tomatoes (including the liquid), and raisins. Simmer for about 10 minutes until the pan contents begin to thicken. Let cool, then purée. Leave as is for a rustic, chutney-like texture, or for a similar mouthfeel to store-bought ketchup, push the purée through a chinois or fine-mesh strainer. Taste for salt, spices, and acid balance, and adjust if desired.

Time
< 30 minutes

Yield
About 1½ cups (slightly less if you strain it)

Plan-Overs
Store refrigerated for 3 to 4 weeks

Piri Piri Piri! Sauce *photo on page 238*

Piri piri sauce has a fresh, zingy acidic finish that you don't find in many sauces. Because it is a cooked sauce, it takes more time and effort to make than blended herb sauces—which makes it impractical for a quick weeknight meal for two, but perfect when you want to grill something unique for a larger group. The most traditional use of the sauce is on grilled chicken (page 172), but it is also a natural pairing for grilled pork chops, shrimp, and cauliflower.

Time
<1 hour

Yield
About 2 cups

Plan-Overs
Because of the high acid content, this sauce will keep in the fridge for 3 to 4 weeks

2 large red bell peppers

1 large tomato, cored

4 garlic cloves, minced

½ large red onion, roughly chopped

¾ cup lemon juice

½ cup apple cider vinegar

10 small fresh red Thai chilis, stemmed, or 10 dried chile de árbol, rehydrated in ¼ cup of water, or in a pinch, 2 fresh serrano chilis

1½ tsp smoked paprika

1½ tsp dried oregano

1½ tsp salt

1 tsp pepper

2 bay leaves

Zest of two lemons

½ cup olive oil

Blacken the red peppers and tomato over a gas burner or barbecue. Transfer to a bag for 5 minutes, then peel off and the discard the skins along with the seeds and stems. Reserve.

To a food processor, add the bell pepper, tomato, garlic, onion, lemon juice, vinegar, chilis, paprika, oregano, salt, and pepper. Purée until smooth.

Transfer the sauce to a medium saucepan over medium heat and add the bay leaves. Bring the sauce to a boil, then reduce to a simmer and cook uncovered for 30 minutes, stirring occasionally to incorporate the bits that sink to the bottom. Sauce should reduce by about 30% to 50%.

Let the sauce cool, remove the bay leaves, and then return the sauce to the food processor.

Add the lemon zest. With the processor running, drizzle in the olive oil until it is all incorporated.

Three-Clove Aioli *photo on page 239*

Homemade aioli is technically mayonnaise with garlic. But it tastes unlike any commercial mayonnaise you can buy in a store because packagers are hesitant to use raw eggs in their products.

Aioli is made possible by the scientific phenomenon known as emulsification, which turns oil and water-based ingredients into a thick, luscious sauce. With its strong garlic kick and creamy texture, aioli is a great accompaniment for a wide variety of foods including grilled veggies, fried foods, and fish. It also plays well with additional flavors ranging from chipotle (page 176) to Pernod (page 165), which allows you align it with the taste profile of whatever you are serving. In truth, even cardboard slathered in aioli would taste delicious.

3 garlic cloves, minced

1 best available egg yolk* + one extra egg as backup

⅛ tsp salt

¼ cup neutral oil + extra as backup

¼ cup olive oil

Zest of 1 Meyer lemon, or 1 conventional lemon

1 Tbsp freshly squeezed lemon juice

1 tsp Dijon mustard

HACK: if you have a squeeze bottle, add both oils to the bottle and use it to drizzle the oil. Otherwise, mix it in a measuring cup, or any other vessel with a pouring lip.

*NOTE: Raw eggs should not be served to anyone with a compromised immune system, or to anyone over 100 years old

FOOD PROCESSOR OR BLENDER METHOD
To a mini food processor or blender, add the garlic, egg yolk, and salt. Purée for 30 seconds.

With the motor running, *slowly*—starting with a few drops at a time—drizzle in the oil. After the first few tablespoons of oil have been incorporated, increase the oil flow slightly and drizzle until all the oil is incorporated and the sauce is thick like mayonnaise. Add the lemon zest, lemon juice, and mustard. Pulse a few times, then add a tablespoon or two of water to thin it out and pulse a few more times. (The aioli will thicken more when it chills.) Taste for salt and acid balance and adjust if desired. Cover and refrigerate.

WHISK METHOD This is best done as a two-person project. One person whisks while the other one drizzles.

To a large bowl, add the garlic, egg yolk, and salt. Whisk the ingredients together for 30 seconds. While whisking, *slowly*—starting with a few drops at a time—drizzle in the oil. After the first few tablespoons of oil have been incorporated, increase the oil flow slightly, and drizzle until all the oil is incorporated and the sauce is thick like mayonnaise. It will take a few minutes of strenuous whisking. Add the lemon zest, lemon juice, and mustard. Continue whisking to incorporate, then add a tablespoon or two of water to thin out and whisk a bit more. (The aioli will thicken more when it chills.) Taste for salt and acid balance and adjust if desired. Cover and refrigerate.

Time
<15 minutes

Yield
About ¾ cup

What to Do If Your Aioli "Breaks"

As you incorporate the oil into the yolk, the sauce is supposed to thicken. If it suddenly breaks—resulting in a runny liquid—it's time to pause and regroup. Remove the broken liquid and reserve it. Add your backup egg yolk to the empty blender or bowl. With the motor running or whisk whisking, drizzle in the broken liquid a few drops at a time. When you have incorporated all of the broken liquid, slowly drizzle in the remaining oil plus an additional ¼ cup (to compensate for the extra yolk). Continue with the recipe.

When in Romesco *photo on page 239*

Nuts, stale bread, tomatoes, and bell peppers anchor this fisherman's sauce from Spain's Catalonian region. It's so thick and complex, you will want to eat it with a spoon. If there is any left, slather it on bread, crispy potatoes, grilled onions, fish, or burgers of any kind.

Time
< 30 minutes

Yield
About 2 cups

2 red bell peppers

1 large tomato

1 very stale slice sourdough bread, broken into pieces

⅓ cup roasted almonds

⅓ cup roasted hazelnuts, skins removed (as much is possible)

3 garlic cloves

1 dried ancho chili, stemmed and seeded, or 1 Tbsp ancho chili powder

¼ cup parsley, stemmed

1 Tbsp smoked paprika, or regular paprika in a pinch

2 Tbsp sherry vinegar, or red wine vinegar in a pinch

½ cup olive oil

Salt and pepper

Blacken the red peppers and tomato over a gas burner or barbecue. Put them in a bag for 5 minutes, then peel off and discard the skins along with the seeds and stems. Reserve.

To a food processor, add the bread, almonds, hazelnuts, garlic, and ancho chili. Purée for 30 seconds. Add the tomato, bell peppers, parsley, paprika, and vinegar. Purée for another 30 seconds. With the processor running, drizzle in the olive oil. Season to taste with salt and pepper. Taste for acid balance and adjust if desired.

Chimichurri Sauce *photo on page 238*

I come by chimichurri sauce honestly. My great-great-uncle emigrated from Romania to Argentina where he became a gaucho and herded cattle across the pampas (plains). During their treks, the gauchos packed dried herbs in their saddlebags to concoct a sauce that they served with one of the cattle that they sacrificed and roasted on an open spit. This version is made with heaps of fresh parsley. In combination with the lemon juice and sherry vinegar, it delivers a bright, herbalicious sauce that will wake up any steak. It's equally as good on other grilled meats or grilled veggies, and as a dip for bread.

Time
< 10 minutes

Yield
About 1 cup

Plan-Overs
Will keep in the refrigerator for up to 5 days

2 cups roughly chopped fresh parsley

1 Tbsp dried oregano

6 Tbsp olive oil

1 Tbsp freshly squeezed lemon juice

2 garlic cloves, minced

1 shallot, minced

1 Tbsp sherry vinegar or in a pinch, red wine vinegar

¼–½ tsp chili flakes

Pinch salt and pepper

Place all ingredients in a food processor or blender and pulse for about 30 seconds until very well chopped but not quite puréed. Taste for salt and acid balance and adjust if desired.

Compound Butters

Compound butters are a great alternative to oils and sauces for finishing proteins and vegetables. They are a snap to make and can be stored in the freezer, waiting on standby, for up to 6 months.

Garlic Butter *photo on page 246*

This classic is great on bread, potatoes, and anything else you want to infuse with the buttery essence of garlic.

1 stick (8 Tbsp) salted butter

6 garlic cloves, minced super finely (HACK: use a Microplane to mince)

¼ tsp pepper

1 Tbsp finely chopped parsley

In a small pot over medium heat, add the butter. When the butter starts to bubble, reduce the heat to a very low simmer. Add the garlic and pepper and cook for 30 seconds, stirring constantly. Remove from the heat and let sit at room temperature for 15 minutes. When the butter begins to solidify, but is still malleable, fold in the parsley.

Set a 10-inch piece of plastic wrap, parchment paper, or aluminum foil on a flat, solid surface. Drop the butter onto the plastic wrap and roll into a log form, about 1 inch in diameter and 6 inches long. Refrigerate or freeze. Cut off slices as needed.

Time
< 30 minutes

Yield
Makes 1 stick (8 ounces)

Plan-Overs
Store in the fridge for 1 month or in the freezer for up to 6 months

Chipotle Lime Butter *photo on page 246*

A match made in heaven for corn on the cob.

1 stick (8 Tbsp) salted butter, at room temperature

Zest of 1 lime + 1 Tbsp lime juice

1 Tbsp puréed chipotle in adobo, or ¼ tsp ground chipotle

¼ tsp pepper

NOTE If you open a fresh can of chipotles in adobe for this recipe, puree the whole can and freeze leftovers in an ice cube tray or log form for future use

To a small bowl, add all of the ingredients. Combine until all ingredients are incorporated into the butter.

Set a 10-inch piece of plastic wrap, parchment paper, or aluminum foil on a flat, solid surface. Drop the butter onto the plastic wrap and roll into a log form, about 1 inch in diameter and 6 inches long. Refrigerate or freeze. Cut off slices as needed.

Time
< 10 minutes

Yield
Makes 1 stick (8 ounces)

Plan-Overs
Store in the fridge for 1 month or in the freezer for up to 6 months

245

GARLIC BUTTER
page 245

CITRUS
BUTTER
page 247

CITRUS

GARLIC

MISO

CHIPO

MISO BUTTER
page 247

CHIPOTLE LIME BUTTER
page 245

Citrus Butter

Perfect for fish, pork, and other delicate proteins.

1 stick (8 Tbsp) salted butter, at
    room temperature
Zest of 1 lime
Zest of 1 lemon
Zest of 1 orange
4 chives (optional), chopped
    finely

To a small bowl, add all of the ingredients. Combine until all ingredients are incorporated into the butter.

Set a 10-inch piece of plastic wrap, parchment paper, or aluminum foil on a flat, solid surface. Drop the butter onto the plastic wrap and roll into a log form, about 1 inch in diameter and 6 inches long. Refrigerate or freeze. Cut off slices as needed.

Time
< 10 minutes

Yield
Makes 1 stick (8 ounces)

Plan-Overs
Store in the fridge for
1 month or in the freezer
for up to 6 months

Miso Butter

Fabulous for baked sweet potatoes, scallops, eggplant, and any other protein or veggie you want to infuse with a rich layer of umami. It's also great on popcorn.

1 stick (8 Tbsp) unsalted butter,
    at room temperature
4 Tbsp miso (white or red)
¼ tsp white pepper, or black
    pepper in a pinch

To a small bowl, add all of the ingredients. Combine until all ingredients are incorporated into the butter.

Set a 10-inch piece of plastic wrap, parchment paper, or aluminum foil on a flat, solid surface. Drop the butter onto the plastic wrap and roll into a log form, about 1 inch in diameter and 6 inches long. Refrigerate or freeze. Cut off slices as needed.

Time
< 10 minutes

Yield
Makes 1 stick (8 ounces)

Plan-Overs
Store in the fridge for 1
month or in the freezer for
up to 6 months

Clarifying Butter

Melt a minimum of ¼ pound of butter (1 stick) in a heavy saucepan over low heat. When the butter is fully melted, remove it from the heat and let stand for 3 minutes. The butter should settle into three layers: a frothy top, a clear yellow middle, and a milky solid bottom. Begin by skimming or spooning the froth off the top. Then carefully and slowly pour out the clear middle layer into a bowl while retaining all of the white solids in the saucepan. Discard the froth and solids. If necessary, repeat the skimming process on contents in the bowl. Store the clarified butter in an airtight container. It will last almost indefinitely in the refrigerator.

Flavored Olive Oils

As noted elsewhere in this book, virtually every cooked protein and vegetable, and a wide range of other dishes, benefit from a drizzle of oil just before serving. You can never go wrong with a good-quality extra-virgin olive oil, but when you really want to make an impression, any one of these oils will add some extra sizzle to your drizzle.

Sicilian-Style Infused Olive Oil

This classic pizzeria-style infused oil is perfect for pizzas, bread, and anywhere else you want to add some well-rounded kick.

Time
< 15 minutes

Yield
Makes 3 cups

Plan-Overs
Always keep refrigerated.
Will keep for up to a month

1 empty 25-ounce bottle (either the original olive oil bottle, or an empty wine or booze bottle with the label removed)

5 garlic cloves, lightly smashed

3 dried chile de árbol, or other small dried chili peppers

3 wide strips of orange peel (use a vegetable peeler or a sharp paring knife to peel off wide strips of the outer, colored layer of the skin, leaving behind as much of the white pith as possible)

3 sprigs fresh rosemary, or 5 sprigs thyme, or some of each

½ Tbsp multicolored peppercorns, or any peppercorns

1 pour spout (optional)

3 cups good-quality extra-virgin olive oil

Clean and dry the bottle thoroughly. Stuff the ingredients into the bottle and use the pour spout to fill the bottle with oil. Seal and refrigerate for a minimum of 2 days before using.

VARIATIONS ON A THEME Add more or less of any of the listed ingredients, other fresh or dried herbs, or other citrus zests.

PARSLEY OIL

page 250

LEMON OIL

page 250

SICILIAN

page 248

GARLIC-HERB

page 250

Lemon-Infused Olive Oil *photo on page 249*

Citrus oils are particularly well suited to fish and shellfish.

Time
< 30 minutes

Yield
Makes 1 cup

Plan-Overs
Will keep in the refrigerator
for up to a month

2 lemons, or Meyer lemons

1 cup olive oil (ideally, one that
is more creamy than peppery
or grassy)

Scrub the lemon skins thoroughly, then dry. Use a Microplane to zest the lemons, or use a vegetable peeler or a sharp paring knife to peel off wide strips of the outer, colored layer of the skin, leaving behind as much of the white pith as possible. Add the zest or peels and oil to a small pot. Over the lowest heat setting, simmer for 15 minutes, or until the oil has taken on a pleasant citrus aroma and flavor. Let cool then strain out the peels.

One-Minute Garlic-Herb Oil *for Everything* *photo on page 249*

For those times when you want to add a little extra somethin' to a simply prepared piece of meat, fish, or chicken, or to grilled veggies, but you don't have the time, energy, or ingredients to make a more complex sauce from scratch, here's the versatile little black dress of herb oils.

Time
1 minute

Yield
Makes about ½ cup

Plan-Overs
Will keep in the refrigerator
for up to a week.

½ cup olive oil

1 large handful of whatever
herb—or mix of herbs—you
have on hand (basil, parsley,
cilantro, dill, fennel tops,
celery tops, chives, mint . . .)

1 garlic clove, smashed

1 Tbsp of lemon juice

Salt and pepper

Toss the olive oil, herbs, garlic, and lemon juice into a blender, hit high, and let the motor run for 30 seconds. Season to taste with salt and pepper. BOOM, done!!!

Parsley or Cilantro Olive Oil *photo on page 249*

These clear green oils are perfect for finishing soups and garnishing plates.

Time
< 15 minutes + 1 hour resting

Yield
Makes 1 cup

Plan-Overs
Will keep in the refrigerator
for up to a month

1 bunch of parsley or cilantro

1 cup olive oil

Blanch your chosen herb in boiling salted water for 10 seconds, then transfer to an ice bath for 2 minutes. Remove the herbs from the ice bath and squeeze out as much water as possible, chop roughly, then add to a blender along with the oil. Blend until smooth, then let sit for an hour. Strain the mixture through cheesecloth or a chinois—or a coffee filter if you have the time.

No-Fuss Stocks

All-Purpose Zero-Waste Chicken Stock

Homemade chicken stock will up your cooking game and help you rescue many items that you would normally toss into the green bin. Any time you buy a rotisserie chicken, or roast or grill a chicken at home, stick the leftover carcass in a plastic bag and freeze it. Ditto for any raw chicken bits (such as backbones or wing tips). And any time you have leftover or "tired" bits of onions, carrots, celery, fennel, garlic, fresh herbs, etc., freeze them. After you have rescued several carcasses, wait for a rainy day, then toss them in a pot with the veggies (in a ratio of roughly 6 parts chicken to 1 part veggie). With minimal effort and a few hours of simmering, you will be rewarded with a deeply flavored multipurpose chicken stock that cost you nothing to make.

About 4 chicken carcasses

Couple of cups of rescued veggies, roughly chopped (e.g. 3 carrots, 2 celery stalks (or the tops of a head of fennel), and 1 onion)

A few tired garlic cloves, roughly chopped

Any leftover herbs, plus a palmful of parsley or cilantro stems, roughly chopped

5 black peppercorns

Bay leaf

Fill a large stock pot with the frozen or fresh, raw or cooked chicken carcasses. Add the veggies, garlic, herbs, peppercorns, and bay leaf.

Fill the pot with water to the point that it covers the chicken and veggies. Bring to a boil, reduce to a simmer, and let simmer, covered, for 4 hours.

Let cool, then strain out the solids, using the back of a ladle to force the remaining liquid out of the detritus in the strainer. Let the stock settle until the fat rises to the top, then use a fat separator or ladle off as much fat as you can.

Before freezing, taste the stock. The intensity will indicate what strength to use it in (using traditional chicken broth from your memory as your benchmark). After 4 hours of simmering, the stock should be intense enough that you can dilute it with an equal amount of water when cooking with it. The more you reduce the stock, the more water you can eventually add.

Freeze in various size containers (leaving some room at the top for expansion) and ice trays, so that you have options when the need for stock arises.

Time
4 hours (mostly inactive)

Yield
Makes 8 to 12 cups, depending on intensity

Plan-Overs
Store in the fridge for 5 days or in the freezer for up to 6 months

Veggie Stock

Vegetable stock is a great way to rescue the various bits of the vegetables that you don't use, as well as "tired" veggies that still have a modicum of life and lots of flavor left in them. Peels (asparagus, carrot, zucchini, onion), stems (mushroom, kale, Swiss chard, parsley, cilantro), bell pepper cores, corn cobs, fresh herbs, etc., will all contribute to a deeply flavored vegetable broth. Store them as you go in a plastic bag in the freezer, then make stock when you have enough to fill a stock pot.

Time
1 hour (mostly inactive)

Yield
Makes about 8 cups

Plan-Overs
Store in the fridge for
1 week or in the freezer for
up to 6 months

4 to 8 cups vegetable scraps
5 black peppercorns
Bay leaf

Add all the ingredients to a stock pot and fill the pot with water to the point it covers the veggies. Bring to a boil, reduce to a simmer, and let simmer, covered, for around 1 hour.

Let cool, then strain out the solids, using the back of a ladle to force the remaining liquid out of the detritus in the strainer. If your freezer space is limited, return the stock to the pot after straining off the solids, and reduce by half. Add more water when using this stock.

Freeze in various size containers (leaving some room at the top for expansion) and ice trays, so that you have options when the need for stock arises.

Stock HACKS

- Cool the stock quickly by putting the pot in a sink filled with ice water.

- As an alternative to ladling off the fat, refrigerate overnight, then skim off the fat cap.

- If your freezer space is limited, return the stock to the pot after straining off the solids and fat, then over high heat, reduce by half. Add more water when using this stock.

Rustic Fried Breadcrumbs

Get into the habit of saving your leftover bits of bread in a paper bag. If you want to make breadcrumbs and don't have any stale bread on hand, put a few slices of rustic bread into a toaster oven or oven at 250°F and bake for approximately 30 minutes, or until rock hard.

1 cup stale bread bits (see above)

2 Tbsp of olive oil or leftover oil from an anchovy tin or jar

Put your stale or oven-dried bread in a plastic bag and smash it with a blunt object until it's reduced to coarse breadcrumbs. Alternatively, you can smash it in a large mortar and pestle. Transfer the breadcrumbs to a pan over low heat. Add the oil. Stir occasionally and watchfully for about 10 minutes, or until the crumbs are golden brown.

Time
15 minutes

Yield
Makes 1 cup

Plan-Overs
Will keep in the refrigerator for 1 month and the freezer for 6 months

Acknowledgments

A heartfelt thank you to Robert McCullough for believing in this project from the beginning, and to Lindsay Paterson for juggling the dueling roles of cheerleader and grim reaper. To Kate Zankowicz for sprinkling her magic dust on my life, and onto every page of this book. To Chris Houston for his big-picture guidance during my formative "bombing" mission. To Elizabeth Karmel for sharing all of her best tricks and recipes with me, and for always being willing to discuss the minutiae that makes all the difference. To Mary Sue Milliken, for her infinite patience in explaining all the things I don't know—because I forgot to get formal culinary training. To Chris McDonald for his suggestions, and for only rolling his eyes when I can't see him. And to David Sanfield for his culinary insights, and the delicious results of our sibling rivalry.

My Kitchen Cabinet: Sarah Damson, Matt Zimbel, Rob and Cherry Dickins, Michael Brook, Julie Rogers, Felix Rogers Brook, Joy Harding, Cal and Ellen Shumiatcher, Juila Sweeney and Michael Blum, MP Wachter, Mathias Fain, Mark Wilkinson and Annunziata Gianzero, Keith Mabry, Romily Perry, Carlo Rota, Rachel Gerstein, Clarissa Troop, Bridgette Bacco and Jeff Stettin, Colby Groom, Lauren Groom, Jason Briseño, and Margarita Perez.

To Jordie McTavish and Roseanna Plutino of Plutino Culinary, for helping to keep the boat afloat.

The Photography Crü: The food photography in this book came to life over the course of 12 grueling days during which I turned my living room into a makeshift studio, and my tiny kitchen into command central. All of the food was photographed in natural light, styled organically, and then eaten by the crü, or shared with neighbors, mailpeople, couriers, gardeners, and lost tourists looking for the Hollywood sign. The results are a testament to the keen, artful eye of photographer Suzi Q. Varin, the wisdom of digital sparkle pony Alina Prax, and the indefatigable spirit of sous chef/assistant stylist Lindsey Hedrick. Special thanks to the unknown chef to whom I handed my iPhone, for snapping the candid duck head portrait on page iix.

And a final thank you goes to you—yes you—for buying and/or reading this book. I am humbled to have the opportunity to share the lessons of my life's journey with you.

Index

Notes

"Whether you're just beginning your journey in the kitchen, or are already an experienced cook, *Flavorbomb* will up your game. It is chock-full of useful information, insider tips, and all the tools you need to take your food to the next level. And, like Bob, it never takes itself too seriously."

JASON PRIESTLEY—actor, director and cooking enthusiast

"Flavorbomb is full of boundless creativity, fresh ideas and intuitive advice for making the most of every minute you spend in your kitchen."

MARY SUE MILLIKEN —chef and recipient of the Julia Child Award